TRANSFORM YOUR HOME INTO A FORTRESS OF ABSOLUTE SECURITY TO FACE ANY CRISIS

DAVID RUSH

Copyright © 2024 by David Rush.
All rights reserved. No part of this book may be reproduced, distributed, or transmitted in any form or by any means, including photocopying, recording, or other electronic or mechanical methods, without the prior written permission of the author, except in the case of brief quotations embodied in critical reviews and certain other noncommercial uses permitted by copyright law.

Disclaimer

This book is a work of non-fiction based on the author's experiences and research. The information provided is for educational and entertainment purposes only. The author and publisher have made every effort to ensure the accuracy and completeness of the information contained in this book. However, they make no representations or warranties of any kind, express or implied, regarding the completeness, accuracy, reliability, suitability, or availability of the information, products, services, or related graphics contained in this book.

The strategies, ideas, and suggestions in this book are not intended to be a substitute for professional advice. The author and publisher specifically disclaim any liability, loss, or risk, personal or otherwise, which is incurred as a consequence, directly or indirectly, of the use and application of any of the contents of this book.

Legal Disclaimer: This book is not intended to provide legal, financial, medical, or professional advice. Readers are encouraged to consult with appropriate licensed professionals before taking any action based on the information contained herein.

Medical Disclaimer: The information in this book is not intended to be a substitute for professional medical advice, diagnosis, or treatment. Always seek the advice of your physician or other qualified health provider with any questions you may have regarding a medical condition.

Financial Disclaimer: The financial information in this book is for general informational purposes only and should not be considered as financial advice. Always consult with a qualified financial advisor before making any investment decisions.

Risk Assumption: By reading this book, you agree that the author and publisher are not responsible for any losses or damages that may result from your use of, or reliance on, the information contained in this book. You assume full responsibility for your actions and decisions.

Limitation of Liability: In no event shall the author or publisher be liable for any direct, indirect, punitive, incidental, special, or consequential damages arising out of, or in any way connected with, the use of this book or the information contained herein, whether based on contract, tort, strict liability, or otherwise, even if the author or publisher has been advised of the possibility of damages.

Personal Use: This book is for personal use only. It may not be resold, reproduced, or distributed without the written permission of the author. No part of this book may be used or reproduced in any manner whatsoever without written permission, except in the case of brief quotations embodied in critical articles and reviews.

Trademarks: All trademarks, service marks, trade names, product names, and logos appearing in this book are the property of their respective owners. Any rights not expressly granted herein are reserved.

Updates and Revisions: The information in this book is current as of the publication date. However, the author and publisher reserve the right to make changes to the information contained herein without notice.

To Reiterate, By reading this book, you agree to the following:

1. You understand that the author and publisher are not providing professional advice of any kind.
2. You acknowledge that the author and publisher are not liable for any loss or damage, including without limitation, indirect or consequential loss or damage, or any loss or damage whatsoever arising from the use of information contained in this book.
3. You agree to use the information in this book at your own risk and understand that the techniques and practices described may be dangerous if not executed properly or in appropriate circumstances.
4. You will not hold the author or publisher responsible for any injuries, losses, or damages that may occur as a result of following the information in this book.
5. You understand that this book is for personal use only and may not be resold, reproduced, or used for commercial purposes without express written consent from the author.
6. You acknowledge that the author and publisher do not warrant the performance, effectiveness, or applicability of any websites or resources mentioned in this book.
7. You agree that any perceived slights of specific persons, peoples, or organizations are unintentional.

By continuing to read this book, you acknowledge that you have read, understood, and agree to be bound by these terms and conditions. If you do not agree with these terms, please do not use or read this book.

TABLE OF CONTENTS

INTRODUCTION 9
    The Decision to Stay: Why Bugging-In is the Safest Option 9
    The Significance of the Bugging-In Strategy 9
    Survival Lessons: Key Strategies and Tactics 9

CHAPTER 1: 10
ESTABLISHING A SECURE HOME ENVIRONMENT 10
    Transforming Your Home into a Sanctuary 10
    NATURAL THREATS: EVALUATION AND PREPARATION 11
    MAN-MADE RISKS: PREVENTION AND RESPONSE 12
    HOME SAFETY EVALUATION 13
    DEVELOPING YOUR PERSONAL BUG-IN STRATEGY 15

CHAPTER 2: 17
LONG-TERM FOOD STORAGE FOR EMERGENCIES 17
    The Importance of Nutrition for Survival 17
    Cooking Techniques for Off-Grid Living 17
        Fermentation of Foods in Jars 18
        Constructing a Smokehouse 19
        Portable Cooking Solutions 20
        Reflector Oven 21
        Earth Oven 23
        Thermal Oven 23
        Candle Oven 24
        Solar Cooking 24
        Barbecue Grill 24
        Constructing a Root Cellar 26
        Constructing a Solar Dehydrator 27
        Zeer Pot (Clay Pot Refrigerator) 28
        Fermentation of Food in Crocks 29
        Preserving Meat and Fish with Salt and Sugar 31
        Understanding Aquaponics 32
    H.O.S. Recipes 35
        Solar-Cooked Beef Jerky with Lettuce and Arugula 35
        Dried Salmon with Spinach and Watercress, Served with Yogurt and Mint Sauce 35
        Stuffed Zucchini with Dried Beef Cooked in a Solar Oven 36
        Light Vegetable and Dried Salmon Soup Heated with Candles 36

Dried Chicken and Lettuce Heated in a Candle Oven	37
Lettuce boats with beef jerky, gently warmed with candles:	38
Zucchini stuffed with dried turkey cooked slowly underground:	39
Beef dried in chard leaves, slow cooked in an earth oven:	40
Hearty Stew of Dried Meat and Vegetables Cooked in an Earthen Oven	40
Smoked Meat with Green Onions	41
Cooking on a Charcoal Grill:	42

Weekly Meal Plan — 42

CHAPTER 3: — 44

FUTURE PLANS: UNDERSTANDING THE IMPORTANCE OF WATER IN CRISIS SITUATIONS — 44

The Critical Role of Water During System Failures — 44

Preparations Prior to a Crisis — 44

Ensuring Water Security at Home — 45

Assessment of Household Water Requirements — 45

Understanding Water Management for Home Security — 45

Solutions for Safe Water Conservation — 46

Securing a Consistent Water Source — 46

Identifying Water Sources — 47

Water Storage Solutions — 48

Calculating Total Water Storage for Non-Drinking Use — 48

Choosing the Right Water Storage Containers — 49

Water Conservation and Reuse — 51

Water Sources to Avoid — 53

Risks of Water Contamination — 53

Assessing Water Quality — 54

Identifying Hidden Water Reserves — 54

Finding Water Sources in Emergency Situations — 55

Filtration Methods — 56

DIY Water Filtration Systems — 57

Advanced Water Purification Methods — 60

— 63

DIY Water Collection System — 63

Stream or River Water Collection System — 64
Solar Distiller for Water Collection — 66
Constructing a Manual Water Pump — 67

Constructing a Homemade Water Filter 68
Chemical Water Disinfection 69

CHAPTER 4: 72

ENERGY GENERATION AND CONSERVATION AT HOME 72

Generate Your Own Energy 72

Energy Requirements During Emergencies 73

Understanding Off-Grid Energy Solutions 73
DIY Solar Panel Installation 74
Building a Wind Turbine 75

Wind-Powered Lighting 76

DIY Project: Construct a Wind-Powered Streetlight 77

DIY Project: Construct a Wind-Powered Streetlight 78
Constructing a Pedal Generator 79

Core Concepts of Energy Storage 80
Setting Up a Battery Bank 81
Constructing a Solar Charger 82

Long-Term Solutions for Lighting 84

Emergency Lighting Options 84
Battery-Powered Lighting Solutions 85
Chemical Glow Sticks 86

Creating Emergency Lighting Solutions 86

DIY Emergency Light Project 86
DIY Project: Constructing Solar Lights for Your Driveway 87

Creating Candles and Oil Lamps 89

Constructing Reflectors for Fire-Based Lighting 90

Off-Grid Energy Solutions: Generators, Wind Power, and Solar Energy 92

Fuel Safety and Management 92

CHAPTER 5: 94

SECURITY MEASURES AND ALARM SYSTEMS FOR HOMES 94

Perimeter Protection 94

Erecting Fences and Barriers 94

Natural Barriers with Thorny Vegetation 95

Implementation of Motion Sensors 95

Defense Tools and Strategies 96

Tools and Techniques for Home Defense 96

Techniques for Sustainable Construction ___ 96

Selecting Suitable Natural Materials ___ 97

Insulation and Thermal Mass ___ 97

Building an Off-Grid Cabin ___ 98

Crafting a Sustainable Cabin ___ 98

Selecting the Ideal Site and Layout ___ 98

Foundation Options for Off-Grid Cabins ___ 98

Enhancing Home Defense ___ 99

Strengthening the Home's Structural Integrity ___ 99

Bulletproof and Blast-Resistant Protections ___ 100

CHAPTER 6: ___ 101

COMMUNICATION ___ 101

Effective Communication and Navigation Techniques ___ 101

The Importance of Communication During Emergencies ___ 101
Constructing a HAM Radio ___ 101
Installation of Two-Way Radios ___ 103
Installation of a Solar-Powered Radio ___ 105

Selection of Solar Panels ___ 107

Battery Selection ___ 107

Connecting Communication Devices ___ 107

Advantages of Solar-Powered Communications ___ 107

Choosing Solar Panels for Communication Devices ___ 107

Battery Backup Solutions for Communication Devices ___ 108
Constructing a Solar Device Charger ___ 108
Constructing an Emergency Beacon ___ 109

Connectivity Solutions ___ 111

Satellite Internet Alternatives ___ 111

Data Management and Bandwidth Optimization ___ 111

Ensuring Network Security ___ 112

CHAPTER 7: ___ 113

EMERGENCY MEDICAL SUPPLIES AND PERSONAL WELL-BEING ___ 113

Medical Supplies and First Aid Essentials ___ 113

Key Elements of a First Aid Kit ___ 113

Essential First Aid Techniques _____ 114

Building a Comprehensive First Aid Kit _____ 115

   DIY First Aid Kit _____ 116

Managing Common Off-Grid Injuries _____ 117

Herbal Remedies and Natural Approaches _____ 118

Integrating Herbal Solutions _____ 118

   Cultivating a Medicinal Herb Garden _____ 118

Herbal Medicine _____ 120

Cultivating Medicinal Plants _____ 120

Cultivating Medicinal Herbs _____ 121

Crafting Herbal Remedies _____ 122

Storage and Utilization of Herbal Medicines _____ 122

DIY Project: Establishing an Herbal Medicine Garden _____ 123

CHAPTER 8: _____ 124

PERSONAL HYGIENE AND WASTE MANAGEMENT _____ 124

Health and Hygiene _____ 124

Sustaining Health Off the Grid _____ 124

Hygiene Strategies _____ 125

   Composting Toilet _____ 125

   Construction of an Off-Grid Shower System _____ 126

   Homemade Soap and Detergent _____ 127

   Creating Your Own Toothpaste _____ 129

Off-Grid Sanitation Solutions _____ 130

Gray Water Management _____ 130

Constructing a Composting Toilet _____ 130

Gray Water Treatment Systems _____ 131

Establishing a Humanure System _____ 131

Constructing a Humanure Compost Bin _____ 131

Creating a Gray Water System _____ 132

Off-Grid Waste Management _____ 132

Off-Grid Waste Incineration Solutions _____ 133

Types of Incineration Systems _____ 133

Building a Basic Incinerator _____ 133

Establishing an Off-Grid Recycling System _____ 134

Creating a Recycling Station 134

CHAPTER 9: 136

Home Survival: Techniques for Off-Grid Heating and Cooling 136

Solar Heating Techniques 136

Passive Solar Heating 136

Insulation 136

Building Orientation and Window Configuration 137

Optimal Orientation 137

Window Placement 137

Thermal Mass and Insulation 137

Understanding Thermal Mass 137

Importance of Insulation 137

DIY Project: Constructing a Solar Heater 138

Wood Stoves and Biomass Heating Solutions 140

Varieties of Wood Stoves 140

Firewood Collection and Storage 140

Safety and Maintenance 141

"Rocket" Thermal Mass Heaters 141

Designing and Constructing a Thermal Mass Bench 142

Cooling Techniques 142

DIY Project: Constructing a Solar-Powered Ventilation System 144

DIY Project: Constructing a "Rocket" Thermal Mass Heater 146

Sustainable Refrigeration Solutions 149

CHAPTER 10: 151

ESTABLISHING A COMMUNITY NETWORK 151

The Role of Community Networks in Emergencies 151

Steps for Building a Community Network 151

CHAPTER 11: 154

STRESS MANAGEMENT 154

.... 154

Mental Readiness: Equally Vital as Physical Preparation 154

FINAL THOUGHTS 157

INTRODUCTION

The Decision to Stay: Why Bugging-In is the Safest Option

Opting to remain at home during a crisis, a practice known in emergency preparedness as "bugging-in," is widely recognized by experts as one of the safest and most effective strategies. While the instinct may be to evacuate or find shelter elsewhere during emergencies, bugging-in offers numerous advantages in terms of safety, control, and self-reliance.

The Significance of the Bugging-In Strategy

The bugging-in approach revolves around preparing, protecting, and managing resources within your home, transforming it into a secure refuge capable of enduring critical situations. Choosing to stay put is especially advantageous when leaving would pose a greater risk than remaining. For instance, during natural disasters like severe storms or hurricanes, evacuating can expose you to unpredictable hazards, whereas fortifying your home provides essential protection against external threats.

Home defense is a vital component in any crisis scenario. Experts emphasize that bugging-in allows individuals to maintain complete control over their surroundings. Unlike evacuation, which may lead to unfamiliar or crowded environments, staying home enables you to utilize known resources within a familiar setting. This approach mitigates the uncertainty of congested roadways and the dangers associated with hasty escapes.

Moreover, bugging-in facilitates a more organized and effective defense strategy. In situations that require you to leave your residence, adequately protecting yourself and your family from threats such as looters or intruders can prove challenging. Conversely, remaining at home grants you the time to prepare and establish defenses by enhancing locks, securing doors and access points, and implementing security measures like surveillance cameras or alarms.

Survival Lessons: Key Strategies and Tactics

Navigating emergency situations necessitates meticulous preparation and strategies that extend beyond conventional solutions. Field experts with extensive training in high-risk scenarios offer invaluable insights on how to convert your home into a secure fortress and respond to crises swiftly and effectively.

Their strategies blend proactive planning with precise tactical actions, potentially distinguishing between vulnerability and safety. A fundamental lesson is the identification and rectification of physical vulnerabilities within the home: reinforcing doors and windows, ensuring robust security systems, and closely monitoring access points are essential steps. Visible deterrents, such as security cameras and outdoor lighting, play a crucial role in discouraging potential intruders.

In addition to physical defenses, cultivating a resilient mindset is equally emphasized. The ability to remain calm under pressure, prepare for prolonged scenarios, and establish reliable communication plans are critical elements. Survival training emphasizes practical actions and repetitive emergency drills, ensuring that each family member knows exactly how to respond in various situations.

The importance of self-sufficiency is underscored: maintaining a supply of food and water for extended periods, assembling a comprehensive first aid kit, and having the means to generate energy independently are fundamental to surviving unforeseen events. By embracing these survival lessons, you not only bolster physical safety but also cultivate a mental readiness that empowers you to confront emergencies with confidence and control.

CHAPTER 1:

ESTABLISHING A SECURE HOME ENVIRONMENT

Transforming Your Home into a Sanctuary

Preparing your residence for potential emergencies is an essential duty, particularly in today's world where natural disasters and unforeseen events can arise unexpectedly. This detailed guide will provide you with the necessary information to effectively transform your home into a secure and functional space, even during crises. Viewing preparation not as an exercise in fear but as a responsible measure for yourself, your loved ones, and the community is vital. The aim is to create a household that serves as a safe refuge and a launching point to confront external challenges. Throughout this guide, we will explore comprehensive security strategies, resource acquisition, the application of innovative technologies and tools, and address significant topics including the mental and physical aspects of readiness.

Cultivating a Prepared Mindset
Before diving into the specifics of preparation, it's crucial to adopt the right mindset. Experts assert that during crises, your mental approach is paramount. Their philosophy emphasizes that mental readiness is as crucial—if not more so—than physical or logistical preparedness. The ability to adapt swiftly, maintain composure under pressure, and rely on a well-formulated plan are essential traits. When gearing up your home for emergencies, it is vital to visualize potential scenarios and strategize how to address them. Having a plan in place is important, but equally vital is the practice of executing it, much like professionals do during their mission drills. Engaging all family members in this process ensures that everyone is informed and knows how to respond appropriately.

Assessing Risks
Every home and geographic region comes with its unique vulnerabilities. Prior to initiating your preparedness efforts, conduct a comprehensive risk assessment. This entails evaluating the most probable emergencies based on your location—be it earthquakes, floods, hurricanes, wildfires, power outages, or even social unrest. Each scenario necessitates a tailored approach, and your preparation should reflect these distinctions. For instance, if you reside in an earthquake-prone area, reinforcing the structure of your home and strategically placing heavy objects becomes imperative. Conversely, if you live in a flood-prone zone, considering solutions like water pumps and barriers is essential. Specific strategies for each of these risks exist, including managing adrenaline levels and maintaining focus during intense moments.

Prioritizing Safety
Safety should be the foremost concern when preparing your home for emergencies. It is critical that your residence is outfitted with security systems designed to protect inhabitants from both internal and external threats. Prevention is always superior to reaction, making a proactive assessment of your home's vulnerabilities a foundational step.
- **Exit Routes:** Each household should have multiple clearly marked escape routes for both external emergencies (like a fire) and internal crises (such as structural failure). All family members should be familiar with these routes and trained to navigate them efficiently. Conducting regular drills is a beneficial practice to maintain preparedness.
- **Safe Zones:** In the event of disasters such as earthquakes, knowing which areas of your home are safest, like those away from windows and under sturdy structures, is crucial. Designate safety zones in every room.

- **Designated Gathering Spot:** It's also important to establish a safe meeting point outside the home where family members can regroup after evacuating. This location should be sufficiently distanced from potential hazards while remaining easily accessible.

Inventory and Resources: The Two-Week Rule
A vital lesson in survival is the ability to sustain oneself with minimal resources for extended periods. In terms of home preparation, this means having enough essential supplies to last at least two weeks. This not only enables survival during isolation but also provides time for a prolonged response or to await assistance.
- **Non-Perishable Food:** Assemble a stockpile of non-perishable food items sufficient to sustain your family for at least fourteen days. Focus on items that are easy to prepare and do not rely on external energy sources. Ideal choices include canned goods, energy bars, freeze-dried meals, and foods with long shelf lives.
- **Water Supply:** Aim to maintain at least 4 liters of water per day for each person, covering both drinking and basic hygiene needs. Investing in durable water containers and purification filters or tablets is advisable, especially if your available water source may not be potable.

Identifying Potential Risks
Every residence, regardless of location or size, may encounter a variety of emergencies, from natural disasters to human-made incidents. The key to effectively managing these situations lies in preparation, which hinges on recognizing potential risks and developing a focused action plan. Effective preparation always starts with situational awareness and an understanding of the specific threats that could arise in your environment.

Recognizing the Importance of Risk Assessment
Before formulating a thorough home preparedness strategy, it's essential to pinpoint potential risks that could impact your residence and locality. This identification process fosters awareness and helps prioritize your preparations.
Risks can be categorized into two primary types:
1. **Natural Risks:** These encompass events such as earthquakes, hurricanes, floods, wildfires, snowstorms, landslides, and other disasters tied to geographic conditions.
2. **Anthropic Risks (Human-Caused):** This category includes technological incidents, such as explosions, power outages, or failures in essential services (like water, gas, or electricity), along with more targeted threats such as terrorist attacks, social unrest, or health crises.

The cornerstone of effective preparation is a comprehensive understanding of the specific risks in your area, coupled with the ability to assess the potential impact of an emergency on your home, family, and assets.

NATURAL THREATS: EVALUATION AND PREPARATION

Seismic Activity
Earthquakes rank among the most unpredictable and destructive natural hazards, striking without warning and inflicting substantial damage on properties. Areas susceptible to seismic activity, especially those situated near significant tectonic faults, necessitate targeted measures to minimize damage and safeguard family members.
In order to enhance your home's earthquake resilience, it is crucial to reinforce its structure and mitigate internal hazards. This involves securing furniture and heavy items to walls, implementing window security measures, and ensuring that the building complies with earthquake safety standards.
Additionally, identifying "safe zones" within your residence—such as spaces adjacent to load-bearing walls or beneath sturdy tables—will provide refuge during seismic events. Familiarity with escape routes is equally important, as is formulating a family evacuation plan. Regular drills will help ensure everyone can react promptly in the event of an earthquake.

Flood Risks
Floods represent another significant natural disaster that can inflict severe damage, particularly on homes situated in low-lying areas or adjacent to rivers, lakes, or coastlines. Here too, preparation and risk assessment are essential.
Understanding your geographical vulnerability to flooding is the first step. Local authorities typically offer flood risk maps, which help identify which parts of your home might be affected in the event of a flood. Subsequently, you can implement preventive measures, such as deploying water barriers or installing sump pumps in critical areas.
Having an evacuation strategy is vital, as rapidly rising waters can trap individuals inside their homes. It's essential that every family member is familiar with the plan, including escape routes and designated safe meeting points.

Hurricanes and Storms

Residents in coastal areas and regions susceptible to tropical storms must be equipped to handle hurricanes and severe windstorms. These extreme weather events can result in extensive structural damage and jeopardize personal safety.

To prepare your home for a hurricane, reinforce doors and windows with protective coverings or fortified shutters, and ensure that trees are trimmed to prevent branches from falling onto your property. Establishing an interior safe space, away from windows and outside walls, is standard practice in such situations.

You should carefully strategize your hurricane response, ensuring you have adequate food and water supplies for at least two weeks, as help may be delayed. Having a backup generator is also critical for maintaining electricity during prolonged outages.

Wildfire Risks

Wildfires pose a significant threat in rural or suburban regions surrounded by dry vegetation. The rapid spread of flames can devastate entire communities in mere hours.

To mitigate the risks of wildfires, it's vital to create a "defensive zone" around your home by clearing away dry vegetation and flammable materials. Homes in these areas should be constructed using fire-resistant materials and equipped with sprinkler systems for extinguishing fires.

For regions at high risk of wildfires, timely evacuation is crucial. Be prepared to leave your home on short notice, and ensure your emergency plan includes clearly defined escape routes and an emergency kit to take with you.

Snowstorms

In colder, mountainous regions, snowstorms present a significant risk to both safety and the continuity of essential services. Heavy snow, ice, and strong winds can cause structural damage, power outages, and block transportation routes, leaving residents isolated for days or even weeks.

To prepare for a snowstorm, it is essential to keep your home properly insulated and have an alternative heating source, such as a wood stove or portable heater. Stockpile enough food and water to cope with potential service interruptions. Additionally, ensure you have a shovel on hand to clear entrances and escape routes in case of heavy snowfall.

As with any emergency, understanding the importance of resilience and adaptability is vital. During an isolation caused by a snowstorm, remaining calm and utilizing your stored resources will help you navigate the crisis more smoothly.

MAN-MADE RISKS: PREVENTION AND RESPONSE

Disruptions in Essential Services

Interruptions in crucial services such as electricity, potable water, or gas can occur unexpectedly and have devastating impacts, particularly during emergencies.

To address these possibilities, it's important to devise an alternative plan for managing energy and household resources. A portable generator or solar panels can ensure a consistent power supply, while storing drinking water in proper containers helps mitigate potential shortages.

One of the most critical takeaways is the need for self-sufficiency and readiness to handle unforeseen events. This principle is integral to home preparation, ensuring you have alternatives for every vital service.

Terrorist Threats and Social Unrest

Though less common than natural disasters, terrorist attacks or social unrest can pose genuine threats in certain areas. Political tensions, civil disturbances, or other forms of instability can create hazardous situations for individuals and their homes.

Preparing for such emergencies entails formulating a plan to ensure safety within your home. Reinforcing doors and windows, maintaining a functioning alarm system, and having access to alternative communication devices—such as two-way radios—can be essential.

In a potentially dangerous environment, it's crucial to maintain a low profile and minimize exposure to external risks. Preparing your residence as a secure haven with sufficient supplies will enable you to confront challenging situations without compromising safety.

Technological and Domestic Incidents

Emergencies stemming from technological failures or domestic accidents, such as gas leaks or electrical fires, are serious risks that require adequate preparation. Although these incidents might seem less catastrophic than natural or human-made disasters, they can still result in life-threatening situations.

Conducting regular inspections of home security systems, including electrical wiring and gas lines, is an essential step in accident prevention. Adopting a routine of periodic checks and installing safety devices such as smoke detectors or carbon monoxide alarms can avert emergencies.

Developing a Family Emergency Plan
Once potential risks have been identified, the subsequent step is to create a comprehensive emergency plan that addresses various scenarios.

HOME SAFETY EVALUATION

Ensuring a Secure Living Environment
In an increasingly unpredictable world, safeguarding your home has become a paramount concern. Conducting a home safety evaluation is the initial step in ensuring that your residence can endure various emergencies, whether natural or man-made. This preparation involves strategic planning, thorough risk analysis, and the implementation of effective protective measures.

Your home should serve not only as a sanctuary but also as a well-functioning operational center during crises. The notion of home security encompasses more than mere physical protection; it also involves safeguarding individuals, preserving essential resources, and ensuring effective communication and prompt action. By adopting this comprehensive approach, you can develop a clear strategy to maximize safety in your home environment.

Confront threats with discipline, precision, and thorough mental and physical readiness. These attributes are equally relevant when assessing and enhancing home security. A methodical approach involves diligent preparation, crafting emergency plans, and paying close attention to detail—all of which can be instrumental in safeguarding your residence.

Home Security Evaluation: A Methodical Approach
The assessment of home security unfolds in several stages, each aimed at pinpointing vulnerabilities, fortifying existing defenses, and preparing for potential emergencies. This process considers various factors, including the geographical location of your home, possible natural and human-made threats, structural integrity, and available resources.

Step 1: Analyze Structural Integrity
The first phase in assessing home security is a comprehensive examination of your house's structure. This evaluation is crucial for determining how well your home can endure extreme events like earthquakes, hurricanes, floods, and wildfires.

1.1 **Structural Soundness**
The primary focus should be on the stability of the supporting framework. While modern homes are typically built to meet safety standards, older residences may lack the necessary fortifications to withstand severe forces. Review the following aspects:
- **Foundations**: These are the cornerstone of your home's stability. Ensure that there are no cracks or signs of settling. If any doubts arise, consult a professional for a thorough assessment and potential reinforcement.
- **Load-Bearing Walls**: Inspect the integrity of load-bearing walls for any signs of sagging or damage. In earthquake-prone regions, utilizing flexible materials and seismic-resistant construction can be crucial.
- **Roof**: A strong roof is essential for safeguarding your home. Confirm that it is in sound condition, free of leaks, and structurally sound to withstand storms or seismic activity.

1.2 **Enhancements for Security**
After identifying any weaknesses in the structure, take proactive measures to bolster your home's security. Consider your residence as a base of operations and implement the following strategies to enhance safety:
- **Securing Furniture**: In the event of an earthquake, heavy furniture can pose a danger if unsecured. Fastening cabinets, bookshelves, and appliances to the walls can prevent accidents.
- **Reinforcing Walls and Windows**: Installing shatter-resistant windows or temporary barriers (like those used during hurricanes) can protect your home from harsh weather. Fortifying doors with security bars can help deter break-ins.
- **Regular Structural Inspections**: Even homes built with durable materials need routine checks. Regular inspections help identify minor issues before they escalate into emergencies.

Step 2: Access Security and Perimeter Defense

Once you've ensured structural integrity, the next focus is on securing access points and perimeter protection. This involves examining entryways (doors, windows, garages) and safeguarding the surrounding property.

2.1 Securing Entry Points
Doors and windows serve as the primary access points and the first line of defense against intrusions. Ensuring they are robust and equipped with reliable security systems is essential.
- **Entry Doors**: Exterior doors should be solid, ideally constructed from steel or heavy-duty wood, and fitted with high-grade locks. Installing deadbolts or double locks can further enhance security.
- **Windows**: Ground-level windows can be particularly vulnerable. Intrusion-resistant windows with reinforced glass or security grilles can deter break-ins. During extreme weather, using protective shutters or barriers is critical.
- **Lock Mechanisms**: Ensure that all locks are modern, functional, and secure, avoiding outdated or easily compromised systems.

2.2 Perimeter Security Measures
Securing the perimeter is vital in any protective strategy, including your home. The outer boundary should be fortified to deter potential intruders and enhance surveillance.
- **Fencing**: A solid fence can act as a deterrent to unwanted visitors. High fences equipped with secure locks and surveillance systems such as cameras or motion sensors add an extra layer of protection.
- **Exterior Lighting**: Properly illuminated perimeters reduce blind spots and complicate unauthorized entry. Installing motion-activated lights can discourage intruders.
- **Surveillance Cameras**: A comprehensive camera system is one of the most effective tools for monitoring the perimeter. It provides continuous observation and can deter potential threats.
- **Automated Gates**: If your property allows, installing automated gates with electronic access systems can provide an additional level of security.

Step 3: Internal Emergency Preparedness
Once external defenses are established, it's crucial to focus on internal readiness. Since advance planning can significantly influence outcomes, it's essential to take a structured approach to potential emergencies within the home.

3.1 Emergency Supply Kit
Every household should be equipped with a comprehensive emergency kit that contains all necessary items for managing critical situations.
- **Medical Supplies**: Ensure you have a well-stocked first aid kit containing pain relievers, bandages, antiseptics, gloves, scissors, and any necessary medications for minor injuries. If anyone in your household requires specific medications, maintain an adequate supply.
- **Food and Water**: In case of service interruptions, it is essential to have enough non-perishable food and drinking water to last at least two weeks. Stock sealed water bottles, jerry cans, and portable water purification devices.
- **Versatile Tools**: A quality multi-tool (such as a Swiss Army Knife) is indispensable. Include flashlights with extra batteries, a hand-crank or battery-operated radio, waterproof matches, and a repair kit.
- **Emergency Clothing**: Keep thermal blankets, waterproof attire, and sturdy footwear readily available for extreme conditions.

3.2 Fire Safety Systems
A common yet frequently overlooked risk is the potential for house fires. Installing smoke detectors and sprinkler systems is crucial for protecting your family.
- **Smoke and Carbon Monoxide Detectors**: Install detectors in every room, especially in kitchens and sleeping areas, and regularly check their functionality. Ensure a carbon monoxide detector is in place, particularly if using gas heating systems.
- **Fire Extinguishers**: At least one fire extinguisher should be readily accessible within the home. Position them in high-risk areas like kitchens or garages.
- **Evacuation Plans**: Every family member should be familiar with escape routes in case of fire. Regular evacuation drills will ensure everyone knows their roles and actions during emergencies.

3.3 Safe Heating and Ventilation Systems
Accidents related to heating and ventilation can lead to serious emergencies, including fires or carbon monoxide exposure.
- **Inspection of Heating Systems**: Ensure that heating systems are correctly installed and receive regular maintenance. For gas systems, routinely inspect pipes and valves for leaks.
- **Proper Ventilation**: Confirm that there is adequate airflow throughout your home. Stagnant air can lead to humidity and mold issues, as well as increase poisoning risks.

- **Automatic Shut-off Systems**: Some heating systems can be equipped with automatic shut-off features in emergencies, preventing potential fires or more severe failures.

Step 4: Mental and Physical Readiness
It's essential to emphasize the importance of being mentally prepared in addition to being physically equipped to handle emergencies. This mental fortitude can significantly influence your ability to protect yourself and your family effectively.

4.1 Mental Preparedness
The capacity to maintain composure and clarity in high-stress situations is crucial for any expert. In the context of home preparation, developing this ability is equally important.
- **Crisis Visualization**: Train yourself to imagine various emergency scenarios and envision your responses. This mental rehearsal will enhance your ability to react swiftly and calmly during unexpected events.
- **Problem-Solving Drills**: Emergencies often demand rapid and creative responses. Engage your family in exercises that simulate crises, thereby honing your ability to think on your feet and make informed decisions.

4.2 Physical Conditioning
Physical fitness and endurance can greatly assist in navigating challenging situations, such as quickly evacuating a residence or moving heavy items.
- **Strength Training**: Maintain physical fitness through strength and endurance exercises. Bodyweight workouts, including push-ups, squats, and sit-ups, can be incredibly effective.
- **Cardiovascular Endurance**: The capacity to sustain energy levels during physical stress is crucial. Engage in running, walking, or other aerobic activities to enhance your stamina.

DEVELOPING YOUR PERSONAL BUG-IN STRATEGY

Transforming Your Residence into a Secure Retreat
The concept of "bugging-in" involves the decision to stay in your home during emergencies, turning it into a sanctuary that shields you from external threats. This approach proves invaluable during situations like natural disasters (e.g., snowstorms, hurricanes), utility outages (extended power failures), or civil unrest (social upheaval, pandemics).

Defining a Bug-In Strategy
A bug-in strategy is a meticulously crafted and organized plan designed to navigate a crisis without leaving your home. This includes preparing essential resources, securing your property, managing medical situations, and adapting to scenarios where power, water, or communication services may be unavailable. It's not merely about stockpiling supplies; it's about understanding how to utilize them and being mentally and physically equipped to confront any situation. The primary focus is on achieving self-sufficiency and being prepared to tackle challenges with limited resources.

Essential Elements of a Bug-In Strategy
Creating a tailored and effective bug-in strategy requires consideration of various factors. Every household and family situation is unique, and your plan should address the specific needs of your environment and loved ones. Here are the key components to consider:
1. **Identifying Specific Risks**: Determine which emergencies are most likely in your area, such as earthquakes, floods, wildfires, hurricanes, pandemics, or civil disturbances. Understanding these risks will help you prepare the necessary resources and safeguards.
2. **Home Structure**: Evaluate whether your home is adequately equipped to serve as a secure refuge. The location and construction of your home are critical to ensuring your and your family's safety.
3. **Family-Specific Needs**: Assess the medical requirements, dietary restrictions, and unique needs of each family member. Your preparations should encompass resources for infants, elderly individuals, or those with disabilities.
4. **Anticipated Duration of Emergencies**: Emergencies may last from a few days to several weeks or months. Your bug-in strategy should be flexible and adaptable according to the expected length of the event.
5. **Resource Inventory**: Ensure you are equipped with a sufficient supply of water, food, medical supplies, and other essential survival resources.
6. **Home Defense**: Protecting your home during a crisis is of utmost importance. Implement security measures to safeguard against intrusions or damage from external threats.

7. **Mental Well-being and Stress Management**: Bugging-in involves not just physical survival but also managing stress and maintaining mental health for you and your family members.

Risk Evaluation and Emergency Scenarios
The first step in any preparedness plan is evaluating risks and developing a strategy. You cannot effectively prepare for a bug-in situation without a clear understanding of the potential threats. Each emergency scenario has its unique features, and your strategy should reflect those specifics.
1. **Local Risk Evaluation**
   Begin by identifying the most common emergencies in your geographic region. Consult local authorities, review historical data on natural disasters, and examine crime or technological accident statistics. Some examples of situations necessitating a bug-in include:
- **Natural Disasters**: If you reside in an area susceptible to earthquakes, hurricanes, tornadoes, or snowstorms, ensure your home is fortified against these events. For instance, reinforce windows against hurricane winds or verify that your roof can bear heavy snow loads.
- **Utility Crises or Prolonged Blackouts**: Power outages can arise from storms, cyberattacks, or failures in the power grid. Be ready to endure without electricity for extended periods by having generators, solar batteries, or LED lamps on hand.
- **Civil Disturbance**: In instances of social unrest or riots, remaining indoors may be the safest course of action. In these scenarios, strengthen doors, install security systems, and ensure your home is well-protected against potential intrusions.
2. **Duration Evaluation**
   One of the most challenging aspects of preparing for a bug-in is estimating the duration of the emergency. Some crises might only last a few days, such as a storm, while others may extend for weeks or months, like a pandemic. Plan with flexibility to ensure your resources are adequate for both short-term and long-term scenarios.
- **Short-Term (2-7 Days)**: During brief emergencies, you'll likely need basic supplies of food, water, medications, and strategies to keep your home safe and comfortable.
- **Medium-Term (8-30 Days)**: If the crisis persists, you'll need to address challenges such as resource shortages, mental health considerations, and ongoing safety measures.
- **Long-Term (Over 30 Days)**: In extended emergencies, your focus will shift to sustainability, which may include growing food, using alternative energy sources, and maintaining both physical and mental health.

Developing the Right Mindset for Bug-In Preparedness
Formulating a personalized bug-in plan is not solely about logistical readiness; it also involves fostering a resilient and disciplined mentality. By embracing the right principles, you can create a robust and tailored bug-in plan that empowers you to safeguard yourself, your family, and your home during any emergency. Preparing for potential challenges does not imply living in fear but rather equipping yourself to face the unexpected with confidence and resolve. With a solid strategy, adequate resources, and a proactive mindset, you will be ready to navigate any crisis from the safety of your home, transforming it into a reliable base of operations capable of handling any adversity.

CHAPTER 2:

LONG-TERM FOOD STORAGE FOR EMERGENCIES

The Importance of Nutrition for Survival

Food is a fundamental component for survival in emergency situations, making it essential to develop the ability to procure and store it safely over the long term. In this chapter, we will explore various traditional techniques that enable us to gather and preserve food effectively, allowing us to navigate the challenges of our environment. It's not merely about surviving; it's about thriving outside conventional systems. It's important to note that the techniques discussed here are not limited to extreme scenarios such as natural disasters or apocalyptic events. The skills you gain in this context can be applied to various aspects of daily life. Whether your goal is to increase self-sufficiency, save money, or have greater control over your food quality, these methods will prove invaluable. Mastering these techniques will not only equip you for survival but also lead to a healthier and more conscious lifestyle. When you embrace this way of living, the surrounding environment significantly influences the food resources you have access to. Even with refrigerators and freezers at your disposal, you must always consider the worst-case scenarios to devise effective solutions. Picture a situation where electricity is limited, and the conveniences of daily life become scarce. You will need to find alternative cooking and preservation methods, allowing you to remain indoors, safe, and adequately supplied to survive.
In addition to foraging for food, it is essential to learn how to store it properly, especially in the absence of refrigeration. Techniques like dehydration, fermentation, and curing can prolong the shelf life of food while preserving its nutritional value. Proper food storage decreases reliance on store-bought products and enhances self-sufficiency, a vital asset during emergencies or in remote settings. We will also delve into various food preservation methods, including the construction of a root cellar, which utilizes the earth's insulating properties to keep produce fresh, and creating a solar dehydrator, a simple and cost-effective system harnessing solar energy to remove moisture from food, thus extending its shelf life. For those interested in advanced techniques, building a smokehouse can allow you to preserve meat and fish by infusing them with a smoky flavor while also extending their longevity without refrigeration. This ancient practice, rooted in traditional food preservation methods, employs heat and smoke to dehydrate food and shield it from bacteria and spoilage agents. Other preservation methods, such as curing with salt or sugar, allow for the natural preservation of meat and fish by drawing out moisture and inhibiting bacterial growth. Curing also enhances the flavor of food, making it an excellent approach for those looking to preserve large quantities. Although these techniques were originally developed for emergencies or self-sufficiency scenarios, they offer intrinsic benefits in everyday life by enabling you to gain greater control over your food sources and manage your diet effectively.
To navigate situations without power successfully, preparation encompasses not just stockpiling resources but also acquiring and practicing new skills. Learning to cook using alternative methods is crucial. The best advice is to practice these techniques before a crisis arises. Don't wait for disaster to strike to explore unfamiliar cooking methods; learn how to cook both indoors and outdoors, keeping in mind that some techniques may be safer outside, while others may require indoor cooking, especially during inclement weather.

Cooking Techniques for Off-Grid Living

When it comes to cooking methods, there is no single best option; the best approach depends on what you intend to prepare. Familiarity with different techniques and ensuring you have the necessary fuels for each method is essential.

Fermentation of Foods in Jars

Estimated Cost: $52 - $145
Difficulty Level: Moderate
Time Required: Initial Setup 1-2 Hours; Fermentation Period 1-4 Weeks

Fermentation is a natural preservation method that fosters the growth of beneficial bacteria, which not only aids in food preservation but also enhances its digestibility and nutritional content. Foods like sauerkraut and pickles provide significant benefits for gut health, and this environmentally friendly process allows you to preserve your harvest without refrigeration. Using jars for fermentation is particularly suitable for vegetables like cabbage, cucumbers, and carrots.

Necessary Materials
1. **Fermentation Jar**: A non-reactive container made of ceramic or food-grade plastic with a capacity of 2 to 5 gallons and a wide opening for packing vegetables.
2. **Vegetables**: Approximately 5-10 pounds of fresh produce. Cabbage, cucumbers, carrots, and beets work well for fermentation.
3. **Sea or Kosher Salt**: 1-2 cups to create brine. Avoid iodized salt, as it can negatively impact fermentation.
4. **Water**: Non-chlorinated water is crucial since chlorine can inhibit the fermentation process. Filtered or spring water is preferred.
5. **Jar Weights**: Glass or ceramic weights to keep the vegetables submerged in the brine.
6. **Cover**: A lid or plate to cover the jar and maintain an anaerobic environment.
7. **Knife or Mandoline**: To cut vegetables evenly; a mandoline is ideal for achieving uniform slices.
8. **Large Bowl**: For mixing the vegetables with salt.
9. **Clean Cloth or Towel**: To cover the jar and protect its contents from dust and insects, while allowing fermentation gases to escape.

Instructions
1. **Prepare the Vegetables**
Thoroughly wash 5-10 pounds of fresh, firm vegetables. Using crisp vegetables ensures better fermentation quality and extended shelf life. For cabbage, slice it into thin strips, while other vegetables like cucumbers and carrots can be cut into rounds or sticks. Ensure uniformity in size for even fermentation.
2. **Salt the Vegetables**
Combine the sliced vegetables in a large bowl and add salt, using about 1 to 2 tablespoons of salt for every pound of vegetables. Salt is vital for extracting moisture and creating a natural brine essential for fermentation.
3. **Massage the Vegetables**
Massage the vegetables with your hands for 5-10 minutes to release their natural juices, forming the brine. During this process, the vegetables will soften and release liquid.
4. **Prepare the Jar**
Once the vegetables are ready, pack them into the fermentation jar. Press down on the vegetables firmly after each layer to eliminate air pockets and release additional juice. Continue adding vegetables until the jar is filled, leaving about 3 inches of space below the top edge.
5. **Add Weights**
Place weights on top of the packed vegetables to ensure they remain submerged in the brine. If specific weights are unavailable, use a clean plate with a heavy object (like a water-filled jar) on top to keep the vegetables submerged.
6. **Cover the Jar**
Cover the jar with a lid or plate to prevent dust and insects from contaminating the food. Alternatively, use a clean cloth tied around the edge with string or a rubber band to let fermentation gases escape while protecting the contents.
7. **Fermentation**
Store the jar in a cool, dark location with a stable temperature between 18°C and 24°C (65°F - 75°F). Fermentation times vary: leafy vegetables like kale may ferment in 1-2 weeks, while root vegetables like carrots can take up to 4 weeks. Higher temperatures will accelerate the process.
8. **Monitor Fermentation**
Check the jar every few days to ensure the vegetables remain submerged in the brine. If any mold appears on the surface, remove it promptly—this is common and harmless, as it does not penetrate the brine.
9. **Taste and Store**

After 1-4 weeks, depending on the vegetables and your taste preferences, begin tasting. Once the flavor meets your liking, transfer the fermented vegetables to clean jars with tight lids. Store them in the refrigerator or a cool, dark place. Fermented vegetables will continue to develop flavor and can last for several months.

Maintenance Guidelines
- Ensure that all utensils, containers, and hands are impeccably clean to prevent contamination.
- Keep vegetables completely submerged in the brine to avoid spoilage and maintain the anaerobic conditions necessary for fermentation.
- Regularly inspect for mold or changes in brine levels. Immediately remove any mold to ensure the fermentation process remains healthy.
- Store fermented foods in a cool, dark location to maintain their freshness and crunch over time.

Constructing a Smokehouse

Estimated Cost: $50 - $100
Difficulty Level: Moderate
Time Required: 4-8 Hours for Construction, 6-12 Hours for Smoking

A smokehouse is an invaluable tool for those interested in preserving meats, fish, and other foods naturally while imparting a rich, smoky flavor. This ancient preservation method has been utilized for centuries across various cultures to extend food shelf life without refrigeration. The smoking process involves exposing food to low heat and smoke over an extended period, which dehydrates it and infuses it with protective compounds derived from wood. Follow this guide to build a durable smokehouse that will allow for sustainable food storage, no matter where you are.

Required Materials
1. **Large Metal Drum or Barrel (55-gallon capacity)**: This will serve as the main chamber of the smoker. Ensure the barrel is clean and free of chemical residues.
2. **2-3 Metal Racks**: These will support the food inside the barrel. Choose racks that fit snugly within the barrel.
3. **Hardwood Chips (10-20 lbs)**: Use hardwoods such as oak, hickory, or applewood for a rich smoky flavor. Soak the chips prior to use to prevent them from burning too quickly.
4. **Charcoal (10-15 lbs)**: Charcoal will provide a consistent heat source to generate smoke from the chips.
5. **Meat or Fish (10-20 pounds)**: Lean cuts of meat or fish are optimal for smoking, as they dry well and absorb smoke evenly.
6. **Meat Thermometer**: This tool is vital for monitoring the internal temperature of the meat to ensure safe smoking.
7. **Basic Tools**: Drill with a 1/2 inch bit, saw, screwdriver, and heat-resistant gloves.
8. **4-6 Bricks**: These will be used to create a simple hearth at the base of the barrel.
9. **High-Temperature Sealant (optional)**: This can be applied to seal any cracks, improving heat and smoke retention.

Instructions
1. **Prepare the Barrel**
   Begin by thoroughly cleaning the metal barrel, ensuring it is free from debris, rust, or chemical residues. A clean barrel is crucial for preventing contamination during the smoking process. Use a saw to cut a 12x12-inch door on one side of the barrel for easier access to food and fire management. Drill 8-10 holes in the bottom of the barrel using a 1/2-inch drill bit to ensure proper ventilation and maintain a consistent temperature.
2. **Install the Racks**
   Inside the barrel, position 2-3 metal racks at regular intervals. The first rack should be placed approximately 12 inches from the bottom, with subsequent racks spaced 12 inches apart. These racks will hold your food during the smoking process.
3. **Set Up the Hearth**
   Construct a hearth inside the barrel using 4-6 bricks arranged in a square shape. This area will contain the charcoal and wood chips. Ensure that the hearth is stable and positioned directly beneath the lowest rack to promote even heat distribution.
4. **Prepare the Wood Chips**

Soak 10-20 pounds of wood chips in water for a minimum of 30 minutes. Soaking helps to prolong the burning of the chips and enhances smoke production. After soaking, drain any excess water and set the chips aside for use.
5. **Ignite the Fire**
Light 10-15 pounds of charcoal in the firebox and allow it to burn until it turns to white ash, indicating it is ready for smoking. Evenly distribute the charcoal within the firebox and add a handful of soaked wood chips on top to initiate smoke generation.
6. **Smoke the Meat or Fish**
Arrange 10-20 pounds of meat or fish on the racks, ensuring that the pieces do not touch each other to facilitate proper smoke circulation. Close the barrel door to retain smoke and heat. Use the meat thermometer to monitor the internal temperature, which should remain between 160°F and 200°F for safe smoking.
7. **Monitor the Smoking Process**
Regularly check the internal temperature of your meat or fish with the thermometer. Ensure the pieces reach a safe internal temperature, typically around 145°F for fish and 165°F for meat, to ensure proper smoking.
8. **Cool and Store**
Once the meat or fish has reached the desired temperature and smoky flavor, remove it from the smoker using heat-resistant gloves. Allow the food to cool completely before transferring it to airtight containers or vacuum bags. Store smoked items in a cool, dry place to maximize their shelf life.

Maintenance Guidelines
- **Regular Cleaning**: After each use, clean the barrel and racks of ash, grease, and food residues to maintain hygiene.
- **Periodic Inspections**: Regularly examine the barrel and firebox for signs of rust or damage. Repair or replace any compromised components to ensure safety and efficiency.
- **Storing Smoked Foods**: Once smoked, meat and fish should be stored in a cool, dry area, away from direct sunlight to prevent spoilage.
- **Ventilation**: Ensure that ventilation holes remain clear of obstructions to allow adequate airflow and smoke production during smoking.
By following these guidelines, you can construct an effective smokehouse and use it to naturally preserve your food in a sustainable manner.

Portable Cooking Solutions

Understanding the Camping Stove
Camping stoves can be powered by various fuels, including gas (propane, butane, or isobutane) or alcohol (ethanol or pure methanol). If you opt for a gas stove, it's important to note that not all models are suitable for indoor use; therefore, you should verify their certification and ensure proper ventilation. While butane stoves might be convenient, they can become costly over time. Many users prefer alcohol stoves, but they require considerable practice to manage the heat effectively. Additionally, portable wood stoves are available that require minimal wood and maintain heat well, though mastering their use also requires some experience.

Utilizing a Wood Stove
If you have a wood stove, it can be utilized for cooking, provided it is correctly installed and properly ventilated. To cook effectively on a wood stove, you must learn to control the heat by identifying the hottest areas for quick cooking and cooler spots for slower cooking. The choice of wood is also significant, as thinner logs burn more quickly and produce greater heat.

Instructions for Building a DIY Wood Stove
Creating a DIY wood stove can be a rewarding project, particularly for DIY enthusiasts looking for a cost-effective and eco-friendly way to heat spaces or cook outdoors. Below is a straightforward method to construct a DIY wood stove using readily available materials like a metal can or barrel.

Required Materials
- A metal container or steel jerrycan (approximately 20-50 liters) or a metal barrel.
- A smoke exhaust pipe (approximately 10 cm in diameter).
- A grill or perforated sheet (for the base of the combustion chamber).

- Metal hinges and a door handle.
- Heat-resistant paint (optional).
- Tools: drill, saw or angle grinder, screwdriver, pliers, protective gloves, and a face mask.

Step 1: Preparing the Container
1. **Clean the Container**: If using a barrel or jerrycan that has previously held other substances (like fuel or liquids), ensure it is thoroughly cleaned and free from flammable residues.
2. **Cutting the Top**: Using a saw or grinder, remove the top of the container to create the main opening for adding wood and allowing heat to escape.

Step 2: Creating the Door
1. **Cutting the Door**: With the grinder or a saw, cut a rectangular opening near the bottom of the container; this will serve as the door for wood loading. Ensure the door is large enough for easy insertion of wood pieces.
2. **Attaching Hinges**: Secure the metal hinges to the cut door and the container, using screws and bolts. Ensure the door opens and closes smoothly.
3. **Adding a Handle**: Install a heat-resistant handle to facilitate easy operation of the door.

Step 3: Installing the Exhaust Pipe
1. **Cutting the Exhaust Hole**: At the top of the container, create a circular hole that matches the diameter of the exhaust pipe (about 10 cm).
2. **Inserting the Pipe**: Insert the exhaust pipe into the hole and secure it using screws or metal clamps. The pipe must be firmly attached to allow the combustion fumes to escape.
   - **Safety Note**: If the stove will be used indoors, ensure that the exhaust pipe directs fumes outside to avoid carbon monoxide buildup.

Step 4: Creating the Combustion Grate
1. **Wood Support**: Place a metal grill or perforated sheet at the bottom of the container (above the door) to hold the wood. This will facilitate air circulation beneath the wood for efficient combustion.
2. **Securing the Grate**: Weld the grate to the container's sides or create internal supports using metal bars.

Step 5: Adding Ventilation
1. **Air Holes**: Drill several holes near the bottom of the container, just below the grate or around the door, to allow air to enter. Adequate airflow is essential for sustaining the fire and ensuring effective combustion.
2. **Air Regulator**: You may install a sliding plate or a simple door to adjust the airflow, thereby controlling the fire's temperature.

Step 6: Finalizing and Protecting
1. **Painting**: To protect your stove from rust and enhance its appearance, consider applying heat-resistant paint; this step is optional.
2. **Inspecting Connections**: Ensure all connections are secure and stable. Verify that the door, exhaust pipe, and ventilation holes function correctly.

Step 7: Usage and Safety
- **Starting the Stove**: Begin by placing small pieces of wood on the grate and lighting them. Once the fire is established, add larger logs.
- **Controlling the Fire**: Utilize the door and air regulator to adjust the fire's intensity. Increase airflow to intensify the flame, or decrease it to lower the heat.
- **Extinguishing**: When finished, allow the fire to die out naturally. Avoid pouring water directly onto it, as this could damage the stove's metal structure.

Safety Precautions
- **Ventilation**: Always ensure adequate ventilation, especially if using the stove indoors. Combustion gases can be hazardous.
- **Regular Replacement**: If any signs of wear or holes appear in the structure, repair or replace the stove immediately.
- **Maintenance**: Regularly clean the exhaust pipe of soot buildup to maintain good airflow and prevent chimney fires.

Building a DIY wood stove is a relatively straightforward project that can be extremely beneficial for heating small spaces or cooking sustainably

---

Reflector Oven

Building a Reflector Oven

Another option is to construct a reflector oven using a simple sheet of metal along with a baking tray. This type of oven utilizes the radiant energy from a fire to cook food, but it requires some practice to maintain a consistent temperature.

Instructions

Creating a reflector oven from sheet metal and a baking tray is a relatively straightforward project that can be accomplished with basic materials. Follow these steps to construct your own reflector oven and learn how to operate it effectively.

Materials Needed
- A sheet of metal (aluminum or stainless steel, rectangular, approximately 1 mm thick)
- A baking tray
- A stand or easel to secure the metal sheet
- A fire or heat source (such as a campfire or embers)
- Heat-resistant tongs or gloves
- Tools for bending sheet metal (like a vise or rubber mallet, if necessary)
- A kitchen thermometer (optional, for monitoring temperature)

Step 1: Preparing the Metal Sheet
- **Dimensions**: The metal sheet should be large enough to effectively reflect heat. A good starting size is approximately 60x90 cm.
- **Bending the Sheet**: Bend the metal sheet along the edges to create a concave shape. This will serve as a reflector, concentrating the radiant energy of the fire towards the food. A bend of around 30-45 degrees along the long sides is typically sufficient.

Step 2: Constructing the Support
- **Inclined Stand**: The reflector oven should be angled towards the fire to capture and reflect heat efficiently. Utilize a wooden or metal easel to hold the sheet at an angle, typically between 30-45 degrees from the ground, depending on the fire's position.
- **Distance from Fire**: Position the reflective sheet about 30-50 cm away from the fire, depending on the heat intensity. While a closer position increases heat, it also poses a risk of overheating or burning the food.

Step 3: Positioning the Tray
- **Baking Tray**: Set the tray in the area where the heat reflected from the sheet will be focused. It can be elevated on rocks, a small metal stand, or any other raised structure near the fire. Ensure the tray is lifted and not in direct contact with the flame to prevent burning.

Step 4: Controlling Temperature
- **Monitoring Temperature**: If you have a kitchen thermometer, use it to check the internal temperature of the baking dish. Maintaining a consistent temperature is a key challenge with a reflector oven. If it becomes too hot, reposition the reflector further from the heat or reduce the flame intensity.
- **Food Placement**: Place food on the baking tray and allow it to cook gradually with the reflected heat. It's important to rotate the food or reposition it if you notice one side cooking faster than the other.

Step 5: Adjusting the Oven
- **Modifying Position**: You may need to slightly adjust the oven's position during cooking to maintain even heat distribution. Since the fire's intensity can fluctuate, it's essential to tweak the angle and position of the reflector as needed.
- **Practice Regulating**: It's common to require some practice to learn how to keep a consistent temperature. You'll need to adjust the distance from the fire and the incline of the metal sheet multiple times throughout the cooking process.

Step 6: Safety Precautions
- **Heat-Resistant Gloves**: Always use gloves or tongs when handling the reflective sheet and baking tray, as they will become very hot during use.
- **Stability**: Ensure the metal sheet and baking tray are stable and securely positioned to prevent accidents or food spills.

Additional Suggestions
- **Experimenting with Reflection**: Try different angles and distances of the sheet to observe how the temperature varies.
- **Food Types**: Dishes that require slow, steady cooking, such as bread and pastries, are ideal for a reflector oven. Avoid foods that necessitate very high temperatures or quick cooking.

With practice, this reflector oven will become an invaluable tool for efficiently cooking outdoors using the energy of fire!

Earth Oven

For those with outdoor space, constructing an earth oven can provide a more stable and durable cooking solution. This oven, made from clay and sand, requires time to build but yields excellent results, including the ability to bake bread and pizza. Though it necessitates advance preparation and suitable materials, once completed, it serves as an excellent option for cooking without traditional fuels.

Thermal Oven

Another intriguing alternative is the thermal oven, or "hay box," which employs residual heat for slow cooking. This technique conserves fuel and requires prior planning. You can create a DIY thermal oven using simple materials, such as an old thermal bag or an insulated box.

Instructions for Constructing a DIY Thermal Oven

Creating a DIY thermal oven is a straightforward project that enables you to retain heat for cooking food without additional energy, utilizing thermal insulation. It's perfect for those seeking to cook in an eco-friendly manner or while camping. The principle behind the thermal oven is to hold onto the heat generated by food or a hot pot to complete cooking gradually and evenly.

Required Materials
- A cardboard box (large enough to accommodate the pot you intend to use)
- A wool sack or an old sleeping bag (for thermal insulation)
- Aluminum foil (to reflect heat)
- A lid or cushion to cover the top of the oven
- Strong adhesive tape (to secure materials)
- A pot with a lid (designed to retain heat effectively)

Step 1: Preparing the Box
1. **Selecting the Box**: Choose a cardboard box that is spacious enough to fit the pot comfortably but not excessively large to prevent heat loss.
2. **Lining the Inside**: Line the interior of the box with aluminum foil to reflect heat and ensure even distribution around the pot. Use strong adhesive tape to keep the foil securely attached to the inner walls of the box.

Step 2: Adding Insulation
1. **Incorporating Insulation**: Use wool sacks, old towels, wool blankets, or a sleeping bag to create a layer of insulation surrounding the pot. The goal is to fill the space inside the cardboard box to maintain heat effectively.
    - **Bottom Layer**: Start with a layer of wool or sleeping bag material at the bottom of the box to protect the base of the pot from losing heat downward.
    - **Side Walls**: Ensure there is enough insulating material on the sides of the box to cover the pot and create a thermal "nest."
2. **Top Insulation**: Prepare a cushion or insulating lid (which can be a folded or padded piece of cloth) to cover the top of the box when the pot is inside. This is crucial to prevent heat from escaping from above.

Step 3: Operating the Thermal Oven
1. **Preheating Food**: Cook your food in the pot as you normally would (for instance, boil a broth or simmer a stew for 10-15 minutes on the stove). The goal is to elevate the temperature of the food before placing it in the thermal oven.
2. **Inserting the Pot**: Once the food is heated, remove the pot from the heat (keeping the lid on to retain warmth) and place it at the center of the insulated box, resting on the wool or sleeping bag base.
3. **Closing the Thermal Oven**: Fill any remaining space around the pot with additional insulating material (towels or blankets) and close the box with the lid or insulating cushion you prepared. Ensure there are no gaps where heat can escape.

Step 4: Cooking Time
- The thermal oven will continue cooking by utilizing the heat retained by the pot and food. While the cooking duration will be longer than with direct heat, the food will cook evenly and slowly without the risk of burning.
- **Cooking Duration**: The time required varies based on the type of food, but dishes like rice, stews, or legumes typically take about double the time they would normally take on the stove.

Recommendations
- **Opt for Slow-Cooking Foods**: Dishes such as stews, soups, rice, or legumes are ideal for a thermal oven, as they benefit from gradual, even cooking.
- **Enhance Insulation**: To improve the thermal oven's efficiency, consider using superior insulating materials, like polystyrene or sheep's wool padding, which can better retain heat.
- **Use Thick-Bottomed Pots**: Thick-bottomed pots, such as those made from cast iron or stainless steel, help to retain heat more effectively.

Benefits of the Thermal Oven
- **Energy Efficiency**: By utilizing the heat generated during initial cooking, you won't need additional energy for the rest of the process.
- **Even Cooking**: The thermal oven cooks food gradually and uniformly, reducing the risk of burning or drying out meals.
- **Portability**: This thermal oven can be easily transported anywhere, making it perfect for camping or situations with limited energy.

This DIY thermal oven is economical, straightforward to construct, and highly effective for those seeking to cook sustainably or without constant energy sources.

Candle Oven

Utilizing a Candle Oven
Candle ovens, also known as HERCs, provide an alternative method for cooking food using the heat generated by several tea light candles. Although this is a slower cooking method, it serves as a practical solution to consider in emergencies.

Solar Cooking

Another viable option is solar cooking, which relies on sunlight and does not require any fuel. However, it is effective only when the UV index is above 7. You can purchase pre-made solar ovens or create your own using cardboard boxes and aluminum foil.

Barbecue Grill

The barbecue grill is one of the most convenient solutions during power outages, especially if you have an ample supply of charcoal. It is a straightforward method that many are already familiar with.

Instructions
Constructing a DIY barbecue grill can be an enjoyable and practical project, allowing you to personalize your grill using reclaimed or readily available materials. Here's a step-by-step guide to building your own grill with simple materials.

Materials Required
- A metal barrel (preferably a 200-liter drum or similar, clean and free of toxic substances).
- A metal grate (sized appropriately for the barrel).
- Bricks or cinder blocks (for support, if not constructing with metal legs).
- Metal tubes or rods (for legs or the structure of the internal grill).
- Drill and bits suitable for metal.
- Angle grinder or jigsaw with a metal blade.
- Metal hinges (for the top of the barbecue if you want to create a lid).

- Stainless steel screws and bolts.
- Heat-resistant paint (optional).

Step 1: Preparing the Barrel
1. **Selecting the Barrel**: Ensure the metal barrel is in good condition and thoroughly cleaned. If it has contained chemicals, clean it extensively, burning off any residue inside before using it for cooking.
2. **Cutting the Barrel**: With an angle grinder or jigsaw, slice the barrel in half lengthwise. You'll have two halves: one will serve as the base for charcoal or wood, while the other can be utilized as a lid if you desire a closable barbecue.
    - **Note**: If a lid isn't desired, simply use one half of the barrel.

Step 2: Building the Support
You have two options for grill support:
- **Option 1: Support with Concrete Blocks or Bricks**:
    1. Position concrete blocks or bricks beneath the barrel to create a stable foundation. Ensure the base is secure and the barrel rests firmly on the blocks.
    2. Space the bricks adequately to allow enough room beneath the grate for wood or charcoal.
- **Option 2: Metal Legs**:
    1. Utilize steel tubing or metal rods to construct four legs that will attach to the sides of the barrel. Drill holes in the barrel's ends and use heavy-duty bolts to secure the metal legs.
    2. The legs should be tall enough to raise the barbecue to a comfortable working height (typically around 80-100 cm from the ground).

Step 3: Adding the Grill
1. **Purchasing or Creating a Metal Grill**: The grill can be sourced in stainless steel or wrought iron. Ensure it fits the top half of the barrel correctly.
2. **Installing the Grill**: Secure the grill inside the barrel. You can do this by using metal rods or tubes attached to the inner sides of the barrel to support the grate, or simply rest the grate on the barrel's edges.
    - If you wish to adjust the grill's height, consider installing multiple supports at varying heights to accommodate your cooking needs (closer for quick grilling, further away for slow cooking).

Step 4: Creating the Lid (Optional)
1. **Attaching Hinges**: If you've cut the barrel in half and intend to add a lid, attach sturdy hinges along one of the long sides of the barrel using screws and bolts to secure them.
2. **Installing the Lid Handle**: Add a heat-resistant handle to the top of the lid for easy opening and closing.

Step 5: Adding Vents
1. **Ventilation Holes**: To ensure adequate airflow for keeping the flame alive, drill several holes (approximately 1-2 cm in diameter) in the bottom of the barrel, underneath the area where charcoal will be placed.
2. **Air Regulation Option**: You can install a movable plate or an adjustable valve above the holes to manage the airflow entering the barbecue and consequently control the fire's temperature.

Step 6: Finalizing and Protecting (Optional)
1. **Painting**: If you want to safeguard the barbecue against rust and environmental factors, consider applying heat-resistant paint. Ensure you use paint specifically designed for high temperatures.
2. **Cleaning**: Thoroughly clean the inside of the barbecue before its first use, burning off any residual oils or materials in the barrel.

Step 7: Testing the Barbecue
1. **Lighting the Fire**: Place charcoal or wood in the bottom of the barrel and ignite the fire. Allow the heat to stabilize before beginning to cook. Ensure adequate airflow to sustain a consistent flame.
2. **Cooking**: Now you're set to start cooking! Adjust the grill height or the amount of charcoal to regulate cooking temperatures.

Additional Suggestions:
- **Thermometer**: If you wish to keep track of the internal temperature of your grill, consider installing an oven thermometer on the side of the barrel.
- **Secondary Grill**: You can incorporate a second, taller grill to reheat food or for slow cooking.

- **Cleaning**: After each use, clean the grill and remove ashes to extend the barbecue's lifespan.

With these straightforward steps, you can create a DIY barbecue grill that is not only functional but also budget-friendly and customizable to your preferences.

Food Preservation Techniques

The significance of food preservation has grown increasingly important in an era marked by unpredictability and climate change, which can affect both the availability and quality of our food supply. Preparing for future challenges involves discovering effective methods to keep food resources secure and accessible for extended durations. This practice not only enhances food safety but also helps minimize waste, leading to a more sustainable utilization of our planet's resources.

Food preservation has ancient roots, originating from when early humans recognized the necessity of maintaining food quality during times of scarcity. While modern techniques are based on centuries of experimentation and advancement, the primary objective remains unchanged: to prolong the lifespan of food by shielding it from spoilage factors such as microorganisms, oxidation, and fluctuations in temperature and humidity.

Refrigeration is a common method that retards food spoilage by lowering temperatures, thereby inhibiting bacterial and microbial growth. However, it has its limitations; not all food remains fresh for extended periods in the refrigerator, and power outages can result in swift spoilage.

Drying is another time-honored technique that extracts moisture from food, making it less conducive to bacterial and mold growth. This method, whether done naturally through sun exposure or using electric dryers in controlled environments, is effective for preserving fruits, vegetables, meats, and fish.

Constructing a Root Cellar

Estimated Cost: $100 - $300
Difficulty: Moderate
Time Required: 3-5 Days

A root cellar serves as an underground storage solution tailored for fruits, vegetables, and other perishable items, capitalizing on the natural properties of the soil. The earth offers natural thermal insulation, maintaining a cool, stable temperature with high humidity levels. These conditions are ideal for long-term food storage, eliminating the need for electricity or refrigeration. Thus, building a root cellar presents a practical and sustainable option for efficiently storing your harvest.

Essential Materials
1. **Cinder Blocks or Wood Planks**: Approximately 50 cinder blocks or equivalent wood planks are needed to construct the cellar walls. Concrete is a more durable choice, while pressure-treated wood resists rot and insects.
2. **Plywood or Wood Sheets**: About 4-6 sheets of plywood (4x8 feet) will be used for the roof and interior shelving. Opt for exterior-grade plywood, which offers enhanced moisture resistance.
3. **Gravel or Sand**: You will need 5-10 bags of gravel or sand, each approximately 0.5 cubic feet, for drainage. Gravel is preferable, as it facilitates better water flow within the structure.
4. **Ventilation Pipes**: Two PVC pipes, each 4 to 6 feet long and 4 inches in diameter, are required to ensure proper airflow within the cellar, maintaining an optimal environment for food storage.
5. **Door and Hinges**: A sturdy hardwood door (approximately 2x6 feet) with two heavy-duty hinges will provide access. The door must be thick and well-insulated to protect food from temperature variations.

Construction Steps
1. **Excavation and Site Preparation**: Begin by selecting a suitable location and digging an underground space large enough to accommodate your produce. Ideally, position the cellar on slightly sloped terrain to promote natural drainage. After excavating, lay down a layer of gravel or sand at the base to create a drainage foundation, preventing moisture accumulation.
2. **Building the Walls**: Once the base is prepared, construct the walls using cinder blocks or treated wood planks. Concrete blocks are more durable and require less maintenance, while wood offers a more natural appearance but may need treatments to resist insects and rot.
3. **Installing the Ventilation System**: To maintain a constant airflow inside the cellar, install the ventilation pipes. Place one pipe near the floor and the other at the top of the structure to ensure adequate air circulation. This setup helps maintain humidity levels and prevents mold growth.

4. **Constructing the Roof**: After erecting the walls, use moisture-resistant plywood or wood planks for the roof. Ensure the roof is well-sealed to prevent rainwater and external elements from entering. It should be slightly sloped to facilitate water drainage.
5. **Door Installation**: Secure the solid wood door at the cellar entrance, using robust hinges for safe and stable operation. A well-insulated door is vital for maintaining a consistent internal temperature.
6. **Creating Shelving**: Inside the cellar, construct racks or shelves to organize your food. The shelving should be sturdy and well-ventilated to allow for proper airflow around the stored items.

Benefits of the Root Cellar
- **Energy Efficient**: As an underground structure, the cellar utilizes the earth's natural properties to maintain a stable temperature, eliminating the need for electrical devices.
- **Extended Food Storage**: By controlling temperature and humidity, items such as potatoes, carrots, apples, and other vegetables and fruits can be stored for months without spoilage.
- **Sustainability**: The use of natural materials and the fact that the cellar operates without electricity make it an eco-friendly choice for food preservation.

With a properly constructed root cellar, you can store fruits and vegetables throughout the winter, reducing waste and ensuring access to fresh produce even in colder months. Additionally, this structure enhances your self-sufficiency, limiting reliance on modern and costly storage solutions.

Constructing a Solar Dehydrator

Estimated Cost: $50 - $100
Difficulty Level: Moderate
Time Required: 1-2 Days

A solar dehydrator is an eco-friendly appliance that enables food preservation utilizing solar energy. This drying process extracts moisture from fruits, vegetables, herbs, and meats, thereby decreasing the likelihood of bacterial, yeast, and mold development. Building your own solar dehydrator is a practical and economical way to prolong the shelf life of food without depending on electricity.

Essential Materials
1. **Plywood or Wooden Planks:** Approximately 4 sheets of untreated plywood (4x8 feet each) to construct the frame, back panel, and shelves. Untreated wood is crucial to avoid chemical contamination of food.
2. **Clear Plastic Sheet or Glass Panel:** A piece measuring 2x3 feet for the roof, allowing sunlight to penetrate and trap heat inside. Glass is more durable, while plastic is lighter.
3. **Wire Mesh or Food-Safe Drying Racks:** Sufficient material to create 3-4 drying surfaces, each around 3x2 feet. Ensure these materials are safe for food use.
4. **Hinges and Latch:** Two robust door hinges and a latch to securely close the dehydrator.
5. **Black Paint (Optional):** Non-toxic and heat-resistant paint to enhance internal heat absorption.
6. **Thermometer (Optional):** To monitor the internal temperature during the drying process.
7. **Screws, Nails, and Basic Tools:** Includes a saw, hammer, drill, screwdriver, measuring tape, and level. Use weatherproof screws and nails for durability.

Construction Steps
1. **Frame Assembly**
    - Cut four pieces of plywood for the frame: two pieces measuring 2x3 feet and two pieces measuring 1x3 feet for the top and bottom. Assemble these using screws and nails, creating a rectangular frame. Use a level to ensure the structure is even and robust enough to support the drying racks and the clear cover.
2. **Back Panel Installation**
    - Cut a piece of plywood to fit the back of the frame (2x3 feet). Attach this panel securely with screws to provide additional support and act as the back wall for the dehydrator.
3. **Installing Drying Surfaces**
    - Measure and cut chicken wire or prepare food drying racks measuring 3x2 feet. Secure these surfaces to the inside of the frame at different heights, marking 3-4 evenly spaced points on the

inner sides to support the racks. Ensure adequate space between shelves for optimal air circulation.
4. **Attaching the Clear Cover**
   - Cut the plastic sheet or glass panel to fit the top of the frame. This cover must seal heat effectively within the dehydrator. Secure it using screws or nails, sealing the edges with silicone caulk to prevent heat loss.
5. **Creating Ventilation Holes**
   - Drill 3-4 small holes (1 inch in diameter) near the bottom and top of the side panels to facilitate airflow. Cover these holes with fine mesh to keep insects out of the dehydrator.
6. **Interior Painting (Optional)**
   - To improve heat absorption, paint the interior of the dehydrator with non-toxic, heat-resistant black paint. Ensure it is completely dry before proceeding.
7. **Constructing the Door**
   - Cut a piece of plywood to fit the front opening (2x3 feet). Attach the door to the frame using sturdy hinges, and install a lock to keep it securely closed. Ensure the door fits snugly to minimize heat loss.
8. **Positioning the Dehydrator**
   - Once completed, place the dehydrator in a location that receives direct sunlight for most of the day. Tilt it slightly toward the sun to maximize exposure and heat retention.
9. **Monitoring Temperature (Optional)**
   - Use a thermometer inside the dehydrator to keep track of the internal temperature, which should ideally be between 120°F and 140°F. If the temperature exceeds this range, adjust the ventilation holes to release excess hot air.

Food Drying Process
Cut fruits, vegetables, herbs, or meats into thin slices and distribute them evenly on the drying racks. Ensure the food pieces do not overlap to promote even drying. Close the door and allow the food to dehydrate under the sun's heat. Drying time varies based on the type of food, slice thickness, and weather conditions; monitor progress regularly.

Maintenance Tips
- **Cleaning:** Regularly wash drying surfaces with hot, soapy water to eliminate food residue, and thoroughly dry them before reuse.
- **Inspection:** Periodically check the structure, clear cover, and door for signs of wear or damage. Replace any damaged parts to ensure optimal functionality.
- **Ventilation:** Keep ventilation holes free from obstructions like dust or debris to guarantee sufficient airflow.
- **Storage:** When not in use, store the dehydrator in a dry, sheltered area to protect it from environmental elements, ensuring increased durability over time.

By following these guidelines, you can construct a DIY solar dehydrator that harnesses the sun's power to preserve food in an environmentally friendly, economical, and sustainable manner.

Zeer Pot (Clay Pot Refrigerator)

Estimated Cost: $20 - $50
Difficulty Level: Easy
Time Required: 2-4 Hours

The Zeer Pot, often referred to as a clay refrigerator, is an evaporative cooling system that keeps food fresh without electricity. This device proves particularly effective in hot, dry climates, leveraging the natural evaporation process to lower internal temperatures. Building a Zeer Pot is a simple, accessible, and sustainable project, ideal for off-grid living. Here are the steps to create your own Zeer Pot.

Essential Materials
1. **Large Unglazed Clay Pot:** Approximately 14 inches in diameter and 16 inches tall, with no drainage holes.
2. **Small Unglazed Clay Pot:** A second pot, about 10 inches in diameter and 12 inches tall, that fits snugly inside the larger pot, also without drainage holes.
3. **Fine Sand:** About 15-20 pounds (7-9 kg) of damp sand to fill the gap between the two pots.
4. **Water:** 1-2 gallons to moisten the sand and maintain humidity levels.

5. **Cloth:** A cotton towel or sackcloth measuring 24x24 inches to cover the pots.
6. **Lid or Dish:** A dish that fits snugly over the opening of the smaller pot, approximately 10 to 12 inches in diameter.
7. **Basic Tools:** A shovel, small spade, and measuring cup for managing sand and water.

Construction Steps
1. **Selecting Clay Pots**
    - Choose two unglazed clay pots: the larger should be about 14 inches in diameter and 16 inches tall, while the smaller should be around 10 inches in diameter and 12 inches tall. Ensure the smaller pot fits snugly inside the larger one, allowing space for sand in between. Both pots must have no drainage holes.
2. **Preparing the Sand**
    - Moisten the sand gradually with water until it is damp but not muddy, mixing it thoroughly for even moisture distribution. This step is essential for the evaporative cooling process to function effectively.
3. **Assembling the Zeer Pot**
    - Place the larger pot in your chosen location, then carefully insert the smaller pot into it, ensuring an even gap between the sides. Fill the space between the two pots with damp sand, packing it lightly to eliminate air pockets, and allowing the sand to reach the tops of both pots.
4. **Adding Water**
    - Pour water into the sand until it is thoroughly saturated. Ensure that the water level does not exceed the top of the sand to prevent seepage into the smaller pot. Refill as the water evaporates to maintain consistent humidity levels, vital for the cooling effect.
5. **Covering the Inner Pot**
    - Use a lid or plate that fits snugly over the opening of the smaller pot to keep dust, insects, and other contaminants out, ensuring the contents remain fresh.
6. **Covering the Entire Structure**
    - Wrap the Zeer Pot with wet cotton cloth or sackcloth, covering both the tops and sides. This fabric will enhance the evaporative surface area, improving cooling efficiency. Keep it moist but avoid soaking it excessively.
7. **Positioning in a Cool, Shaded Area**
    - For optimal performance, place the Zeer Pot in a well-ventilated, cool, shaded location. Adequate air circulation will further enhance evaporation and cooling.

Zeer Pot Maintenance
To keep your Zeer Pot functioning efficiently, adhere to these straightforward steps:
- **Refill Water:** Regularly check the water level in the sand and refill as needed. The evaporative cooling system only works if the sand remains adequately moist.
- **Moisten the Cloth:** Ensure the cloth covering the Zeer Pot remains damp to facilitate continuous evaporation, especially during hot days.
- **Cleaning:** Keep the lid of the inner pot clean to prevent dust and dirt from contaminating the food stored inside.

Benefits of the Zeer Pot
- **Sustainability:** Functions without electricity, making it ideal for off-grid living or situations with limited access to power.
- **Affordability:** The materials are inexpensive and readily available, making this project accessible to everyone.
- **Effectiveness:** Works best in hot, dry climates but can also be used in other conditions with appropriate precautions.

The Zeer Pot offers a simple yet effective method for food preservation that utilizes natural processes to keep food fresh. It serves as an excellent solution for individuals in hot or arid regions, providing an eco-friendly alternative to conventional refrigerators. The construction process requires only a few hours and basic materials, making it a practical project for anyone seeking to reduce reliance on electricity.

Fermentation of Food in Crocks

Estimated Cost: $52 - $145
Difficulty Level: Moderate
Time Required: Initial Setup 1-2 Hours; Fermentation Period 1-4 Weeks

Fermentation is a natural preservation method that fosters the growth of beneficial bacteria, enhancing not only the preservation of food but also its digestibility and nutritional value. Fermented foods, such as sauerkraut and pickles, offer significant benefits for gut health and represent an eco-friendly way to preserve your harvest without refrigeration. Fermenting in crocks is particularly effective for preserving vegetables like cabbage, cucumbers, and carrots.

Required Materials
1. **Fermenting Crock:** A non-reactive ceramic or food-grade plastic container with a capacity of 2 to 5 gallons and a wide opening for packing vegetables.
2. **Vegetables:** Approximately 5-10 pounds of fresh produce. Ideal choices include cabbage, cucumbers, carrots, and beets.
3. **Sea or Kosher Salt:** 1-2 cups of salt for brine preparation. Avoid iodized salt, as it can adversely affect fermentation.
4. **Water:** Non-chlorinated water is essential, as chlorine can hinder the fermentation process. Filtered or spring water is recommended.
5. **Crock Weights:** Glass or ceramic weights to keep vegetables submerged in the brine.
6. **Lid or Dish:** To cover the crock and maintain an anaerobic environment.
7. **Knife or Mandolin:** For cutting vegetables evenly; a mandolin is particularly useful for achieving uniform slices.
8. **Large Bowl:** Needed for mixing vegetables with salt.
9. **Clean Cloth or Towel:** To cover the crock and protect the contents from dust and insects while allowing gases produced during fermentation to escape.

Phases of Construction
1. **Vegetable Preparation**
   Begin by thoroughly cleaning 5-10 pounds of fresh, firm vegetables. Using crisp, fresh produce ensures higher quality fermentation and an extended shelf life. For cabbage, slice it into thin strips, while cucumbers and carrots should be cut into rounds or sticks. Ensure uniformity in the slices to promote even fermentation.
2. **Salting the Vegetables**
   Transfer the sliced vegetables to a large bowl and add salt, using approximately 1 to 2 tablespoons per pound of vegetables. Salt is crucial for drawing out moisture from the veggies and creating a natural brine, which is vital for the fermentation process.
3. **Massage the Vegetables**
   Gently massage the vegetables by hand for about 5-10 minutes. This action will help extract the natural juices, forming the brine. During this time, the vegetables will soften and release their liquid.
4. **Prepare the Fermentation Crock**
   Once the vegetables are ready, begin placing them into the fermentation crock. After adding each layer, press the vegetables down firmly using a tamper or your hands to remove air pockets and release additional juices. Continue adding until the crock is filled, ensuring to leave around 3 inches of space from the top edge.
5. **Add Weights**
   Position fermentation weights on top of the packed vegetables to guarantee they stay fully submerged in the brine. If you lack specific weights, a clean plate with a heavy object (like a jar filled with water) on top can also be used to keep the veggies submerged.
6. **Cover the Crock**
   Secure the crock with a lid or plate to shield the contents from dust and insects. Alternatively, you can cover it with a clean cloth tied around the edge with string or a rubber band, allowing fermentation gases to escape while keeping the food protected.
7. **Fermentation Process**
   Store the crock in a cool, dark location with a consistent temperature between 18°C and 24°C (65°F - 75°F). The duration of fermentation varies: leafy vegetables like kale may ferment in 1-2 weeks, while root vegetables like carrots can take up to 4 weeks. Warmer temperatures can accelerate the process.
8. **Monitor Fermentation**

Check the crock every few days to ensure the vegetables remain submerged in the brine. If mold develops on the surface, promptly remove it; this is common and harmless as it does not penetrate the brine.
9. **Taste and Store**
After 1-4 weeks, depending on the vegetables and your taste preferences, begin tasting. Once you achieve the desired flavor, transfer the fermented vegetables to clean jars with secure lids. Store them in the refrigerator or a cool, dark space. Fermented vegetables will continue to develop flavor and can be preserved for several months.

Maintenance Recommendations
- Ensure all utensils, containers, and hands are completely clean to prevent contamination.
- The vegetables must remain entirely submerged in the brine to avoid spoilage and maintain the necessary anaerobic conditions for fermentation.
- Regularly inspect for mold or changes in brine levels. Remove any mold immediately to keep the fermentation healthy.
- Store fermented foods in a cool, dark location to maintain their freshness and crunch over time.

Fermenting food in crocks is an ancient, natural technique for preserving food sustainably and healthily. By following these straightforward steps, you can relish fermented vegetables rich in flavor and nutrients while enhancing your food self-sufficiency.

Preserving Meat and Fish with Salt and Sugar

Estimated Cost: $20 - $50
Difficulty Level: Moderate
Time Required: 1-3 weeks

Curing meat and fish with salt or sugar is a time-honored preservation technique that effectively extracts moisture from these foods, inhibiting the growth of bacteria and extending their shelf life. This method not only helps keep food for longer but also enhances its flavor while preserving nutritional content. In this guide, you'll learn various techniques for curing meat and fish, ensuring delicious and enduring results.

Required Materials
1. **Meat or Fish (10-20 pounds):** Choose fresh cuts such as pork belly, beef, or fatty fish like salmon or mackerel. Ensure the quality is high, with no blemishes or discoloration.
2. **Coarse Salt (3-4 pounds):** Use non-iodized salt such as kosher or sea salt to draw out moisture and preserve the food. The salt should comprise about one-third of the total weight of the meat or fish.
3. **Sugar (1-2 pounds, optional):** White or brown sugar can be added to counterbalance the saltiness, particularly effective for bacon or fish. Use roughly 1/4 to 1/2 the amount of salt.
4. **Spices (optional):** Enhance flavor by adding spices like 2-3 tablespoons of ground black pepper, crushed garlic, bay leaves, or dried herbs such as thyme or rosemary.
5. **Airtight Containers:** Select glass, ceramic, or food-safe plastic containers that can hold the food completely covered by the seasoning mixture.
6. **Gauze or Muslin:** These fabrics will be used to wrap the meat or fish, protecting them during the drying phase and allowing for proper air circulation.
7. **Cool, Dry Storage Area:** The best environment for curing is one with a stable temperature of 10-15°C and low humidity, with good ventilation and no direct sunlight.

Steps to Follow
1. **Prepare the Meat or Fish**
Begin by washing the meat or fish (10-20 pounds) with paper towels. Trim away any excess fat or bones that may hinder the curing process. If using whole fish, ensure the innards and scales are removed. Cut the meat into manageable portions if necessary.
2. **Prepare the Seasoning Mixture**
In a large bowl, combine 3-4 pounds of coarse salt with 1-2 pounds of sugar (if included). This will form your basic seasoning mixture. Adjust the spices according to your preferences, adding items like black pepper, garlic, bay leaves, and dried herbs.
3. **Apply the Mixture**

Place the meat or fish on a clean surface and thoroughly coat each piece with the curing mixture, ensuring complete coverage of all surfaces, including crevices and edges. Use about 1/4 inch of mixture per side for even coverage.

4. **Refrigeration and Care**
   After coating, place the food in airtight containers in a single layer. If stacking pieces, intersperse layers of the seasoning mixture. Refrigerate for 1-3 weeks, depending on thickness. Turn the meat or fish every 2-3 days to ensure even curing and drain any accumulated liquid.
5. **Rinsing and Drying**
   Upon completion of the curing process, remove the meat or fish from the containers and rinse them under cold water to eliminate excess salt and curing mixture. Pat dry thoroughly with a clean cloth or absorbent paper. The food should feel firm, indicating successful curing.
6. **Further Maturation**
   Wrap the meat or fish in cheesecloth or muslin to protect them and allow for breathing. The wrapping should be snug yet not overly tight, allowing air circulation. Hang or store the food in a cool, dry, well-ventilated area for an additional 1-2 weeks. This process enhances flavor and improves texture.
7. **Slice and Store**
   After the curing period, remove the cheesecloth or muslin and thinly slice the meat or fish with a sharp knife. Thin slices optimize flavor and texture. Store the slices in airtight containers or vacuum bags and keep them in a cool, dry place or refrigerator for prolonged shelf life.

Maintenance Guidelines
- **Storage Area Inspection:** Ensure the storage area is well-ventilated and clean to prevent moisture or contaminants from accumulating.
- **Monitoring:** Regularly check for signs of spoilage, such as mold or off odors. Discard any compromised food immediately.
- **Hygiene:** Always utilize clean hands and utensils when handling meat or fish throughout the process to avoid contamination.
- **Food Rotation:** Frequently check seasoned foods and use the oldest pieces first to maintain a fresh and safe supply.

By adhering to these guidelines, you'll be able to effectively season meat and fish, preserving and enhancing their flavor for extended periods.

Aquaponic Systems: A Sustainable Food Production Method
Aquaponics is a sustainable approach to food production that integrates aquaculture (fish farming) with hydroponics (growing plants without soil). This system offers a relatively low-cost initial investment and a moderate level of difficulty, making it an effective solution for food sustainability and autonomy. In situations where you may need to remain at home, creating an aquaponic system can guarantee a steady supply of fresh produce while decreasing reliance on external resources.

Understanding Aquaponics

The aquaponic system harnesses the natural nutrient cycle: fish waste is broken down by beneficial bacteria into nutrients that plants can utilize, while the plants filter and purify the water, returning it to the aquatic environment. This closed-loop system significantly reduces water usage and eliminates the need for chemical fertilizers.
- **Estimated Cost:** $200 - $500
- **Difficulty Level:** Moderate
- **Time Required:** 2-4 days

Aquaponics combines aquaculture and hydroponics, allowing for integrated and self-sufficient production of both plants and fish. For our purposes, the focus will be on the plant aspect of the aquaponic system.

Required Materials
1. **Aquarium:** A minimum 50-gallon tank made of food-grade plastic or glass that is durable and non-toxic.
2. **Grow Bed:** A sturdy tray or container with a capacity of 10-15 gallons to hold soil and water.
3. **Water Pump:** A submersible pump with a capacity of 300-500 GPH (gallons per hour) to facilitate water circulation between the aquarium and grow bed.
4. **Pipes and Fittings:** Approximately 10 feet of 1/2 inch PVC pipe for water flow and 5 feet of 1 inch pipe for drainage, along with various fittings (elbows, tees, connectors).

5. **Growing Medium:** About 50 liters of expanded clay, gravel, or another inert material to support plant roots and filter water.
6. **Plants:** 10-15 seedlings (e.g., lettuce, herbs, tomatoes) suitable for aquaponic systems.
7. **Air Pump and Air Stones:** An air pump equipped with two air stones to enhance aeration, particularly in larger systems.

Construction Steps
1. **Select the Location:** Choose a spot with sufficient natural or artificial light for the plants. Ensure the area has a stable temperature and good ventilation, and that the surface can support the weight of the filled aquarium and grow bed.
2. **Set Up the Aquarium:** Position the aquarium in the designated area, fill it with water, and allow it to sit for 24 hours to dissipate any chlorine.
3. **Install the Water Pump:** Place the submersible pump in the aquarium and connect it to the grow bed using the 1/2 inch PVC pipe. The pump should be powerful enough to ensure adequate water circulation.
4. **Prepare the Grow Bed:** Set the grow bed on top of the aquarium and fill it with the growing medium. This inert material will support the plants while acting as a biological filter for the water. Ensure the structure is sturdy enough to handle the weight of the filled bed.
5. **Create the Water Flow System:** Install the PVC pipes and fittings to establish proper water circulation. You can implement a bell siphon or a continuous flow flood and drain system. Confirm that there are no leaks and that water flows freely between the aquarium and the grow bed.
6. **Plant in the Grow Bed:** Insert the seedlings into the grow bed, selecting varieties appropriate for aquaponics, such as lettuce, spinach, basil, or tomatoes. Space the plants adequately for optimal growth and light access.
7. **Monitor and Adjust:** Use a water quality test kit to monitor pH levels (ideal range: 6.8-7.0), ammonia, nitrites, and nitrates. Adjust water parameters as necessary to maintain optimal conditions, and keep a log of the results to track system health.
8. **Aeration (Optional):** If required, utilize an air pump and air stones to enhance oxygenation, promoting plant growth. Position the stones strategically for even oxygen distribution.
9. **Maintain the System:** Regularly inspect the pump, hoses, and grow bed to prevent clogs.

Maintenance Guidelines
- **Regular Water Changes:** Perform partial water changes of 10-20% every 2-4 weeks to maintain system balance.
- **Health Checks:** Inspect plants for diseases or pests and remove any infected specimens.
- **Pruning and Harvesting:** Regularly trim plants to prevent overcrowding and ensure adequate airflow and light penetration.
- **System Cleaning:** Periodically clean the pump and tubing to prevent algae buildup and maintain efficient water flow.
- **Temperature Monitoring:** Keep track of water temperature, adjusting with heaters or chillers as necessary.

By following these guidelines, you can successfully create and sustain an aquaponic system that provides you with fresh and sustainable food over the long term.

Maintaining Your Aquaponic System
1. **Monitor Water Quality:**
    - Regularly test for pH, ammonia, nitrite, and nitrate levels.
    - Keep pH between 6.8 and 7.2 to promote the health of both fish and plants.
2. **Fish Nutrition:**
    - Feed fish the appropriate amount of food, avoiding overfeeding to prevent water contamination.
3. **Plant Pruning:**
    - Remove any dead or diseased leaves to stop the spread of illness and encourage healthy growth.
4. **System Cleaning:**
    - Regularly clear out debris from the tank and plant containers.
    - Replace water as needed while maintaining recirculation.

Helpful Tips for Emergency Situations
- **Recycled Materials:** Use plastic containers, bottles, and reclaimed materials to minimize the need for new purchases.

- **Electrical Needs:** If electricity is limited, consider using energy-efficient pumps or manual systems for water recirculation.
- **Water Sources:** Use potable water from home, avoiding stagnant or contaminated sources.
- **Adaptability:** Stay flexible in emergencies, adapting the system as resources allow.
- **Fish Protection:** Safeguard the tank from potential domestic predators or extreme conditions (excessive light or extreme temperatures).

Benefits of Aquaponics in Emergencies
- **Food Self-Sufficiency:** Provides a continuous supply of protein (fish) and fresh vegetables.
- **Waste Reduction:** Utilizes organic fish waste as natural fertilizer.
- **Water Efficiency:** Employs minimal water through continuous recirculation.
- **Ease of Management:** Once established, the system requires minimal ongoing maintenance.

Potential Challenges and Solutions
- **System Balancing:** Initially, it may be challenging to maintain balance among fish, bacteria, and plants. Monitor carefully and adjust as needed.
- **Fish Health:** Ensure good water quality and avoid overcrowding the tank.
- **Plant Growth:** Make certain plants receive adequate light and nutrients.

By following these steps, you'll be equipped to establish and manage an effective aquaponic system, providing you with fresh, sustainable food.

1. Leafy Greens
Leafy greens are among the simplest crops to cultivate in an indoor aquaponics setup, as they require minimal space and grow rapidly.
- **Lettuce**
- **Spinach**
- **Arugula**
- **Kale**
- **Swiss Chard**
- **Watercress**

2. Culinary Herbs
Herbs thrive exceptionally well in aquaponic systems and are easy to grow.
- **Basil**
- **Parsley**
- **Mint**
- **Cilantro**
- **Chives**
- **Rosemary** (note that it requires a bit more space)

3. Fruiting Vegetables
Certain fruiting vegetables can flourish in aquaponics but may need additional care regarding space and light.
- **Tomatoes** (preferably dwarf or determinate types)
- **Peppers** (both sweet and spicy)
- **Zucchini** (selecting compact varieties)
- **Cucumbers** (opt for dwarf or compact types)

4. Legumes
- **Green Beans**
- **Peas**

5. Root Vegetables (With Care)
Root vegetables can also be grown in aquaponics; however, it's crucial to ensure the substrate is suitable for proper root development.
- **Radishes**
- **Carrots** (dwarf varieties)
- **Beets**

6. Additional Plants
- **Cauliflower and Broccoli** (these require more space and may grow slowly)
- **Green Onions**

Important Considerations
- **Lighting:** Providing high-quality artificial light, such as specialized LED grow lights, is vital to compensate for the lack of natural sunlight indoors.
- **Space:** Quick-growing, compact vegetables like lettuce and herbs are most suited for limited spaces.
- **Nutrients:** Aquaponic plants rely on fish waste for nutrients, so careful management of the fish-to-plant ratio is necessary.

With proper management, an indoor aquaponics system can yield a diverse range of fresh vegetables throughout the year.

H.O.S. Recipes

Here are some easy-to-make recipes that utilize cooking methods suitable for emergency situations, featuring simple and preserved ingredients:

Solar-Cooked Beef Jerky with Lettuce and Arugula

Ingredients:
- 50 g of dried beef
- 50 g of fresh lettuce (about 3-4 large leaves)
- 30 g of fresh arugula
- 1 tablespoon of extra virgin olive oil
- 1 tablespoon of fresh lemon juice
- A pinch of salt (optional)
- A pinch of black pepper (optional)

Instructions:
1. **Prepare the Beef:** Cut the dried beef into thin strips for easier tenderizing. Arrange them on a plate.
2. **Prepare the Vegetables:** Wash and dry the lettuce and arugula. Place the whole lettuce leaves on the plate and top with the arugula.
3. **Make the Dressing:** In a small bowl, combine the olive oil and lemon juice. Season with a pinch of salt and pepper if desired.
4. **Solar Cooking:**
   - If you have a solar oven or a similar device, place the dish inside and allow the beef to soften while the vegetables warm slightly for about 20 to 30 minutes, depending on sunlight and oven strength.
   - If you lack a solar oven, cover the dish and leave it outdoors in the sun, monitoring to prevent overheating.
5. **Assemble and Serve:** Once the beef is softened and the vegetables are warmed through, drizzle the lemon-oil dressing on top. Serve immediately.

This dish is light, nutritious, and perfect for sustainable cooking in various situations.

Dried Salmon with Spinach and Watercress, Served with Yogurt and Mint Sauce

Ingredients:
- 50 g of dried salmon
- 40 g of fresh spinach (about a handful)
- 20 g of fresh watercress (about half a handful)
- 2 tablespoons of plain Greek yogurt
- 4-5 fresh mint leaves, chopped
- 1 tablespoon of fresh lemon juice
- 1 teaspoon of extra virgin olive oil
- A pinch of salt (optional)
- A pinch of black pepper (optional)

Instructions:
1. **Prepare the Salmon:** Cut the dried salmon into small pieces or thin strips and arrange on a plate.

2. **Prepare the Vegetables:** Wash and dry the spinach and watercress. Arrange them on a plate, creating a base with the spinach and topping with the watercress.
3. **Make the Sauce:**
   - In a small bowl, combine the Greek yogurt with lemon juice, chopped mint leaves, olive oil, and a pinch of salt and pepper. Mix until smooth and creamy.
4. **Solar Cooking:**
   - If you have a solar oven, place the plate with the dried salmon, spinach, and watercress inside to heat slightly for 20-30 minutes, ensuring the salmon softens and the vegetables warm without wilting.
   - Alternatively, if you lack a solar oven, set the dish outdoors under a clear cover to heat naturally.
5. **Assemble and Serve:** Once the salmon has softened and the vegetables are warm, pour the yogurt-mint sauce over the dish. Serve immediately for the best fresh and delicate flavors.

This dish is refreshing, light, and bursting with flavor, making it ideal for a quick and healthy meal!

Stuffed Zucchini with Dried Beef Cooked in a Solar Oven

Ingredients:
- 1 medium zucchini
- 40 g of dried beef, chopped into small pieces
- 1 tablespoon of fresh parsley, chopped
- 1 tablespoon of fresh basil, chopped
- 1 tablespoon of extra virgin olive oil
- 1 tablespoon of breadcrumbs (optional, for added crunch)
- 1 teaspoon of fresh lemon juice
- A pinch of salt (optional)
- A pinch of black pepper (optional)

Instructions:
1. **Prepare the Zucchini:**
   - Wash the zucchini and cut it in half lengthwise. Use a teaspoon to gently hollow out the inside, creating a boat.
   - Set aside the zucchini pulp to incorporate into the filling.
2. **Prepare the Filling:**
   - In a bowl, combine the shredded dried beef, chopped zucchini pulp, parsley, basil, olive oil, breadcrumbs (if using), lemon juice, and season with salt and pepper to taste. Mix all the ingredients well.
3. **Stuff the Zucchini:**
   - Fill the hollowed zucchinis with the prepared mixture, pressing lightly to ensure it is well packed.
4. **Solar Cooking:**
   - Place the stuffed zucchinis on a baking tray or heatproof plate.
   - Position the tray in the solar oven and let it cook for about 1-2 hours, until the zucchinis are tender and the filling is well integrated.
   - Cooking times may vary based on sunlight intensity and the type of solar oven used. Check for doneness after about an hour.
5. **Serve:**
   - Once the zucchinis are thoroughly cooked, remove them from the solar oven and allow them to cool slightly before serving.

This simple yet delicious recipe is perfect for a light, nutritious meal, utilizing solar energy for cooking

---

Light Vegetable and Dried Salmon Soup Heated with Candles

Ingredients:
- 30 g of dried salmon, chopped into small pieces
- 250 ml of vegetable broth (homemade or store-bought)
- 30 g of fresh spinach (approximately a handful)
- 20 g of fresh arugula

- 1 tablespoon of extra virgin olive oil
- 1 clove of garlic, minced
- A pinch of salt (optional)
- A pinch of black pepper (optional)

Instructions:
1. **Prepare the Broth:**
   - In a small saucepan, combine the vegetable broth with a tablespoon of olive oil and the minced garlic.
   - Bring the mixture to a boil, then lower the heat and let it simmer for a few minutes to allow the garlic to infuse its flavor.
2. **Add the Vegetables:**
   - Stir in the spinach and arugula, allowing the broth to simmer for about 2-3 minutes until the greens soften slightly.
3. **Incorporate the Dried Salmon:**
   - Add the pieces of dried salmon to the broth and vegetables.
   - Mix thoroughly and let everything warm together for about 5-10 minutes over low heat, utilizing the candle oven to maintain a gentle and consistent temperature. The salmon will gradually rehydrate.
4. **Adjust Seasoning:**
   - Taste the soup and, if needed, season with a pinch of salt and black pepper according to your preference.
5. **Serve:**
   - Once the salmon is adequately softened and the broth has absorbed the flavors of the vegetables, ladle the soup into bowls and serve hot.

This light and nutritious soup, featuring the delicate taste of dried salmon and the freshness of greens, makes for a healthy and simple meal.

Dried Chicken and Lettuce Heated in a Candle Oven

Ingredients:
- 50 g of dried chicken, sliced into thin strips
- 60 g of fresh lettuce (about 3-4 large leaves)
- 1 tablespoon of toasted pumpkin seeds
- 1 tablespoon of extra virgin olive oil
- 1 teaspoon of fresh lemon juice
- A pinch of salt (optional)
- A pinch of black pepper (optional)

Instructions:
1. **Prepare the Chicken:**
   - Slice the dried chicken into thin strips for easier reheating. Place these strips on a heatproof plate.
2. **Reheat the Chicken:**
   - Use a candle oven to warm the dried chicken. Position the dish over the candle and allow it to heat slowly for approximately 15-20 minutes, stirring occasionally to ensure even heating. The gentle heat will soften the chicken while enhancing its flavor.
3. **Prepare the Lettuce:**
   - Wash and dry the lettuce leaves, arranging them on a serving plate.
   - In a separate pan, lightly toast the pumpkin seeds over low heat for a few minutes until they are golden and crunchy.
4. **Assemble the Plate:**
   - Once the dried chicken is warm and slightly softened, place it on top of the fresh lettuce leaves.
   - Sprinkle the toasted pumpkin seeds over the dish for added crunch.
5. **Season the Dish:**
   - In a small bowl, whisk together the olive oil and lemon juice. Season with a pinch of salt and pepper to taste.
   - Drizzle the dressing over the chicken and lettuce.
6. **Serve:**
   - Serve the dish warm, featuring the slightly heated chicken, the fresh crunch of lettuce, and the delightful texture of the toasted pumpkin seeds.

This meal is light yet satisfying, perfect for a quick and nutritious option, showcasing the contrast between the tender dried chicken and the fresh vegetables.

Lettuce boats with beef jerky, gently warmed with candles:

Ingredients:
- 50g dried beef, cut into small pieces
- 3-4 large lettuce leaves (to make boats)
- 30 g of fresh rocket
- 20 g cherry tomatoes, cut into cubes
- 1 tablespoon extra virgin olive oil
- 1 teaspoon fresh lemon juice
- A pinch of salt (optional)
- A pinch of black pepper (optional)

Procedure:
1. Preparation of beef jerky:
   - Cut the dried beef into small pieces or thin strips, to make it easier to stuff the lettuce boats.
2. Preparation of vegetables:
   - Wash and dry the lettuce leaves and rocket.
   - Cut the cherry tomatoes into small cubes.
   - Mix together the arugula and cherry tomatoes in a bowl with a pinch of salt and pepper.
3. Assembling the boats:
   - Arrange the lettuce leaves on a plate, so that they form small "boats".
   - Fill each lettuce leaf with a portion of beef jerky, and add the arugula and cherry tomato mixture on top.
4. Heating with candles:
   - Place the plate with the lettuce boats over a candle oven to gently heat everything, without letting the lettuce leaves wilt. Let heat for 10-15 minutes to blend the flavors and tenderize the beef slightly.
5. Seasoning:
   - In a small bowl, mix the olive oil with the lemon juice.
   - Pour the dressing over the lettuce boats with the beef and vegetables.
6. Serve:
   - Serve the reheated lettuce boats immediately, enjoying the contrast between the crunch of the lettuce and the tenderness of the dried beef.

This dish is light, fresh and full of flavor, perfect for a healthy and easy to prepare meal.

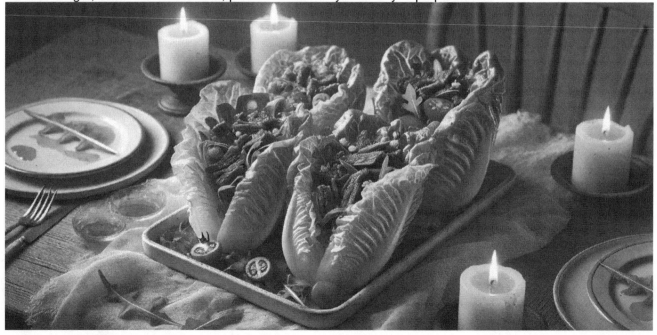

Zucchini stuffed with dried turkey cooked slowly underground:

Ingredients:
- 1 medium courgette
- 40 g dried turkey, cut into small pieces
- 1 tablespoon chopped onion (optional)
- 1 tablespoon chopped fresh parsley
- 1 tablespoon extra virgin olive oil
- 1 teaspoon fresh lemon juice
- A pinch of salt (optional)
- A pinch of black pepper (optional)
- 1 tablespoon breadcrumbs (optional, to add crunch)

Procedure:
1. Preparation of the courgettes:
   - Wash the courgette and cut it in half lengthwise. With a teaspoon, delicately empty the inside of the courgette, leaving an edge of about 1 cm to form a boat.
   - Keep the internal pulp of the courgette aside, finely chopped, to add to the filling.
2. Preparation of the filling:
   - In a bowl, mix the chopped turkey jerky, chopped zucchini pulp, fresh parsley, chopped onion (if using), olive oil, and lemon juice.
   - Add a pinch of salt and pepper to taste.
   - If you want to give a crunchier texture, you can add breadcrumbs to the mixture.
3. Filling the courgettes:
   - Fill the two halves of the emptied courgette with the prepared filling. Press the mixture lightly to fill the spaces well.
4. Cooking in the earthen oven:
   - Dig a hole in the ground and heat some stones until they are red hot.
   - Cover the stuffed courgettes with heat-resistant leaves or aluminum foil, and place them on top of the hot stones.
   - Cover everything with earth to keep the heat in and cook slowly for about 1-2 hours, depending on the temperature of the stones and the depth of the hole.
5. Serve:
   - Once cooked, remove the courgettes from the earthen oven and let them cool slightly before serving.
   - Serve the stuffed courgettes with a drizzle of raw olive oil on top, if desired.

This rustic and nutritious dish uses traditional earthen oven cooking to bring out the natural flavors of turkey jerky and courgettes.

Beef dried in chard leaves, slow cooked in an earth oven:

Ingredients:
- 50g dried beef, cut into strips
- 2-3 large chard leaves
- 1 tablespoon extra virgin olive oil
- 1 clove garlic, finely chopped
- 1 teaspoon fresh lemon juice
- A pinch of salt (optional)
- A pinch of black pepper (optional)

Procedure:
1. Preparation of the beef:
   - Cut the beef jerky into thin strips, so that it is easier to wrap it in the chard leaves.
2. Preparation of the chard leaves:
   - Wash the chard leaves well and dry them gently. If the leaves have very thick stems, cut off part of the stems, leaving only the tender portion of the leaves.
3. Preparation of the filling:
   - In a small bowl, mix the beef jerky with the minced garlic, a tablespoon of olive oil, a pinch of salt and pepper, and the lemon juice.
   - Let the beef season for a few minutes.
4. Winding:
   - Take a chard leaf and place a portion of the seasoned beef jerky in the center.
   - Wrap the beef in the leaves, folding the sides inward and rolling up, forming a tight package. Repeat with the remaining chard leaves and remaining beef.
5. Cooking in the earthen oven:
   - Prepare an earth oven by digging a hole in the ground and heating stones until they are red hot.
   - Wrap the chard and beef packets in sturdy leaves or aluminum foil, and place them on top of the hot stones in the earthen oven.
   - Cover everything with soil to keep the heat in and cook slowly for about 1-2 hours, until the chard leaves are tender and the beef is well seasoned.
6. Serve:
   - Once cooked, remove the chard packets from the earthen oven, remove the outer wrapping (if you used extra leaves or foil), and serve hot.

This dish enhances the flavors of the dried beef thanks to the slow cooking under ground, which allows the chard leaves to become soft and full of flavor, making the dish rustic and delicious.

Hearty Stew of Dried Meat and Vegetables Cooked in an Earthen Oven

Ingredients:
- 50 g of dried beef, chopped into small pieces
- 1 medium zucchini, sliced into rounds
- 2 large Swiss chard leaves, cut into strips
- 1 small potato, peeled and diced (optional)
- 1/4 onion, finely chopped
- 1 clove of garlic, minced
- 1 tablespoon of extra virgin olive oil
- 250 ml of vegetable broth or water
- 1 teaspoon of fresh lemon juice
- A pinch of salt (optional)
- A pinch of black pepper (optional)
- 1 sprig of rosemary or thyme (optional, for added flavor)

Instructions:
1. **Prepare the Vegetables:**
   - Wash the zucchini and slice it into rounds.
   - Rinse the Swiss chard leaves and slice them into strips.
   - Peel and dice the potato (if using).

- Finely chop the onion and garlic.
2. **Prepare the Beef:**
    - Chop the dried beef into small pieces. If it's very dry, you can soak it in warm water for 10-15 minutes to soften it slightly (optional).
3. **Assemble the Stew:**
    - In a large mixing bowl, combine the beef, zucchini, Swiss chard, potato (if using), onion, and garlic.
    - Drizzle with olive oil and season with salt, pepper, and lemon juice.
    - Add a sprig of rosemary or thyme if desired for additional flavor.
    - Pour in the vegetable broth or water until the ingredients are just covered.
4. **Cooking in the Earthen Oven:**
    - Prepare the earthen oven by digging a hole in the ground and heating stones until they glow red.
    - Transfer the stew to a heatproof container (like a clay pot or covered aluminum container) and place it on the hot stones.
    - Cover the container with sturdy leaves or aluminum foil, then bury it with soil to retain heat.
    - Allow the stew to cook slowly for about 2-3 hours to blend the flavors and tenderize the ingredients.
5. **Serve:**
    - Once the cooking time is up, carefully remove the container from the earthen oven. Check that the vegetables and beef are tender.
    - Serve the stew hot in a bowl, possibly drizzling with raw olive oil on top.

This rustic stew, cooked underground, enhances the natural flavors of dried meat and fresh vegetables, resulting in a nutritious and delicious dish perfect for those who appreciate traditional and sustainable cooking methods.

Smoked Meat with Green Onions

Ingredients:
- 100 g of smoked meat (beef, pork, or turkey, based on preference)
- 2 green onions (also known as spring onions)
- 1 tablespoon of extra virgin olive oil
- 1 teaspoon of fresh lemon juice (optional)
- A pinch of salt (optional, based on the flavor of the smoked meat)
- A pinch of freshly ground black pepper
- 1 teaspoon of mustard (optional, for serving)

Cooking Method:

Cooking in a Solar Oven:
1. **Prepare the Ingredients:**
    - Slice the smoked meat into thin strips or cubes according to your preference.
    - Wash the green onions and slice them.
2. **Assemble for Cooking:**
    - In a solar cooking pan, pour a tablespoon of olive oil.
    - Add the green onions and smoked meat to the pan. Gently stir to coat the ingredients with the oil.
    - Cover the pan with a lid or clear foil to trap heat and accelerate the cooking process.
3. **Cooking:**
    - Place the dish in the solar oven and let it cook for about 1-2 hours, checking every 30 minutes to ensure the onions soften and the meat warms through.
    - Cooking time may vary based on solar oven power and sunlight conditions, so monitor to avoid drying out the ingredients.
4. **Season and Serve:**
    - Once the meat and onions are fully cooked, drizzle with a little lemon juice (if desired) and season with salt and pepper.
    - Serve immediately, with mustard on the side if preferred.

Cooking on a Charcoal Grill:

1. **Prepare the Grill:**
   - Ignite the charcoal grill and let the coals heat up to medium-low. If possible, use a grill with a lid for more even, slower cooking.
2. **Prepare the Ingredients:**
   - Slice the smoked meat and green onions as described earlier.
3. **Cooking:**
   - Set a cast iron skillet or heavy pan on the charcoal grill.
   - Add a tablespoon of olive oil to the pan and allow it to warm slightly.
   - Add the green onions and smoked meat to the pan and cook for 10-15 minutes, stirring occasionally until the onions caramelize and the meat is heated through.
   - If necessary, cover the grill with the lid to retain heat for more even cooking.
4. **Season and Serve:**
   - Add lemon juice, season with salt and pepper, and serve hot with a hint of mustard on the side.

This dish combines the rich flavors of smoked meat with fresh green onions, offering a satisfying and quick meal.

Weekly Meal Plan

Monday
- Lunch:
  - **Solar-Cooked Beef Jerky with Greens**
    - Dried beef paired with lettuce and arugula, lightly warmed under the sun and drizzled with olive oil and lemon juice.
- Dinner:
  - **Stuffed Zucchini with Dried Beef**
    - Zucchini filled with a mixture of dried beef, parsley, and basil, slow-cooked in a solar oven.

Tuesday
- Lunch:
  - **Dried Salmon with Spinach and Watercress**
    - Spinach and watercress served with dried salmon, topped with a yogurt sauce infused with mint and lemon.
- Dinner:
  - **Vegetable and Dried Salmon Soup**
    - A hearty soup made from vegetable broth, featuring dried salmon, spinach, and arugula, warmed by candlelight.

Wednesday
- Lunch:
  - **Lettuce Wraps with Beef Jerky**
    - Lettuce leaves filled with dried beef, arugula, and cherry tomatoes, gently warmed with candle heat and drizzled with oil and lemon.
- Dinner:
  - **Candle-Cooked Dried Chicken with Lettuce**
    - A dish of dried chicken served on a bed of lettuce, topped with toasted pumpkin seeds and a light lemon dressing.

Thursday
- Lunch:
  - **Zucchini Boats with Dried Turkey**
    - Zucchini stuffed with a mixture of dried turkey, onion, parsley, and breadcrumbs, traditionally slow-cooked underground.

- **Dinner:**
  - **Smoked Meat with Green Onions**
    - Smoked meat served with spring onions, prepared in a solar oven and drizzled with olive oil.

Friday
- **Lunch:**
  - **Rustic Dried Meat Stew**
    - A hearty stew of dried beef combined with zucchini, chard, and potatoes, cooked in an earthen oven.
- **Dinner:**
  - **Beef Wrapped in Chard Leaves**
    - Dried beef enveloped in chard leaves, seasoned with garlic and olive oil, and slow-cooked underground.

Saturday
- **Lunch:**
  - **Dried Salmon with Spinach**
    - Fresh spinach accompanied by dried salmon, served with a refreshing mint Greek yogurt sauce.
- **Dinner:**
  - **Stuffed Zucchini with Dried Beef**
    - Zucchini filled with a mix of dried beef, parsley, and basil, cooked to perfection in a solar oven.

Sunday
- **Lunch:**
  - **Solar-Cooked Beef Jerky with Greens**
    - Dried beef served with lettuce and arugula, dressed with olive oil and lemon juice.
- **Dinner:**
  - **Light Vegetable and Dried Salmon Soup**
    - A delicate soup made from vegetable broth, featuring dried salmon, spinach, and arugula, warmed with candles.

CHAPTER 3:

FUTURE PLANS: UNDERSTANDING THE IMPORTANCE OF WATER IN CRISIS SITUATIONS

The Critical Role of Water During System Failures

In the event of a widespread power outage impacting millions, water supplies can be rapidly disrupted. We often take for granted the systems that deliver water to our homes—timers, valves, pumps, and distribution stations. If these components fail to maintain sufficient pressure, water flow will cease. Humans can typically survive for only about three days without water, making it imperative to secure its availability during emergencies.

Water is such a vital resource that, in our modern lives, we often neglect to appreciate its value. With a simple turn of a tap, we access clean water, readily available in stores. For many, access to water has never posed a significant challenge. However, during emergencies—be it natural disasters, infrastructure failures, or a choice to live off the grid—securing a reliable supply of clean water becomes crucial. This chapter will explore this essential issue, providing you with projects and guidelines to help ensure a sufficient water supply in all situations, allowing for independence from modern distribution systems.

It's vital to recognize that your water needs may exceed your initial expectations. Water scarcity can deeply affect individuals and communities psychologically. Those in regions experiencing water shortages often suffer stress and anxiety due to their inability to access clean water for basic necessities. Research published in *Environmental Research Letters* indicates that water scarcity can contribute to the rise of mental health disorders, including anxiety and depression. Uncertainty regarding access to clean water can instill fear and worsen existing social disparities. Acknowledging the psychological impact of water shortages on mental health underscores the necessity of prioritizing water security and implementing proactive strategies to mitigate these challenges.

Beyond drinking, water is essential for personal hygiene, dishwashing, laundry, and cooking. While our book has previously examined short-term water needs, a prolonged crisis necessitates planning for 20 to 30 liters of water per person each month. It's prudent to lean towards the higher estimate. For instance, a family of four would require approximately 360 liters of water to survive for three months. Thus, careful planning for storage is critical; however, detailed guidance will follow soon.

Preparations Prior to a Crisis

Similar to how you can prepare your home for extreme temperatures, you can also prepare for scenarios that might leave you without water. If you maintain a garden, you likely already collect rainwater. However, even if you don't have a garden, rainwater collection is beneficial for various reasons. If the collected water is to be safe for drinking, purification is essential (a topic we will cover later in this chapter), but some household tasks, like flushing toilets, do not necessitate potable water.

To collect rainwater effectively, five key components are required: a collection surface (like a roof), a system for directing water to the collection area (gutters and downspouts), a filter to remove debris, a container with a lid for storage, and a spout for dispensing the water. The spout should be located near the bottom of the tank and ideally include a diversion system for excess water (many opt for a hose connected to a reserve tank). The good news is that if installed well in advance, complete systems can be purchased at garden or hardware stores.

Another preparatory step is to stockpile water in bottles. This reserve will only be useful for a limited time, so it is advisable to store enough for the initial two weeks of an emergency. Keep water in a cool, dry place, shielded from direct sunlight and away from concrete floors or walls, which can leach chemicals into the water. To prevent leaks, avoid stacking containers too high, and regularly rotate your supply to ensure the water remains in good condition, as single-use plastic can degrade over time. While it might be tempting to reuse old tap water bottles, keep in mind that containers for juice, milk, soda, and water are not designed for repeated use and may release harmful chemicals into the water upon refilling.

Ensuring Water Security at Home

When discussing home security, we often think of alarm systems, strong locks, and outdoor lighting. However, a critical yet frequently overlooked aspect is water safety. Ensuring your home has a reliable, clean water source is vital for safeguarding your family's health and well-being. Water is essential for life; without a dependable and safe supply, every other element of home security loses its significance.

The first consideration is the quality of water supplied to your home. Even in areas served by a public water system, it's important to recognize that contamination can occur during transit. Installing a filtration system is a crucial step to eliminate impurities, such as chlorine, lead, and other heavy metals. Activated carbon and reverse osmosis filters are excellent choices, each offering specific benefits. While activated carbon filters effectively remove organic contaminants and chlorine, reverse osmosis provides broader protection, eliminating even the tiniest particles.

Another vital component of water security involves safeguarding supplies during emergencies or natural disasters. When the water supply may be disrupted, having a reserve of drinking water is essential. Ensure that you maintain at least three days' worth of water for each family member, estimating around four liters per person per day. This supply should be stored in safe containers, away from heat and light sources, and regularly checked to ensure its freshness. Investing in emergency tanks or portable purification solutions can make a significant difference during critical situations.

Preventing flooding and water damage inside your home is also essential. Installing leak detectors and automatic shutoff systems can avert extensive damage to your property and preserve water quality. These systems can identify small leaks that might otherwise go unnoticed but could compromise your home's structural integrity and living conditions over time.

Finally, it's essential not to underestimate the importance of educating family members about water safety practices. Teaching both children and adults the significance of conserving water, promptly reporting leaks or anomalies, and understanding proper procedures for purifying and preserving water is crucial for effectively managing any emergencies. Ensuring access to safe water at home is not merely a matter of prevention but a fundamental responsibility to protect the health and lives of your household. Every precaution taken to ensure that the water entering your home is clean, safe, and readily available reinforces the foundation of home security. There is no room for error regarding your family's health, making water safety a top priority.

Assessment of Household Water Requirements

Understanding Water Management for Home Security

Water management is a crucial aspect of home security. To ensure a dependable water supply, it's essential to plan carefully and comprehend your family's specific needs. Start by evaluating your daily water consumption. Each individual requires a certain amount of water for drinking, personal hygiene, meal preparation, and cleaning. By knowing your average daily water requirement, you can better estimate the amount needed to handle emergencies or supply disruptions. In critical scenarios, such as natural disasters or system failures, having an ample water supply can mean the difference between preparedness and crisis.

Proper water conservation is key; it involves not just having water on hand but also storing it correctly, considering the duration and conditions of storage. Additionally, the unique needs of your household must be assessed. If you have a garden or an irrigation system, or if you use water for heating, these factors will affect your total water requirements. Each home is different, and the evaluation of water needs should be tailored to your specific situation. Regular monitoring of consumption and adjusting reserves is essential to ensure you are never caught off guard.

Infrastructure is vital to effective water management. Well-maintained plumbing, storage tanks, and routine maintenance are crucial for keeping water clean and accessible. Neglecting these aspects can lead to issues like contamination or leaks, compromising the safety of your entire water supply.

Planning and Managing Water Needs

Assessing and managing your home's water requirements necessitates a proactive mindset, leaving no room for oversight. Thoughtful planning and constant readiness will ensure your water supply is sufficient and readily accessible, providing security and peace of mind during emergencies. Remember the fundamental guideline: 1 liter per person per day.

To calculate your family's water needs, you can use the following formula:

Water Requirement = (1 gallon) x (number of people) x (number of days)
This approach will cover your family's needs for drinking and sanitation, but you should also account for water required for cooking and pets. As a general guideline, dogs need approximately 1 ounce of water per pound of body weight daily. Additionally, consider your regional climate; living in hotter areas will necessitate greater water consumption.

Calculating Your Requirements
- **Basic Needs**: Allow 2 liters for drinking and about 2 liters for meal preparation and other necessities. This figure may increase during emergencies.
- **Adjustments for Specific Conditions**: In warmer climates or during strenuous activities, hydration needs may be elevated. It's beneficial to increase your daily estimate according to specific conditions.

Strategic Resource Planning
Effective water resource planning involves calculating not only daily needs but also the duration of the necessary water reserve. For optimal preparedness, aim for a supply sufficient for at least a week.

Inventory Management:
- **Long-Term Estimates**: Calculate the total water needed for the anticipated emergency duration. For a family of four over a week, the reserve should total approximately 112 liters (4 liters x 4 people x 7 days).
- **Monitoring and Refilling**: Regularly check your inventory and plan periodic restocks to maintain adequate reserves.

Solutions for Safe Water Conservation

Regardless of your level of preparedness, neglecting to establish a comprehensive plan for a reliable water supply can turn an emergency into a major crisis. Water is essential for daily survival, health, and hygiene, especially in challenging circumstances. Therefore, developing a robust and dependable storage system is vital for managing unforeseen events.

The first step is to select appropriate water containers. Opt for high-quality, food-safe materials that offer durability. Food-grade polyethylene is an excellent option, known for its strength, lightweight nature, and ability to prevent chemical leaching. Additionally, consider the size of your containers, planning for both immediate needs and extended supplies that could last days or weeks during emergencies.

Container placement is equally important. Store them in a cool, dry location, shielded from direct sunlight to minimize the risk of bacterial growth and extend the water's shelf life. However, merely storing water isn't sufficient. Implementing a rotation system is crucial for ensuring water safety. Regularly inspect containers, confirming they are properly sealed, and replace the water periodically to keep it fresh and safe for consumption.

Accessibility during emergencies is vital. Water reserves should be easily reachable and transportable when needed. An effective emergency plan includes clearly defined routes to water supplies.

Furthermore, consider alternative purification methods, such as portable filters, disinfectant tablets, or gravity systems. These tools are essential for rendering potentially unsafe water sources drinkable, thus protecting your family's health even in extreme conditions.

Effective water management requires meticulous planning and attention to detail. Each element must be evaluated carefully, as any oversight can have significant repercussions during water shortages. Your home should be a secure refuge, where exceptional water management ensures readiness for any challenge. Prioritizing water safety entails ongoing vigilance, thoughtful planning, and a steadfast commitment to resource maintenance.

Securing a Consistent Water Source

In the context of emergency preparedness and complex operations, securing access to a reliable water source is paramount. Water is essential not only for survival but also for maintaining operational efficiency and mental and physical well-being. Ensuring a safe, consistent water supply requires a thorough evaluation of available sources and the necessary measures to keep water free from contaminants.

The first step is to identify water sources that can meet your daily needs. If you live in an area with ample rainfall, rainwater harvesting may be an ideal solution, providing a renewable and sustainable source of fresh water. Setting up a rainwater collection system is relatively straightforward and can be tailored to your family's requirements. This method not only conserves water but also decreases reliance on external sources. If you're near a natural water body, such as a river, stream, or lake, these sources can provide a steady water supply. However, it's crucial to treat and purify water before use, as natural sources can be contaminated by wildlife and environmental factors. In the following section, we'll explore various filtering and purification techniques to ensure that the collected water is safe for consumption.

But what if you lack access to a reliable water source? There are innovative alternatives to consider. Extracting groundwater through wells can be a feasible option if the aquifer is reachable. We will discuss how to locate, dig, and maintain a well to ensure a consistent groundwater supply. For those in arid regions, capturing moisture from the air through solar stills or dew collectors can yield significant amounts of water, turning seemingly barren areas into vital resources. This section will present a variety of projects aimed at helping you secure a dependable water supply for all your essential needs, including drinking, cooking, cleaning, and personal hygiene. We will cover practical and cost-effective solutions tailored to different environments and requirements, assisting you in selecting the best approach for your specific situation and budget. Remember, having a consistent and safe water supply is not just about survival; it's about thriving in your self-sufficient lifestyle.

Identifying Water Sources

1.1 Public Water Supplies
Public water supplies, including those provided by municipal aqueducts, undergo treatment and testing to meet the safety and quality standards set by health authorities. However, these systems can encounter issues. Aging pipes, contamination during transport, and failures in treatment facilities can all jeopardize water quality.

Preventive Measures and Monitoring:
- **Regular Testing:** Conduct routine tests to check for contaminants. Utilize certified laboratories to assess parameters like chlorine levels, heavy metals, and bacteria.
- **Quality Surveillance:** Implement continuous monitoring systems to detect real-time changes in water quality. These systems can issue immediate alerts in case of contamination.

1.2 Private Wells
Water from private wells is a crucial resource in areas without public aqueduct access. The quality of well water can vary based on well depth, soil composition, and local activities. Regular testing and maintenance of wells are essential to ensure the water remains potable.

Well Management:
- **Inspection and Maintenance:** Carry out regular inspections of well pipes and pumps. Preventive upkeep can avert contamination and ensure proper functioning.
- **Contaminant Analysis:** Test the water for the presence of bacteria, nitrates, and heavy metals. The results will inform the necessary actions to improve water quality.

1.3 Natural Water Sources
Natural sources like rivers, lakes, and streams can serve as valuable resources in emergencies. However, these sources are frequently contaminated by various pollutants, including organic waste and chemicals. Purification is vital to make this water safe for drinking.

Purification of Natural Sources:
- **Initial Filtration:** Utilize filters to eliminate solid particles and sediment. This step reduces the contaminant load and prepares the water for further treatment.
- **Chemical Treatments:** Apply disinfection tablets or chlorine solutions to eradicate pathogens. These methods are essential to ensure the water is free from harmful microorganisms.

Man-Made Water Sources
In addition to natural sources, human-made structures can provide potential water supplies. Examples include:
- **Wells:** Wells tap into underground water reserves, with approximately 15 million wells globally. If you have access to one, ensure it is properly maintained and regularly tested for water quality. Having a plan for drawing water from your well during emergencies is critical.
- **Cisterns:** Cisterns are large containers designed to collect and store rainwater or other water sources. They are particularly beneficial in areas with limited fresh water access and can be utilized for future storage.
- **Swimming Pools:** With around 10 million swimming pools worldwide, properly maintained pools can serve as temporary water sources during emergencies. However, water must be treated with suitable disinfectants before consumption or use.

Unconventional Water Sources
In times of extreme water scarcity, it may be necessary to explore unconventional sources, such as:

- **Gray Water:** Gray water is lightly used water from sinks, showers, and washing machines. The average person generates about 30-50 liters of gray water daily. While it's not safe for drinking, it can be treated and reused for irrigation or sanitation, reducing pressure on fresh water supplies.
- **Desalination:** Desalination removes salt and impurities from seawater, making it drinkable. Approximately 21,000 desalination plants operate globally, producing about 95 million cubic meters of fresh water daily. Although it requires specialized equipment, desalination can be a viable solution in coastal areas.

Emergency Water Supplies

While emergency water sources may not be suitable for long-term use, they can provide temporary relief. Consider these options:

- **Water Heaters:** Residential water heaters can store a significant amount of potable water, typically between 40 to 60 gallons. If necessary, drain and collect water safely when other sources are unavailable.
- **Ice and Snow:** In cold climates, melting ice and snow can yield water. One cubic foot of compacted snow can generate about 2-3 gallons of water, but ensure the water is fully melted and purified before consumption.
- **Emergency Water Stock:** It is prudent to have emergency water supplies, such as bottled water or water stored in food-grade containers. A common guideline is to store at least one liter of water per person per day for a minimum of three days. These supplies can sustain you until you can access other sources.

Water Storage Solutions

In addition to your initial supply of bottled water, it's crucial to strategize on how to store water for prolonged periods, allowing for easy replenishment when necessary. Before diving into tips, it's important to note: **avoid gallon jugs.** While inexpensive, they complicate the storage system since they cannot be stacked and are quite fragile—one break can lead to leaks and diminish your supply. Fortunately, there are more reliable and manageable alternatives available.

Storage Capacity

To determine how much water to store for long-term emergencies accurately, follow these steps:

- **Assess the Number of People:** Begin by identifying how many individuals will rely on the stored water during an emergency. Include all family members, pets included.
- **Allocate 1 Liter per Person:** Estimate around 1 liter of water per person per day for consumption. This figure accounts for basic hydration and minimal hygiene during an extended emergency.
- **Separate Containers for Drinking and Non-Drinking Water:** It's advisable to use distinct containers for potable and non-potable water. This ensures the safety of drinking water and enables better management of non-potable needs.
- **Estimate Non-Drinking Water Needs:** Consider additional water requirements for uses that don't necessitate potable water, such as gardening or cleaning. Evaluate your specific situation to determine these needs.

Calculating Total Water Storage for Non-Drinking Use

The primary uses for non-potable water include gardening, which can support a survival vegetable garden and requires water, and toilet flushing. Inefficient drainage can cause health issues due to odors and waste buildup. If alternative washing methods are desired, they can be applied, but this information will be provided from a general perspective. Below are two examples of non-potable water usage with relevant calculations.

Estimation of Non-Drinking Water Needs

- **Gardening Requirements:** Calculate the water needed per square meter per week during the summer. This estimate should cover irrigation needs, ensuring adequate hydration of plants and compensation for evaporation.

Example: Assuming a conservative estimate of 10 liters per square meter weekly, we can calculate the non-potable water requirement for a garden as follows:
   - Water requirement per square meter weekly: 10 liters
   - Total weekly water requirement for a 100m² garden: 10 liters/m² × 100 m² = 1000 liters
   - Approximate daily non-potable water requirement for the garden: 1000 liters ÷ 7 days ≈ 143 liters per day

Based on this, to meet the irrigation needs of a 100 square meter garden in summer, approximately 143 liters of non-potable water is necessary each day.

- **Drinking Water Estimate:** A traditional toilet typically uses about 6-10 liters per flush, but many modern water-efficient toilets use only 4-6 liters.

Example: To estimate the non-potable water needed for toilet flushing, let's use an average of 5 liters per flush. The number of flushes per day will vary based on household size and usage. On average, a person may flush 4-6 times daily. Using a conservative estimate of 4 flushes per person each day, the daily non-potable water requirement for flushing can be calculated as follows:
  - Water requirement per flush: 5 liters
  - Flushes per person daily: 4
  - Approximate daily non-potable water requirement for toilet flushing per person: 5 liters/flush × 4 flushes = 20 liters per day

Choosing the Right Water Storage Containers

When selecting containers for both potable and non-potable water, ensure they are clean, food-safe, and sealed to prevent contamination. Use food-grade plastic containers or designated tanks to keep the water safe for its intended use.

Organization and Labeling
Organize and label your containers clearly to differentiate between potable and non-potable water. This will help prevent confusion and ensure the safety of your drinking water.

Stock Rotation
Implement a rotation system for your water supply to ensure it's used before expiration. Store water in a cool, dark location to keep it fresh and inhibit the growth of algae or bacteria.

Protecting Containers
Keep your storage containers shielded from direct sunlight and extreme temperatures. Use covers or place them in shaded areas to maintain water quality.

Monitoring and Maintenance
Regularly check your storage containers for leaks or signs of contamination. Periodically replace the water to ensure a fresh, safe supply.

Accessibility and Ease of Use
Organize your containers for easy access during emergencies. Ensure they are stored conveniently and are simple to open when needed.

Use of Filters and Purifiers
Consider utilizing filters or purifiers to treat stored water, especially if it comes from non-potable sources. This will add an extra layer of safety, ensuring the water is clean and safe to use.

Implementing Water Rotation Systems
A crucial strategy for maintaining the freshness and quality of stored water is to establish a rotation system.

The Importance of Water Rotation
Stagnant water can foster the growth of bacteria and other contaminants, rendering it unsafe for consumption. Thus, water rotation—regularly using and replacing stored water—is essential for preventing stagnation and preserving quality.

Benefits of Water Rotation Systems
Implementing a water rotation system provides several advantages:
- **Freshness and Safety:** Regularly rotating your water supply ensures a consistently fresh and safe source, vital for long-term storage.
- **Quality Control:** By using and replenishing stored water, you can monitor its quality and detect any contamination or degradation. This allows for timely interventions to maintain the reliability of your water supply.
- **Economic Efficiency:** Water rotation systems help prevent waste by utilizing and replacing water before it expires, minimizing the need for constant supplies and reducing unnecessary costs.
- **Peace of Mind:** A well-managed water rotation system gives you reassurance during emergencies, ensuring the safety and reliability of your water supply so you can focus on other critical preparedness aspects.

Steps to Implement a Water Rotation System
To effectively establish a water rotation system, follow these steps:
- **Set a Rotation Schedule:** Create a regular schedule for using and replacing stored water, considering factors such as storage capacity, household size, and expected water needs during emergencies. A common guideline is to rotate water every three to six months, but tailor it to your specific situation.

- **Label and Date Containers:** Mark each water container with the fill date. This practice helps you adhere to the rotation schedule and ensures the oldest water is used first. You can also include additional details like the water source or expiration date for clarity.
- **Monitor Consumption:** Keep track of your water usage to ensure consistent rotation. This can be as simple as maintaining a journal or using a tracking app to log your consumption over time. Monitoring allows for adjustments to your rotation schedule as needed.

Maximizing Space for Water Storage
Efficiently utilizing space for water storage is crucial, especially in areas with limited capacity or space constraints.
Assessing Available Space
Evaluate the potential areas in your home or property for water storage. Consider the following aspects:
- **Indoor Areas:** Check internal spaces like basements, garages, utility rooms, or closets for suitable spots for water containers. Measure these spaces to determine the maximum size of containers that can fit.
- **Outdoor Areas:** Look at outdoor locations such as patios, balconies, or rooftops that may accommodate water storage solutions.
- **Vertical Space:** Make use of vertical space by installing wall-mounted storage options or shelving systems. This can help effectively utilize the height available.
- **Underutilized Spaces:** Identify areas like crawl spaces, attics, or under-stair spaces that can be repurposed for water storage. Ensure these spaces are structurally sound and suitable for storage.

Options for Maximizing Space
To optimize available space for water storage, consider the following options:
- **Stackable Containers:** Use stackable containers that can be securely stacked. This reduces the footprint and maximizes storage capacity. Ensure the containers are stable to avoid tipping.
- **Wall Storage:** Implement wall shelving systems to vertically store containers, freeing up floor space.
- **Collapsible Containers:** Opt for collapsible containers that can be folded for storage when not in use, conserving space.
- **Vertical Solutions:** Install hooks or supports for hanging containers on walls or ceilings, maximizing vertical space.
- **Container Variety:** Use containers of various sizes to fit different spaces and needs, enhancing storage efficiency.
- **Slim Tanks:** Consider tanks with a narrow profile designed to fit into tight spaces, such as side yards or corners. Position them against walls or fences to optimize available space.
- **Modular Systems:** Explore modular water storage systems that can be customized and expanded based on your available area. These systems consist of interlocking units that can be configured to fit your specific storage dimensions.
- **Overhead Storage:** If your ceilings are high or you have open beams, think about installing overhead storage systems. These utilize tanks or containers suspended from the ceiling, taking advantage of vertical space while keeping the water accessible.
- **Underground Storage:** Cisterns or water bags can be placed underground in your yard or driveway, utilizing sub-surface space while maintaining your property's aesthetics. Ensure adequate sealing to prevent contamination of the stored water.
- **Portable Solutions:** For extremely limited spaces, consider portable storage options like collapsible containers or water bladders that can be filled and stored as needed and rolled up or folded when empty, saving valuable space.

Portable Water Storage Solutions
A more effective option for water storage is portable water containers, typically holding between 5 and 7 liters. While larger options exist, they become cumbersome and harder to manage. A recommended choice is the **Reliance Aquatainer**, which has a 7-gallon capacity. This container is robust, easy to store, and includes a spigot for convenient access. Additionally, it features a water level indicator, which is a practical bonus. These containers can be found at retailers like Walmart and are quite affordable, making them easy to acquire ahead of time. Personally, I appreciate the tap feature, making it ideal for camping: you can place it on a table and use it as needed, minimizing waste, and it's accessible for children as well.

My objective is to store enough water to sustain your family for two months using containers like these. An added advantage is that, even if you have a cistern or barrel, these containers are easily transportable should you need to evacuate your home.

When utilizing these containers, it's essential to replenish them every six months or so, discarding old water and thoroughly cleaning them. This is crucial to prevent bacterial growth, which you want to avoid in emergencies.

Tanks and Storage Barrels

If space permits, a water tank or barrel is an excellent solution. Although they can be pricey, they allow for substantial long-term water storage. Available in various sizes, if you have a garage or basement, you may find a suitable area to house one, storing anywhere from 50 to 250 liters of water.

For an average suburban family, installing a cistern may seem impractical, yet it's still worth mentioning. These tanks can hold several thousand liters of water and are usually installed underground, often connected to rainwater collection systems. If you choose this route, ensure the tank is made from food-safe materials and avoid reusing tanks that previously contained chemicals.

Regardless of whether you opt for a cistern, barrel, or tank, it's vital to take additional precautions for storing large volumes of water—treatment is imperative to prevent bacterial growth. You can purchase water treatment drops (Water Preserver is a trusted brand) and follow the provided instructions.

Aqua Pods and WaterBOB

Another option is to consider devices like the **Aqua Pod** or **WaterBOB**, which are essentially plastic bags designed to fit in the bathtub and fill directly from the faucet. Once filled, they conform to the tub's shape, ensuring the water remains safe and protected. While you could fill the tub directly by turning on the water heater before it's shut off, using these devices provides an advantage: they guard your water supplies against bacteria and unwanted debris in the tub. A **WaterBOB** can hold up to 100 gallons, keeping it fresh for about 16 weeks, while an **Aqua Pod** holds 65 gallons and maintains freshness for approximately 8 weeks.

These containers are intended for one-time use, meaning they cannot be reused once the water runs out. However, they are designed to fill directly from the tap; once that source is unavailable, their usefulness diminishes. Avoid attempts to reuse them later, as bacteria may proliferate, compromising the water's safety.

Personally, I recommend having one of these devices available to maximize your bathroom faucet's use in an emergency. It's a quick way to store water immediately and is more hygienic than simply filling the tub without a protective container.

Water Conservation and Reuse

Implementing Gray Water Recycling

In critical situations, where access to drinking water is scarce, a gray water recycling system can become vital for survival. Gray water, generated from daily activities like dishwashing or showering, can be captured and reused, maximizing available water resources and promoting more efficient management.

Understanding Gray Water and Its Benefits for Survival

Gray water is utilized for non-potable purposes, such as dishwashing or personal hygiene. Recycling it allows for the optimal use of every drop of available water, ensuring resource efficiency. It is important to assess feasibility and available resources, taking into account:

- **Water Sources:** Identify sources of gray water, such as sinks or rain collection systems, prioritizing filtered options to minimize health risks.
- **Storage Capacity:** Evaluate available containers for gray water storage.
- **Treatment Options:** In emergencies, advanced treatment methods may not be accessible.

Main Steps to Implement a Gray Water Recycling System

1. **Collection and Diversion:** Gather gray water using containers, diverting it from freshwater sources to avoid contamination.
2. **Basic Filtration:** Use layers of fabric, sand, or gravel to filter visible debris and impurities.
3. **Storage and Treatment:** Store filtered gray water in sealed containers. If possible, expose it to sunlight for natural disinfection or boil it to eliminate pathogens.

Water-Saving Systems and Devices

In survival scenarios, minimizing water waste is essential. Improving your home plumbing can make a significant impact:

- **Install Low-Flow Showerheads and Faucets:** These fixtures reduce water consumption while maintaining pressure, saving resources during daily activities.
- **Replace Conventional Toilets with Low-Flow or Dual-Flush Models:** These systems consume less water per flush, aiding in water conservation.
- **Address Leaks Promptly:** Small leaks can lead to significant water loss over time. Regularly inspect your plumbing and fix leaks swiftly.

Developing Water-Saving Habits
In critical circumstances, adopting efficient water-saving habits is crucial. Some examples include:
- **Reduce Shower Time:** Limiting the duration spent in the shower saves considerable amounts of water. Use a timer or a song to help manage your time.
- **Turn Off the Tap When Not in Use:** For instance, turn off the water while brushing your teeth or washing your face to significantly reduce consumption.
- **Collect and Reuse Water:** Place a bucket under the faucet or in the shower to capture unused water for other tasks, like flushing toilets or watering plants.

Efficient Management of External Water
Outdoor water usage should also be optimized in survival situations:
- **Water Plants Strategically:** Watering early in the morning or late in the evening minimizes evaporation. A drip irrigation system or using a watering can targeted at the roots helps reduce water loss.
- **Grow Drought-Resistant Plants:** Selecting plants that require minimal water, such as native species, will assist in conserving valuable water resources.

These practices are crucial for optimal management of available water reserves, fostering sustainable and effective usage even in challenging conditions.

Immediate Water Collection
You can also tilt the bathtub to drain water into a bucket. Fill any containers available from sink faucets, using bowls and buckets to gather as much water as possible. The collected water won't be stored for long, but it's useful for meeting immediate needs. The primary goal at this stage is to gather as much water as possible before the water supply runs dry.

Collecting Water from Nature
When discussing "nature," I refer to the fact that water can be found everywhere, not just in natural streams.
Your main source will likely be rainwater. If you already have a water barrel set up, you may have collected water prior to an emergency. However, this water could contain impurities, necessitating filtration and purification. If you lack a rainwater collection system, buckets can still be used to collect rain.
Another potential emergency water source is the hot water heater, which typically contains about 30 liters. To access water, you will need to turn off the power and flow (although they might not function). If you have a gas heater, switch the thermostat to pilot mode. The drain valve is located near the base of the heater. Attach a garden hose to the valve and turn on a nearby hot water faucet. Place the other end of the hose in a bucket before opening the valve. It's wise to prepare several buckets ahead of time, as you may need more than one. You don't have to empty the entire tank at once; you can close the valve and retrieve any remaining water later. Some mineral deposits may be noticed when the water runs out, but these are not harmful and can be easily filtered.
Another water source might be found in your area, such as streams, ponds, rivers, or lakes. Availability will depend on your location, but unless you live in a desert, there is likely water nearby. In this case, water containers become essential, but keep in mind that you will need a way to transport everything you collect. If you have a cart or wheelbarrow, it will make transporting multiple containers much easier.

Water Treatment
All collected water must be treated before consumption. The first option is filtering. An effective example is a water filter like the **Big Berkey**, which is known for its longevity—each filter can treat around 11,000 liters of water. It's ideal for camping since it can purify stream water and is durable due to its steel construction, making it easy to transport without damage. Numerous brands are available, so you have many options to choose from. Just ensure you have a supply of filters on hand. Whatever system you utilize, it's important to remove larger debris first to keep the filter clean and functioning longer.
Alternatively, you can create a natural filtration system. Add a layer of sand to the bottom of a filter container, followed by layers of charcoal and rocks. Pass water through these layers to decrease bacteria levels. However, this method does not eliminate giardia if present.
Another method is to boil the water, which will kill any bacteria. Bring the water to a rolling boil and maintain it for about 10 minutes before allowing it to cool. While the taste might not be optimal, it will be safe to drink and can be used to make tea or other beverages to enhance flavor.
You might also consider using UV pens designed to eliminate bacteria from water. While I can't personally vouch for their effectiveness, many campers report positive experiences with these devices.

Immediate Actions When the Water Supply is Interrupted

When the water supply ceases, the amount you can access won't last long. The first step is to collect as much water as possible from the taps. If you have a WaterBOB or Aqua Pod, now is the time to fill it. If not, plug the bathtub and fill it anyway. Place buckets under downspouts to catch excess rainwater and lay out a tarp outside to collect additional water.

Water Sources to Avoid

When living without electricity for an extended period and your water supplies start dwindling, sourcing additional water becomes imperative. However, it's vital to remember that not all available water is safe for consumption. While some precautions may seem obvious, panic can lead to oversight of these basics, making it essential to reiterate them. Contaminated water can harbor harmful microorganisms, chemicals, and pollutants that pose serious health risks. According to the World Health Organization (WHO), roughly 2.2 billion people globally lack access to safely managed drinking water services. Consuming tainted water can lead to a range of waterborne illnesses with severe health implications. For instance, cholera, a bacterial infection transmitted through contaminated water, results in approximately 95,000 fatalities annually. Similarly, water contaminated with the Giardia parasite can cause giardiasis, characterized by diarrhea, abdominal pain, and weight loss. Recognizing the potential health repercussions of drinking contaminated water underscores the critical need for purification and filtration to safeguard public health.

Avoid drinking water from your cistern, toilet bowl, radiators, swimming pool, or any water bed. Such water may be contaminated and should not be consumed without appropriate treatment. Additionally, refrain from drinking floodwater or well water unless it has been confirmed safe. It's important to note that after natural disasters, well water previously deemed safe may become compromised. Do not rely on it until it has been tested and certified. Lastly, if you reside near the ocean, do not attempt to drink saltwater without first distilling it.

Chlorine bleach is another option but requires caution. While it is technically carcinogenic and may lead to poisoning, it can serve as a useful last resort when no other options are available. Avoid scented bleaches or those with added chemicals, and check the expiration date first, as it is only effective for about six months. Do not use pool chlorine, as it is much stronger than household bleach, which is why you should not drink water from your pool. You will need only 8 drops of bleach per gallon of water, but be sure to filter out any debris first. Shake the container well and let it sit for 30 minutes before using.

Personally, I admit to being somewhat apprehensive about using bleach. I would use it only if I had no other alternatives. If I had to chlorinate water, I would prefer using chlorine dioxide tablets. These tablets are effective against various viruses and bacteria, including giardia, which bleach does not eliminate. They are easy to use: just add the tablets to water and follow the package instructions. Liquid forms are also available; the only difference is that you add drops instead of tablets.

Another option is distillation. This method requires a bit more planning and equipment, but if you're inclined to go that route, it's wise to prepare in advance.

To distill water, you will need a heat source, a heat-resistant container, a condenser, and another container to collect the distilled water. You'll also need a tube (made of food-safe materials) to transport the vapor from the first container, through the condenser, into the second container. Countertop distillers are available for around $200, which could be a worthwhile investment if you're committed to securing clean water.

Keep in mind that the human body requires sodium, so don't overindulge; resist the urge to snack excessively on salty foods. We'll discuss laundry and dishwashing shortly, but this is an area where you can conserve water. Wait until you have a full load before using your valuable water supply. Using disposable cups and plates can also minimize the amount of dishwashing required.

Risks of Water Contamination

Water contamination is a serious issue that can pose significant risks to the health of individuals and communities.

Types of Bacteria and Associated Health Risks

- **Escherichia coli (E. coli):** This common bacterium inhabits the intestines of humans and animals. Its presence in water indicates fecal contamination and presents a major health risk. Symptoms of an E. coli infection include diarrhea, abdominal cramps, and vomiting. In severe cases, it can lead to kidney failure.
- **Salmonella:** Another bacterium associated with fecal contamination, Salmonella can cause food poisoning if ingested via contaminated water or food. Symptoms include diarrhea, fever, and abdominal cramps, and serious cases may require medical attention.
- **Campylobacter:** Frequently found in animal feces, this bacterium can contaminate water sources. Consuming water contaminated with Campylobacter can lead to gastrointestinal illness, with symptoms including diarrhea, fever, and abdominal pain.

- **Vibrio cholerae:** This bacterium causes cholera, a waterborne disease that can lead to severe diarrhea and dehydration if untreated. Cholera outbreaks often occur in areas with inadequate sanitation and contaminated water supplies.

Common Water Pollutants and Their Effects
Many types of pollutants can contaminate water. Here are some examples:
- **Heavy Metals:** Elements such as lead, mercury, and arsenic can contaminate water through industrial pollution or natural deposits. Long-term exposure to these pollutants can lead to numerous health issues, including neurological disorders, organ damage, and developmental problems, particularly in children.
- **Pesticides and Herbicides:** Agricultural runoff can introduce these chemicals into water sources, posing harmful effects on human health, including increased cancer risk, hormonal imbalances, and damage to the nervous system.
- **Industrial Chemicals:** Industries can release pollutants like polychlorinated biphenyls (PCBs) and dioxins into water bodies. These persistent organic pollutants can accumulate in the food chain, leading to long-term health risks, including cancer and reproductive disorders.
- **Pharmaceuticals:** Improper disposal of medications can result in pharmaceuticals contaminating water sources. While concentrations are typically low, prolonged exposure to these substances may present unknown risks to human health.

Assessing Water Quality

Risks of Contamination
Water used daily carries various contamination risks.
- **Water Testing Kits:** These kits allow you to evaluate the quality of water sources and identify potential hazards. A recommended kit is the XYZ Water Quality Test Kit, which includes tests for bacteria, heavy metals, pesticides, and other common contaminants. Follow the kit instructions carefully to collect samples and conduct tests accurately.
- **Local Water Quality Reports:** Review local water quality reports from relevant authorities. These documents often contain information about contaminants present in your area's water sources. Pay attention to advisories or warnings regarding specific pollutants.
- **Professional Water Analysis Services:** For more detailed results, consider using professional testing services. These experts have specialized equipment and knowledge to analyze water samples for a wide range of contaminants, providing a comprehensive assessment of water quality.

Identifying Hidden Water Reserves

Understanding Groundwater
Aquifers are underground layers of permeable rock or sediment that hold water, representing a significant groundwater source. To locate aquifers in your area, it's essential to study local geology and hydrogeology. Consult geological maps or contact hydrogeologists or industry experts familiar with your region.

Surface Indicators
Surface indicators can provide valuable clues regarding underground water reserves. Look for areas where vegetation appears greener or denser than the surrounding landscape, as this may indicate a near-surface aquifer. Additionally, wetlands, natural springs, or seepage areas may also signify the presence of groundwater.

Geophysical Investigations
Geophysical surveys utilize specialized equipment to measure physical properties of the subsurface, such as resistivity or electromagnetic conductivity. By analyzing the collected data, experts can identify potential aquifer formations and pinpoint areas where drilling or excavation could yield water.

Groundwater Exploration Techniques
Several techniques are employed to explore underground water sources. Here are commonly used methods:
- **Test Drilling:** This technique involves drilling small wells at various locations to collect core samples and assess the presence of aquifer formations. Analyzing these samples provides valuable insights into the type and quality of available water.
- **Groundwater Monitoring Wells:** Installing monitoring wells enables continuous observation of groundwater levels and quality. These wells offer valuable data on fluctuations in the water table and the overall health of the aquifer.

- **Remote Sensing and Satellite Imagery:** Remote sensing methods, such as satellite imagery or aerial surveys, help identify geological features and vegetation patterns associated with groundwater reserves. These tools provide a broader perspective and assist in narrowing down potential areas for further exploration.
- **Ground Penetrating Radar (GPR):** GPR employs radar pulses to capture images of underground layers, helping identify aquifer formations and potential obstacles or geological features that may affect water accessibility.

Finding Water Sources in Emergency Situations

Rainwater and Dew Collection
Implementing a system to collect rainwater or dew can be highly beneficial, even outside of emergency scenarios, for several reasons:
- **Decrease Reliance on External Water Supplies:** By collecting rain or dew, you can supplement or even eliminate the need for municipal or groundwater, reducing your dependence on external sources.
- **Water Conservation:** Gathering rainwater or dew helps conserve this precious resource by utilizing a free and plentiful supply. This practice minimizes waste and supports sustainable water management.
- **Lower Water Bills:** Using collected rainwater or dew for non-potable activities like watering plants or cleaning vehicles can significantly decrease your water expenses.
- **Minimize Stormwater Runoff:** Collecting rain or dew helps reduce stormwater runoff, alleviating the burden on drainage systems and preventing soil erosion.

Rainwater Harvesting
To effectively collect rainwater, consider these techniques and practices:
- **Rooftop Collection Systems:** Set up a system to channel rainwater from gutters and downspouts into rain barrels, storage tanks, or cisterns.
- **Rain Barrels:** Position rain barrels under downspouts to capture and store rainwater. Ensure that the barrels are fitted with secure lids to keep out debris and mosquitoes.
- **First Flush Diverter:** Install a first flush diverter to redirect the initial runoff from the roof during rainfall. This device helps eliminate potential contaminants like dust and debris, enhancing the quality of the collected rainwater.

Dew Collection
Dew can be a valuable source of water, especially in dry or desert climates where precipitation is minimal. Here are techniques for collecting dew:
- **Dew Collection Surfaces:** Choose surfaces that are effective for collecting dew, such as grass, plants, or non-absorbent materials like plastic or metal. These surfaces should be cleaned and placed in open areas exposed to the sky.
- **Absorbent Materials:** Utilize absorbent materials such as cloths or sponges to capture dew. Place these on dew-collecting surfaces in the evening or early morning when dew formation is most likely.
- **Squeeze and Collect:** After dew has accumulated on the absorbent materials, wring them out into a clean container. Repeat this process across multiple surfaces to maximize water collection.
- **Prevent Contamination:** Ensure that the collection surfaces and absorbent materials are clean to avoid introducing contaminants. When using dew-harvesting plants, steer clear of areas treated with pesticides or harmful chemicals.

Extracting Water from Plants and Trees
In some situations, you may need to extract water from plants and trees to meet your hydration needs.

The Benefits of Harvesting Water from Plants and Trees:
- **Emergency Water Source:** In survival situations, when traditional water sources are scarce or contaminated, extracting water from vegetation can be a lifesaver.
- **Sustainable and Renewable:** Harvesting water from plants is a sustainable approach, tapping into their natural ability to absorb and store water without depleting other sources.
- **Readily Available:** Plants and trees are found in various ecosystems, making them accessible sources of water regardless of your environment, whether rural, desert, or urban.
- **Connecting with Nature:** Learning how plants and trees can provide water deepens our understanding and appreciation of natural systems, fostering a closer relationship with our environment.

Techniques for Harvesting Water from Plants and Trees
To effectively extract water, consider the following methods:

- **Breathable Bag Method:** This technique involves placing a clear plastic bag over a leafy branch to collect water vapor released through transpiration.

Steps:
1. Choose a healthy, leafy branch.
2. Enclose the branch in a clear plastic bag, sealing it tightly.
3. Secure the bag to prevent air leaks.
4. Allow the plant to transpire, collecting water vapor inside the bag.
5. Collect the water by making a small hole in the bag's bottom corner or by pouring it into a container.

- **Solar Method:** This technique uses sunlight and condensation to extract water from plants and soil.

Steps:
1. Dig a hole deep enough to hold plant material and a container.
2. Place leafy green vegetation in the bottom of the hole.
3. Position a container in the center of the hole, ensuring it's lower than the surrounding soil.
4. Cover the hole with a clear plastic sheet, securing the edges with rocks or soil.
5. Place a small stone or weight in the center of the sheet, above the container.
6. Over time, the sun will heat the hole, causing evaporation that condenses on the plastic and drips into the container.

- **Sponge or Wringing Method:** Some plant parts, like succulent leaves or juicy fruits, can be squeezed to extract water. This method works well for plants or trees with water-rich, easily extractable parts.
- **Natural Water Reservoirs:** Certain trees, like baobabs or palms, store water in their trunks or fronds. Tapping into these sources can yield significant water amounts.

These strategies enable effective implementation of water collection and storage systems, ensuring a dependable water supply during emergencies and in daily life.

Considerations and Precautions
When harvesting water from plants and trees, keep the following considerations in mind:
- **Plant Identification:** Properly identify plants before extracting water. Some may have limited supplies or contain toxins that could be harmful if ingested.
- **Environmental Impact:** Use responsible harvesting techniques to avoid causing excessive damage to plants and trees, which play a vital role in ecosystems and provide habitats for various species.
- **Water Purity:** While methods for obtaining water from plants can provide hydration, the collected water may need purification or filtration to eliminate contaminants. Always treat water appropriately before consumption.
- **Sustainability:** Extract only the amount of water necessary to meet immediate needs, allowing the plant or tree to recover and continue its essential functions.

Filtration Methods

The Importance of Water Filtration
Water filtration is a crucial barrier against harmful substances that may be present in your water supply. Understanding filtration processes is vital for several reasons:
- **Removal of Contaminants:** Filtration methods effectively remove harmful substances, making water safe to drink.
- **Health Protection:** Using proper filtration techniques helps prevent waterborne diseases and safeguards your health.
- **Access to Clean Water:** When clean water sources are scarce, filtration enables you to treat water from potentially risky sources, like streams or rainwater, making it potable.
- **Cost-Effective Solution:** Investing in a reliable filtration system or learning basic methods offers a sustainable, long-term solution that reduces reliance on bottled water, even outside emergencies.

Filtration Principles
To effectively filter water, understanding the underlying principles is important. Here are the main categories:
- **Physical Filtration:** This method uses barriers to capture larger particles and sediment.
    - **Screening:** Water passes through a mesh or cloth, removing visible debris and sediment. This simple technique is particularly useful in emergencies.
    - **Sand Filtration:** Layers of sand and gravel retain impurities as water flows through, improving cleanliness.

- o **Ceramic Filters:** These filters have small pores that allow water to flow while retaining bacteria and larger particles. They can function in both gravity and pressure systems.
- **Biological Filtration:** This focuses on microorganisms, such as bacteria and viruses, that physical filtration may not eliminate.
  - o **Slow Sand Filtration:** This method utilizes a bed of fine sand that develops a biological layer, capturing and metabolizing microorganisms as water flows through.
  - o **Biological Activated Carbon Filters:** This combines activated carbon's absorption capabilities with the biological action of microorganisms to degrade contaminants.
- **Chemical Filtration:** This involves using chemicals to treat and purify water.
  - o **Activated Carbon Filters:** These filters absorb chlorine, chemicals, and organic compounds in water, often used in home filtration systems.
  - o **Chlorination:** Chlorine is a common chemical disinfectant that effectively kills bacteria and viruses, widely employed in municipal water treatment facilities.
  - o **Water Purification Tablets:** These tablets, containing chlorine or iodine, disinfect water by eliminating harmful microorganisms, making them ideal for outdoor activities or emergencies.

Choosing the Right Filtration Method
Selecting the appropriate filtration method depends on various factors, including available resources, contamination levels, and desired water quality. Consider the following:
- **Water Source:** Assess the quality of the water source and identify visible sediment, microorganisms, or chemicals that might require specific filtration techniques.
- **Filtering Capacity:** Evaluate how much water you need to filter and the capacity of the method you choose. Some methods are better suited for small amounts, while others can handle larger volumes.
- **Portability and Accessibility:** If you need a method for outdoor use or emergencies, consider the portability and ease of use of the filtration system. Portable filters or tablets might be the best option in these situations.
- **Maintenance and Costs:** Assess the maintenance and costs associated with the chosen filtration method. Some systems require frequent cartridge replacements, while others may have a higher initial investment but lower long-term maintenance expenses.

DIY Water Filtration Systems

Creating your own water filters offers numerous advantages, making them a practical solution in various circumstances. Here are some key benefits:
- **Accessibility:** DIY filters can be constructed using common materials that are easily sourced, such as buckets, sand, gravel, activated carbon, and fabric. This availability enables you to build a filter even in areas with limited resources.
- **Cost-Effectiveness:** Constructing your own water filter can be significantly less expensive than purchasing a commercial filtration system. Utilizing affordable or readily available materials allows you to save money while ensuring safe drinking water.
- **Customization:** DIY filters can be tailored to meet your specific requirements. You can modify the size, filtration capacity, and experiment with different materials to achieve the desired level of purification.
- **Sustainability:** Making and using DIY water filters supports sustainability by reducing reliance on single-use plastic bottles and minimizing waste. This approach empowers you to manage your water purification needs in a more environmentally friendly manner.

Building a Basic DIY Water Filter
Follow this guide to create a simple yet effective DIY water filter using materials that are easy to find.
Materials Required:
- Two plastic food buckets (one larger and one smaller)
- Drill with a hole saw
- Fine sand
- Gravel
- Activated carbon
- Fine mesh or fabric
- Rubber seal or O-ring

- Source of water to be filtered

Step-by-Step Instructions:
1. **Prepare the Large Bucket:** Drill a hole near the bottom of the larger bucket using the hole saw. Insert the rubber gasket or O-ring into the hole to create a watertight seal.
2. **Layer the Filter Materials:** Begin with a layer of fine sand at the bottom of the larger bucket, followed by a layer of gravel. The sand serves as the initial filtration layer, while the gravel prevents clogging and supports the sand.
3. **Add Activated Carbon:** Layer activated carbon on top of the gravel, as it will help remove impurities, odors, and some chemicals from the water.
4. **Prepare the Smaller Bucket:** Puncture several small holes in the bottom of the smaller bucket to allow water to pass through.
5. **Assemble the Filter:** Place the smaller bucket into the larger bucket, ensuring it sits atop the filter materials. The smaller bucket will collect the filtered water.
6. **Secure the Filter:** Use additional gravel to fill the space between the two buckets, stabilizing the filter. Ensure the buckets fit tightly together to prevent unfiltered water from bypassing the filtration system.
7. **Cover the Filter:** Place a mesh or cloth over the top of the filter to block debris from entering.
8. **Test the Filter:** Pour water into the top of the filter and ensure the filtered water is being collected in the smaller bucket. Address any leaks or blockages in the filtration system.

Maintenance of DIY Filters
To keep your filter functioning effectively, adhere to these maintenance tips:
- **Regular Cleaning:** Replace sand, gravel, and activated carbon as needed, as these materials can become clogged or lose effectiveness over time.
- **Rinse Components:** After each use, rinse the filter components with clean water to remove any accumulated debris or contaminants.
- **Storage:** Store the filter in a dry and clean location to prevent bacteria or mold growth.

Additional Considerations
While DIY filters can effectively remove sediment and some contaminants, they may not eliminate all microorganisms or harmful chemicals. Consider the following for complete purification:
- **Boil Water:** Boiling water for at least one minute can eliminate most harmful microorganisms.
- **Chemical Disinfection:** If you suspect microbial contamination, use water purification tablets or liquid disinfectants, following the manufacturer's guidelines.
- **Water Testing:** Periodically check the quality of the filtered water with specialized kits that can detect contaminants not removed by the DIY filter, which may require further treatment.

Benefits of Portable Water Filtration Systems
Portable water filtration systems offer numerous advantages, making them ideal for emergency or preparedness situations:
- **Portability and Compactness:** These systems are designed to be lightweight and compact, making them easy to carry in a survival kit or backpack, ensuring access to clean drinking water in critical situations.
- **Versatility:** Portable filters are designed to treat water from various sources, transforming potentially unsafe water into drinkable water, which is especially beneficial in unpredictable environments.
- **Durability and Reliability:** Many portable filtration systems are built to endure harsh conditions, making them suitable for survival scenarios. They are often constructed with sturdy materials that can withstand shock, extreme temperatures, and frequent use.

Selecting a Portable Water Filtration System
When choosing a portable water filtration system for survival, consider these factors:
- **Filtration Method:** Portable filters may use different techniques, such as activated carbon, ceramic, or hollow fiber membranes. Each method has its own advantages and limitations. Assess the contaminants that might be present and select a filter that effectively addresses them.
- **Filter Longevity:** Choose filters with a long lifespan and a high processing capacity. During extended emergencies, relying on a durable filter is crucial to avoid frequent cartridge replacements.
- **Ease of Use:** Ensure the system is straightforward to operate and does not require complicated installation or maintenance procedures.

Using Your Portable Filter System
Once you have selected the appropriate filter system, it's important to know how to use it properly:
- **Filter Preparation:** Before first use, carefully read the manufacturer's instructions and follow the recommended procedures, such as priming the filter or rinsing it with clean water.
- **Choosing a Water Source:** Aim to source clear, flowing water, avoiding potential contamination from stagnant ponds or polluted areas.
- **Prefiltration:** If the water has visible debris or sediment, use a cloth or pre-filter to remove these particles before passing it through the portable filter. This step helps prevent clogging and extends the filter's lifespan.
- **Filtering Process:** Submerge the filter inlet in the water source, ensuring it is fully submerged. Follow the manufacturer's instructions to pump or squeeze the water through the filter, collecting the purified water in a container.
- **Maintenance and Storage:** After each use, clean and dry the portable filter according to the manufacturer's instructions. Proper maintenance prevents bacterial or mold growth, ensuring the filter remains effective.

Advantages of Ceramic and Activated Carbon Filters
Ceramic filters are renowned for their efficacy in removing bacteria, protozoa, and sediment from water. Key benefits include:
- **Microscopic Pores:** Ceramic filters are crafted from porous material featuring tiny pores that serve as a barrier to contaminants, allowing only clean water to flow through. The pore size varies, but most ceramic filters block particles larger than 0.2 microns.
- **Durability:** Ceramic filters have a long lifespan. When properly maintained, they can purify thousands of gallons of water, making them a cost-effective choice for prolonged use, particularly in survival or camping scenarios where replacement filters may be hard to find.
- **Simple Maintenance:** Cleaning ceramic filters is straightforward. Remove the filter element and gently scrub it with a sponge or soft brush to eliminate accumulated sediments, maintaining the filter's efficiency.

Portable Filtration Solutions
Portable filtration systems, along with ceramic and activated carbon filters, provide a practical and dependable way to ensure access to safe drinking water, especially in challenging environments or emergency situations. With appropriate selection, usage, and maintenance, these filters can become crucial tools for survival and preparedness.

Benefits of Activated Carbon Filters
Activated carbon filters, typically used in combination with ceramic filters, excel at removing chemical contaminants, unpleasant odors, and undesirable tastes from water. Here are several reasons why they are a great choice for enhancing your water filtration system:
- **Adsorption Capabilities:** Activated carbon is composed of a vast surface area filled with tiny pores, enabling it to absorb a wide range of impurities, including chlorine, pesticides, herbicides, volatile organic compounds (VOCs), and some heavy metals. This ability significantly improves the taste and smell of water.
- **Chemical Contaminant Reduction:** These filters are particularly effective at reducing chemical pollutants found in both tap and natural water sources. They can eliminate chlorine, chloramine, and other disinfectants typically used in water treatment, ensuring the water is free from potentially harmful substances.
- **Synergy with Ceramic Filters:** When paired with ceramic filters, activated carbon filters provide comprehensive filtration. Ceramic filters tackle physical contaminants, while carbon filters focus on chemical impurities, delivering a dual-action purification process that guarantees clean, refreshing water.

Selecting the Right Filtration System
Choosing the appropriate filtration system relies on your unique requirements and the quality of the water sources you plan to utilize. Consider the following factors when making your selection:
- **Filtration Capacity:** Assess how much water you will need to filter. Opt for a system that meets or exceeds your filtering requirements.
- **Longevity and Replacement:** Review the expected lifespan of ceramic and carbon filters. It's essential to choose filters capable of processing a substantial volume of water before needing replacement.

- **User-Friendliness:** Select filtration systems that are easy to operate, requiring straightforward installation and minimal maintenance.

Maintenance and Replacement of Filter Components

Filter components play a crucial role in any filtration system, as they eliminate impurities and ensure the water remains safe for consumption. To maximize system efficiency and maintain a steady supply of purified water, it's vital to understand how to properly care for and replace these elements. Here are some practical tips to keep your filters in excellent shape:

Cleaning the Filter Components

Regularly cleaning filter components is crucial to remove accumulated sediment and debris. Here's a step-by-step guide:
1. **Consult the Manufacturer's Guidelines:** Each filtration system has specific requirements, so refer to the manufacturer's instructions for detailed cleaning procedures.
2. **Shut Off the Water Supply:** Before cleaning, turn off the water supply to the filter system to prevent water flow during maintenance.
3. **Remove the Filter Elements:** Carefully detach the filter components from their housing, following the manufacturer's directions for safe disassembly.
4. **Rinse the Filters:** Clean the filter components with fresh water to remove dirt and sediment. Use a gentle flow of water to avoid damaging the material, starting from the clean end.
5. **Soak in Cleaning Solution (if necessary):** For stubborn stains or persistent contaminants, soak the filter components in a cleaning solution as directed by the manufacturer, or use a mild detergent. Allow the filters to soak for the specified duration.
6. **Scrub with a Brush:** Utilize a soft brush or sponge to gently scrub the dirtiest areas, being careful not to apply too much pressure that could damage the filter.
7. **Final Rinse:** After cleaning, thoroughly rinse the filters with clean water to ensure all traces of cleaning solutions are removed.
8. **Inspect for Damage:** Carefully examine the filters for any tears, cracks, or signs of wear. Significant damage may necessitate filter replacement.
9. **Reassemble and Test:** Once the filters are cleaned and dried, reassemble the filtration system according to the instructions. Restore the water supply and test the system to ensure proper operation.

By following these maintenance steps, you can prolong the life of your filters and ensure a continuous supply of purified water, maintaining a high level of filtration efficiency.

Filter Element Replacement

Despite regular maintenance, filter components will eventually require replacement. Consider the following indicators to determine when to replace them:
- **Manufacturer Recommendations:** Adhere to the manufacturer's guidelines regarding filter lifespan and replacement schedules, as these are based on filter specifications and capacity.
- **Reduced Water Flow:** A noticeable decline in water flow may indicate clogged filters that can no longer effectively remove impurities, suggesting that replacement is necessary.
- **Taste and Smell Changes:** If the filtered water has an unusual taste or odor, even after cleaning the filters, it may indicate that the filters are not functioning correctly.
- **Visible Wear:** Inspect filters for evident signs of deterioration, such as cracks or tears. If you observe such damage, replacement is needed.
- **Maintenance Records:** Keep a log of cleaning and maintenance dates to help track the frequency and determine when replacement is due.
- **Water Quality Changes:** Any visible changes in the appearance of filtered water, such as cloudiness or particles, may signal that the filters are no longer effectively retaining impurities.

Advanced Water Purification Methods

The Power of Solar Disinfection

Solar disinfection (SODIS) is a straightforward, cost-effective, and eco-friendly method that utilizes solar energy to eliminate harmful microorganisms in water. This technique is beneficial both in situations where drinking water is scarce and as an additional purification step. Here's how to effectively harness this method.

How Solar Disinfection Works:

The SODIS process involves placing water in clear polyethylene terephthalate (PET) bottles and exposing them to sunlight, allowing solar radiation to disinfect the water.
- **UV Radiation:** UV-A rays from sunlight damage the DNA of microorganisms, inhibiting their growth and reproduction, thus making the water safer for consumption.
- **Heat:** The heat generated by solar rays also aids in inactivating pathogens, enhancing the disinfection process.

Implementing Solar Disinfection (SODIS)
To effectively use the SODIS method, follow these steps:
1. **Select Clear PET Plastic Bottles:** Use clean PET bottles, as this material allows UV-A radiation to pass through for effective disinfection.
2. **Fill the Bottles:** Pour water into the bottles, leaving some space at the top to allow for expansion as the water heats.
3. **Position in Direct Sunlight:** Place the bottles in a sunny location, preferably on a reflective surface like aluminum foil, to maximize sun exposure.
4. **Exposure Duration:** The time required for exposure varies based on factors like solar intensity and water quality. Generally, at least six hours of exposure is needed on clear, sunny days, but in areas with less sunlight, you may need to extend the exposure time.
5. **Weather Considerations:** Since solar disinfection relies on sunlight, if it's cloudy, you may need to increase exposure time or repeat the process on a clearer day.
6. **Temperature Considerations:** Higher temperatures facilitate disinfection. In cooler climates, try the process during warmer months or consider using additional heat sources to raise the water temperature.
7. **Handling and Storage:** Once disinfection is complete, securely close the bottles to prevent recontamination. Store the purified water in a cool, shaded area, away from direct sunlight, until you're ready to use it.

By following these techniques, solar disinfection can serve as an effective means of ensuring access to safe drinking water, leveraging a natural and abundant resource like the sun.

Benefits of Solar Disinfection (SODIS)
Solar disinfection presents several advantages that make it an appealing method for purifying water:
- **Accessibility and Simplicity:** SODIS is a cost-effective approach that requires minimal equipment, making it easily applicable in areas with limited resources. The only necessary items are clear PET plastic bottles, sunlight, and time.
- **User-Friendly:** The simplicity of SODIS allows individuals with minimal technical skills to implement it. The process is straightforward and easy to understand, making it valuable for communities struggling to access clean water or in emergency scenarios.
- **Eco-Friendly:** SODIS does not involve the use of chemicals or energy-consuming devices, thus making it an environmentally sustainable option. It reduces reliance on non-renewable resources and minimizes waste generation.
- **Scalable Approach:** This method can be easily scaled to treat large volumes of water by utilizing multiple bottles exposed to sunlight simultaneously.
- **Complementary Treatment:** SODIS can be combined with other water purification techniques, such as filtration or chemical disinfection, to enhance water safety and quality.

Chemical Water Treatment Implementation
Chemical treatment involves using disinfectant agents to eliminate microorganisms present in water. Below are common substances, the bacteria they target, and their recommended dosages:
- **Chlorine:** Effective against bacteria like E. coli and Salmonella. **Dosage:** Add 2 drops (8 mg) of liquid sodium hypochlorite or 1/4 teaspoon (1.5 grams) of solid calcium hypochlorite per liter of water.
- **Iodine:** Works well against bacteria such as Campylobacter and Giardia. **Dosage:** Use one iodine tablet or 5 drops (8 mg) of iodine crystals per liter of water.
- **Chlorine Dioxide:** Effective against a broad spectrum of bacteria. **Dosage:** Use one chlorine dioxide tablet per liter of water.
- **Potassium Permanganate:** Effective against certain strains of E. coli. **Dosage:** Add 4-5 crystals (200-250 mg) of potassium permanganate per liter of water.

Steps for Proper Chemical Water Treatment

1. **Assess Water Quality:** Observe the clarity, color, and odor of the water. If needed, use a pre-filter to remove larger particles.
2. **Select Appropriate Treatment:** Choose the chemical based on the specific contaminants present and your requirements.
3. **Follow Manufacturer Instructions:** Adhere carefully to the guidelines provided for dosage and contact time.
4. **Add Disinfectant:** Use precise measuring tools to ensure accurate dosing of the disinfectant.
5. **Allow for Contact Time:** Each chemical requires a specific duration to work effectively. Ensure that you follow the recommended time.
6. **Neutralization:** If the treated water has residual taste or odor, consider using activated carbon filters or neutralizing tablets.
7. **Water Storage:** Store treated water in clean, sealed containers, labeling them with the treatment date for proper rotation.

Advantages of Chemical Water Treatment
- **Portability:** Disinfectant chemicals are lightweight, compact, and easy to transport, making them ideal for travel, outdoor adventures, and emergencies.
- **Broad-Spectrum Efficacy:** Substances like chlorine, iodine, and chlorine dioxide eliminate a wide range of bacteria, ensuring the water is safe for consumption.
- **Affordability:** Chemical treatments are generally inexpensive and accessible, providing a viable solution for a diverse user base.
- **Simplicity:** These methods do not require special technical skills, and instructions are typically easy to follow.
- **Longevity:** These products have a long shelf life, making them suitable for those preparing for extended emergencies.

Utilizing Distillation for Pure Water
Distillation employs varying boiling points to separate water from impurities. By heating water to 100 degrees Celsius (212 degrees Fahrenheit), it evaporates, leaving behind impurities like minerals and bacteria. The vapor is then condensed back into pure water.

Steps for Implementing Distillation
1. **Set Up the Distiller:** Choose either a countertop distiller or a solar still, ensuring it's in good condition.
2. **Prepare the Water:** Use a relatively clean water source and pre-filter if necessary.
3. **Fill the Distiller:** Pour water into the boiling chamber, avoiding overfilling.
4. **Heat the Water:** Apply heat to bring the water to a boil. It typically takes 4-6 hours to distill a full chamber.
5. **Collect the Steam:** The vapor rises and moves into the condensation system, where it cools and is collected in a clean container.
6. **Dispose of Residue:** After distillation, discard the remaining residue in the boiling chamber.

Advantages of Distillation
- **Comprehensive Removal of Contaminants:** Distillation effectively removes a wide range of impurities, including bacteria, heavy metals, and minerals, ensuring safe drinking water.
- **Long-Term Reliability:** Distillers are durable and reliable devices suitable for extended use with proper care.
- **Versatility:** Distillation can be applied to various water sources, including seawater, making it an effective method for obtaining pure water in various circumstances.
- **Elimination of Volatile Compounds:** Distillation can also remove some volatile compounds responsible for unpleasant taste and odor. To enhance the flavor of distilled water, aerate it by pouring it back and forth between clean containers or add a small amount of mineralized water.
- **Energy Consumption Considerations:** Depending on the heat source, distillation can be energy-intensive, especially on a larger scale. If energy efficiency is a concern, consider alternative or more energy-efficient purification methods.

Reverse Osmosis (RO) Systems
Reverse osmosis systems are highly effective in purifying water for safe consumption. They utilize a semi-permeable membrane to eliminate impurities and contaminants by applying pressure, thereby removing dissolved solids, bacteria, viruses, heavy metals, chlorine, fluoride, pesticides, and pharmaceutical residues.

Benefits of RO Systems
- **Enhanced Water Quality:** RO systems ensure safe, clean water by eliminating harmful contaminants.
- **Convenience and Cost Savings:** While the initial installation of an RO system can be pricey, it ultimately reduces the need for bottled water, making it cost-effective in the long run.
- **Environmental Benefits:** RO systems help minimize plastic waste associated with bottled water, providing an eco-friendly solution for water purification.

Installing an RO System
1. **Assess Water Quality:** Test the quality of your water source prior to installation to identify specific contaminants.
2. **Select the System:** Evaluate filtration capacity, water waste ratio, and the space available for installation.
3. **Conduct Maintenance:** Follow the manufacturer's directions for regular upkeep, including replacing filters and disinfecting the system to ensure optimal performance.

Troubleshooting and Remineralization
- **Common Issues:** If you notice decreased water flow or an unusual taste, check for clogged filters or water pressure issues.
- **Adding Minerals:** Consider using a remineralization filter to restore essential minerals to purified water, enhancing hydration.

UV Light Water Sterilization
UV sterilization is a method that employs ultraviolet light to destroy or inactivate microorganisms such as bacteria, viruses, and parasites in water without the use of chemicals. UV light damages the DNA of these organisms, preventing them from reproducing.

Advantages of UV Sterilization
- **Safety and Eco-Friendliness:** This method does not involve chemicals, making it an environmentally safe option for disinfecting water.
- **Preservation of Water Quality:** Unlike chemical methods, UV sterilization does not alter the water's taste, smell, or color.

Installing a UV System
1. **Water Assessment:** Prior to installation, test the water quality to determine any contaminants that need addressing.
2. **Select the System:** Evaluate the required flow rate and UV dose necessary for effective disinfection. Ensure compatibility with your existing plumbing system.
3. **Conduct Maintenance:** Adhere to the manufacturer's guidelines for regular replacement of the UV lamp and cleaning of the quartz sleeve to maintain system effectiveness.

UV System Maintenance
- **Lamp Replacement:** UV lamps lose effectiveness over time, requiring regular replacement as per the manufacturer's recommendations.
- **Cleaning the Quartz Sleeve:** Mineral deposits can accumulate on the sleeve surrounding the lamp, diminishing sterilization efficiency, so periodic cleaning is essential.
- **O-ring Inspection:** Regularly check O-rings for leaks, replacing them if they show signs of wear or damage.

DIY Water Collection System

In the context of emergencies, it's important to plan ahead and construct a do-it-yourself system for collecting water, whether from rain or natural sources like streams or rivers.
Estimated Cost: $100 - $300
Difficulty Level: Moderate
Time Required: 4-6 hours

Rainwater harvesting is an effective and sustainable way to accumulate water. This method captures rainwater from rooftops and stores it in tanks for later use. It's particularly beneficial in areas with consistent rainfall, providing significant water for household activities, gardening, and even human consumption, provided adequate filtration is implemented.

Necessary Materials
- **Large Food-Grade Barrel:** A barrel of at least 55 gallons, constructed from food-safe plastic or metal to avoid contamination.
- **Gutters and Downspouts:** Sufficient aluminum or vinyl gutters to cover the roof edge (approximately 10-20 feet per side).
- **Debris Filter:** A fine mesh screen to fit over the downspout.
- **First Flush Diverter:** A unit correctly sized for your roof area (usually 3-4 inches in diameter).
- **PVC Pipes and Fittings:** 10 feet of 1-inch PVC pipe with various fittings (elbows, tees, connectors). Use Schedule 40 PVC for longer durability.
- **Tap:** A brass or plastic tap with threaded ends to secure the hose.
- **Teflon Tape:** A roll of plumber's tape for sealing threaded connections.
- **Concrete Blocks or Sturdy Support:** 4-6 standard concrete blocks or a wooden/metal stand that can hold the full barrel.
- **Waterproof Sealant:** A tube of silicone-based sealant for outdoor use.
- **Tools:** Ladder, drill, screwdriver, hacksaw or PVC cutter, and level.

Procedure
1. **Select the Container:** Choose a large food-grade barrel for water collection. A 55-gallon barrel is standard, but larger containers can be used if needed. Ensure the barrel has a secure lid to prevent contamination and insect growth, placing it where it can receive direct rainwater and is easily accessible for maintenance.
2. **Install Gutters and Downspouts:** Attach gutters along the roof edge to direct rainwater to downspouts. Measure your roof's length to determine the necessary gutter length. Use brackets to secure the gutters every 60-90 cm, ensuring a slight downward slope (about 0.6 cm for every 3 meters) for proper water flow. Connect downspouts to the gutters, directing them toward the collection container.
3. **Add a Debris Screen:** Install a screen at the top of the downspout to filter out larger debris. Cut the screen to size and secure it with screws or adhesive. This will help keep the water clean in the barrel and reduce maintenance frequency.
4. **Install the First Flush Diverter:** Attach a first flush diverter to the downspout to redirect the initial water flow, which may contain contaminants like dust, bird droppings, and leaves, away from the storage container. Follow the manufacturer's instructions for secure installation.
5. **Connect PVC Pipes:** Use PVC pipes to connect the downspout to the collection barrel. Measure and cut pipes as necessary, using elbows and connectors to guide the water into the barrel. Assemble the pipes dry before applying PVC cement to secure the connections, and apply waterproof sealant around joints to prevent leaks.
6. **Install the Faucet:** Drill a hole near the base of the downspout, about 2 inches from the bottom, for the faucet. Wrap Teflon tape around the faucet threads to ensure a leak-proof connection. Insert the tap into the hole and secure it with a washer and nut inside the downspout, applying waterproof sealant around the edges.
7. **Elevate the Container:** Place the barrel on concrete blocks or a sturdy stand to elevate it. This allows gravity to assist in water flow, making it easier to fill buckets or connect pipes for water distribution. Ensure that the stand is stable and level to prevent tipping when the barrel is full.
8. **Seal and Protect:** Ensure all connections are well-sealed to prevent leaks and contamination. Check the stability of the downspout on its support. Make sure the lid is properly secured and that there are no openings for insects or debris.
9. **System Testing:** Once the installation is complete, test it during the next rain. Look for leaks, ensure that water flows correctly through the downspout, and verify the functionality of the first flush diverter and debris screen. Make any necessary adjustments to enhance system performance.

This DIY rainwater collection system will provide a reliable and sustainable water source, decreasing reliance on external supplies and aiding in the conservation of water resources.

Stream or River Water Collection System

Estimated Cost: $150 - $400

Difficulty Level: Moderate
Time Required: 1-2 Days

If you reside near a stream or river, establishing a water collection system can provide a consistent supply of water. This method involves redirecting a portion of the water flow into a storage tank, making it particularly beneficial in areas with flowing water, thereby fulfilling significant needs for irrigation and livestock.

Necessary Materials:
- **PVC Pipe:** Obtain 4-inch diameter PVC pipe, preferably Schedule 40 for added durability. The total length should correspond to the distance between the water source and the storage area, typically ranging from 10 to 50 feet. Carefully measure this distance to determine the precise amount needed.
- **Filter Mesh or Fabric:** Acquire sufficient fine-mesh stainless steel mesh or heavy-duty filter fabric to cover the suction end of the PVC pipe (about 1-2 square feet) to prevent debris from entering the system.
- **Hose Clamps:** Use 4-6 large hose clamps to secure the mesh to the PVC pipe and connect it to the vacuum hose.
- **Concrete Blocks or Large Rocks:** Collect 4-6 concrete blocks or large rocks to anchor and stabilize the intake pipe in the stream or river, ensuring stability during fluctuations in water flow.
- **Water Storage Containers:** Choose 2-4 storage containers, like 55-gallon food-grade barrels or larger tanks, depending on your water needs. Ensure these are made from food-safe materials to avoid contamination.
- **Flexible Hose or Garden Hose:** Utilize a heavy-duty garden hose or flexible PVC tubing matching the diameter of the PVC pipe, long enough to connect the intake to the storage containers (typically between 10 and 50 feet).
- **Waterproof Sealant:** Acquire outdoor silicone caulk to protect connections and prevent leaks.
- **Shovel or Digging Tool:** A standard shovel or specialized tool will be needed to dig a shallow trench for the pipe.
- **Water Purification System:** Have a purification system ready, such as chemical disinfectants (e.g., chlorine tablets) or a filtration system (e.g., ceramic filter), to treat the collected water before consumption.
- **Basic Tools:** You'll require a saw for cutting PVC pipes, a drill for making holes in storage containers, and a wrench for tightening hose clamps.

Instructions:
1. **Select a Location:** Find a spot along the stream or river where the water flow is steady and clean. Avoid areas with stagnant water, excessive algae, or potential upstream contamination sources. Look for a location where the water is clear and where both the water source and storage area are easily accessible.
2. **Prepare the Suction Hose:** Cut a section of the 4-inch PVC pipe long enough to reach the bank of the river or stream. Attach a fine mesh screen or filter fabric to one end to prevent debris from entering. Secure the screen using hose clamps or zip ties to ensure it stays in place with the water flow.
3. **Install the Suction Hose:** Insert the suction hose into the stream or river so that the screened end is submerged but not buried in sediment. Use concrete blocks or large rocks to stabilize the pipe, ensuring it remains anchored even during strong water flows.
4. **Connect the Suction Hose to the Transfer Hose:** Use a hose clamp to connect one end of the transfer hose to the suction hose, ensuring a tight, watertight seal. The transfer hose should be long enough to connect the suction point to the storage containers.
5. **Lay the Transfer Pipe:** Dig a shallow trench from the intake pipe to the storage container area, approximately 4 to 6 inches deep to protect the pipe from damage and allow smooth water flow. Place the pipe in the trench, avoiding kinks or sharp bends, and cover it with soil or rocks to secure it and protect it from UV exposure.
6. **Prepare Containers for Storage:** Position the water storage containers on a flat surface near your living area, raising them on a platform or concrete blocks to facilitate gravity-fed flow. Drill a hole near the top of each container to insert the end of the transfer hose, using waterproof sealant around the hole to prevent leaks. If using multiple containers, connect them in series by drilling additional holes and connecting extra tubing.
7. **Collect and Store Water:** After assembly, allow water to flow through the intake hose and into the storage containers. Regularly check the intake hose for blockages and clean the mesh screen as necessary to maintain optimal water flow. Treat the collected water with your chosen purification system before drinking or cooking.

Maintenance Tips:
- **Regular Inspection of the Suction Pipe and Filter Screen:** Periodically check the suction hose and mesh screen for debris, cleaning them as necessary to ensure adequate flow.

- **Monitor Water Flow:** Daily check the water flow to ensure it remains constant and free of obstructions. Adjust the intake hose as needed during changes in water levels or after heavy rainfall.
- **Clean and Sanitize Storage Containers:** Regularly clean and sanitize storage containers to prevent algae growth and contamination. Use a mild bleach solution (1 tablespoon bleach per gallon of water) to clean the interior, followed by thorough rinsing.
- **Regular Water Quality Testing:** Frequently test your water quality using a test kit. Treat the water with your purification system to ensure it is safe for consumption.

This collection system for stream or river water will provide you with a continuous and reliable water source, effectively meeting your water needs in a sustainable manner.

Solar Distiller for Water Collection

Estimated Cost: $10 - $30
Difficulty Level: Easy
Time Required: 30-45 Minutes
Collection Time: Typically 12-24 Hours

A simple yet efficient solar distiller can produce drinking water by harnessing moisture from the soil, plants, or other sources using solar energy. This setup is especially suitable for arid regions where traditional water sources are scarce. The yield of water is influenced by environmental factors such as temperature, humidity, and the moisture content of the soil or plant material. Under optimal conditions, a solar distiller can generate about 1 liter of water daily, though yields may drop under less favorable circumstances.

Necessary Materials:
- **Transparent Plastic Sheets:** 1 sheet, 4 mil thickness, measuring 6 feet x 6 feet. This thickness and size provide durability and sufficient coverage.
- **Water Collection Container:** 1 container with at least a 1-quart (1-liter) capacity. A wide-mouthed container, like a bucket or bowl, maximizes water collection.
- **Small Rock or Weight:** 1 rock weighing approximately 2 lbs, which will create the condensation point by weighing down the center of the plastic sheet.
- **Drinking Tube (Optional):** 1 tube, 3 feet long and 1/4 inch in diameter, for direct drinking without disturbing the distiller.
- **Shovel:** 1 standard shovel for digging the trench.
- **Green Plant Material (Optional):** Leaves, grass, or other non-toxic vegetation to enhance humidity and boost water production.
- **Adhesive Tape or Pegs (Optional):** Sufficient to secure the plastic sheet, using tape or 4-6 stakes to keep the plastic taut.

Instructions:
1. **Select a Location:** Choose an area with direct sunlight for most of the day, preferably a slight depression or sandy spot that can retain moisture. Avoid shaded locations as they reduce distillation efficiency. In very dry settings, gather moist soil or green plant material to improve water output.
2. **Digging the Pit:** Use a shovel to create a circular pit about 3 to 4 feet in diameter and 2 feet deep. Ensure the sides slope inward toward the center to assist in directing condensation water to the collection container. Level the bottom of the pit for proper container placement.
3. **Position the Water Collection Container:** Place the container at the center of the pit to catch any water dripping from the plastic sheet. Ensure it is stable and unlikely to tip over.
4. **Add Green Plant Material (Optional):** If available, place green plant material such as leaves or grass around the container inside the pit. Evenly distribute this material to enhance moisture release and improve the distiller's water production.
5. **Cover the Pit with Plastic Sheet:** Lay the clear plastic over the pit, ensuring it covers the edges with some excess hanging over. Pull the plastic taut to prevent sagging and secure it with soil, rocks, or stakes to maintain an airtight installation, maximizing the greenhouse effect and promoting moisture evaporation.
6. **Create the Condensation Point:** Position a small stone or weight in the center of the plastic sheet, directly above the water collection container. This creates a low point in the plastic, allowing condensed water to drip into the container. Ensure the weight is heavy enough to keep the point low without tearing the plastic.
7. **Optional: Insert a Drinking Tube:** If using a drinking tube, insert one end into the container and extend the other end to the edge of the pit, burying it slightly to secure its position. Ensure the tube extends beyond the plastic covering for easy drinking.

8. **Seal and Wait:** Ensure all edges of the plastic sheet are tightly sealed to prevent air escape and retain as much heat as possible. Let the distiller operate throughout the day, ideally for 12-24 hours. The sun's heat will evaporate moisture from the soil or plant material, condensing it on the underside of the plastic and dripping into the container.
9. **Collecting Water:** Carefully remove the plastic sheet without spilling any collected water. Use a clean cup or drinking tube to access the water in the container. If you wish to continue collecting water, reattach the plastic and replace the rock. Assess the water quality before consumption, as additional purification may be necessary.

Maintenance Tips:
- **Regularly Inspect Plastic Sheets:** Check the plastic for holes or tears that could diminish effectiveness. Periodically inspect the cover and replace it as necessary to maintain a good seal.
- **Remove Debris:** Ensure that no debris accumulates on top of the plastic cover, as this could block sunlight and decrease the distiller's efficiency.
- **Monitor the Condensation Point:** The weight or rock used for the condensation point may shift due to wind or other factors. Regularly check to ensure it remains centered over the container.
- **Clean the Collection Container:** After each use, clean the container to remove any dirt, insects, or contaminants that may have entered during the harvesting process.
- **Rotate the Distiller:** If you observe a decrease in water yield, consider relocating the distiller to an area with more moisture or greater sunlight exposure.
- **Store Materials Properly:** If disassembling the distiller, keep the plastic sheets, container, and other materials in a dry, secure location to prevent damage or loss.

This solar distiller allows for the efficient and economical collection of drinking water, utilizing natural resources while reducing reliance on traditional water sources.

Constructing a Manual Water Pump

Estimated Cost: $50 - $100
Difficulty Level: Moderate
Time Required: 3-5 Hours

A manually operated water pump is a vital tool for extracting water from wells, rivers, or rainwater storage. This pump operates independently of electricity, making it ideal for off-grid living. It provides quick and efficient access to water, ensuring a reliable supply even during emergencies.

MATERIALS REQUIRED:
- **PVC Pipe (1 inch diameter, 10 feet total):** Cut into three sections: two pieces of 4 feet each and one piece of 2 feet. These will form the main structure and handle of the pump.
- **PVC Pipe (1.5-inch diameter, 5 feet total):** Cut into two sections: one 4-foot piece and one 1-foot piece, used for the handle and the drain pipe.
- **PVC Pipe Connectors:** Various types such as elbows, tees, and joints for connecting different sections of PVC.
- **Check Valves (1 inch, 2 units):** Allow water to flow in a single direction, preventing backflow.
- **Rubber Washers (4 for 1 inch PVC):** Used to create a watertight seal inside the pump.
- **Piston Rod (3/8 inch metal rod, 4 feet):** Serves as the piston to draw water. It should be durable and resistant to corrosion.
- **Handle Grip (1):** Provides a comfortable hold for the user, fitting the end of the 1.5-inch PVC pipe.
- **Hose Clamp (1):** Secures the piston rod and ensures a tight seal.
- **PVC Cement (1 can):** Used to bond PVC pipe sections and connectors.
- **Teflon Tape (1 roll):** Ensures watertightness of threaded connections.
- **Pipe Cutter or Saw (1):** For cutting PVC pipes to the specified lengths.
- **Sandpaper (1 pack, assorted grits):** Used to smooth the edges of PVC pipes after cutting.
- **Tools:** Pipe cutter or saw, drill with bits, screwdriver, adjustable wrench, clamps (optional, for holding pieces in place during assembly), safety glasses, and work gloves.

Instructions:
1. **Cut PVC Pipes:** Measure and cut the 1-inch PVC pipe into three sections: two at 4 feet each and one at 2 feet. Measure and cut the 1.5-inch PVC pipe into a 4-foot piece and a 1-foot piece. Use a pipe cutter or saw for clean cuts, sanding any rough edges afterward.

2. **Assemble the Pump Cylinder:** Attach a 1-inch PVC fitting to one end of a 4-foot section of the 1-inch pipe using PVC cement. Install a check valve on this fitting, ensuring the arrow on the valve points away from the pipe to indicate the direction of flow. Place a rubber washer inside the joint to create a seal. Connect the 2-foot section of 1-inch PVC to the other side of the check valve using PVC cement.
3. **Create the Pump Piston:** Drill a hole in the center of the remaining 4-foot, 1-inch PVC pipe, just above the coupling, large enough for the 3/8-inch metal piston rod to pass through. Thread the piston rod through this hole and secure it using a hose clamp and rubber washers to ensure a tight seal. Attach the second check valve to the end of the piston rod inside the PVC pipe, making sure the arrow on the valve points towards the rod to allow water to be pushed up.
4. **Assemble the Pump Handle:** Connect a 1-inch PVC tee to the open end of the 4-foot PVC pipe. Insert the 1-foot section of 1.5-inch PVC into the vertical opening of the tee fitting to serve as a handle for operating the pump. Attach the handle to the end of the 1.5-inch PVC pipe for convenience.
5. **Install the Drain Pipe:** Attach the remaining 4-foot section of 1-inch PVC pipe to the other side of the tee fitting, securing it with PVC cement. This pipe will carry water from the pump to the collection container. Use Teflon tape on threaded connections to ensure watertightness and prevent leaks.
6. **Test the Pump:** Position the pump cylinder into the water source, ensuring the check valve at the bottom is completely submerged. Operate the pump handle by moving it up and down to create suction, drawing water through the cylinder and out the drain pipe. If the pump does not function correctly, inspect for leaks, ensure all connections are tight, and verify that the check valves are correctly oriented.

Maintenance Tips:
- **Regular Inspections:** Routinely check the pump for signs of wear or damage, such as cracks in PVC pipes or leaks at connections. Promptly replace any worn components to maintain functionality.
- **Cleaning:** After each use, especially after drawing from a muddy or contaminated water source, rinse the pump with clean water to eliminate debris, preventing blockages and extending the pump's lifespan.
- **Storage:** When not in use, keep the pump in a dry, shaded area to protect the PVC from UV damage and prolong the life of its components.
- **Seal Checks:** Periodically inspect the seals created by rubber washers and Teflon tape. Replace washers or reapply Teflon tape if leaks are found.
- **Lubrication of the Piston Rod:** If the piston rod starts to stick or moves less smoothly, apply a small amount of food-grade lubricant to ensure smooth operation.

It's essential to recognize that water collected from rain, rivers, streams, lakes, or even wells may contain harmful contaminants. These can include bacteria, viruses, parasites, and chemical pollutants that easily infiltrate natural water sources. Consuming or using unfiltered water in an off-grid scenario poses significant health risks, including waterborne diseases like dysentery, cholera, giardia, and E. coli infections. These illnesses can lead to severe dehydration, gastrointestinal issues, and potentially life-threatening conditions if untreated.

This brings us to the critical next step in off-grid water management: filtration and purification. In connected environments like municipal water systems, the water we use daily is treated and safe for drinking, cooking, cleaning, and bathing. However, in an off-grid situation, the responsibility for ensuring water safety falls entirely on you. It's not merely about having water; it's about ensuring that it is clean and safe.

Failing to properly filter and disinfect water can lead to using contaminated water for essential activities, posing significant health risks that could jeopardize your survival and well-being. There are several reliable methods to ensure your water is safe, each suited to different circumstances and needs. This section will explore various simple and effective techniques, from basic filtration systems you can construct with minimal supplies to advanced purification methods. By understanding and implementing these methods, you can significantly reduce the risks associated with untreated water, ensuring that you and your family remain healthy and hydrated, regardless of the challenges faced off the grid.

Remember, clean water is not a luxury; it is a necessity. By dedicating time to learn and apply these water filtration and purification techniques, you not only meet a basic survival need; you build the foundation for a thriving, resilient off-grid lifestyle.

Constructing a Homemade Water Filter

Estimated Cost: $10 - $30
Difficulty Level: Easy
Time Required: 1-2 Hours

A homemade water filter is a straightforward yet effective method for removing physical impurities from water. This design typically utilizes layers of sand, gravel, and activated carbon to filter out debris, bacteria, and some chemicals. It serves as an excellent way to enhance the quality of water from natural sources such as rivers, lakes, and rainwater collection.

Necessary Materials:
- **Two Large Plastic Bottles:** 2 bottles (1-liter size is sufficient); one will act as the filter, and the other will collect the filtered water.
- **Sand:** 2 cups each of fine and coarse sand. Sand aids in capturing fine particles and impurities in the water.
- **Activated Carbon:** 1 cup. Activated carbon is vital for eliminating chemicals, odors, and toxins.
- **Gravel:** 1 cup of small gravel and 1 cup of large gravel. Gravel traps larger debris and supports the sand layers.
- **Coffee Filters or Fine Mesh Fabric:** 2 pieces needed to prevent the filter medium from falling and to add an additional filtration layer.
- **Scissors or Knife:** 1 pair of scissors or a knife for cutting the plastic bottles.
- **Elastic Bands or Cords:** 2 rubber bands or cords to secure the coffee filters or fabric to the bottle.
- **Container for Collecting Filtered Water:** 1 clean container, such as a jar or bowl, to hold the filtered water.

Instructions:
1. **Prepare the Bottles:** Take one of the large plastic bottles and cut off the bottom about 2 inches from the end. This will serve as the filtration unit. Remove the cap to allow water to drain. Keep the second bottle intact to collect the filtered water.
2. **Create the Filter Layer:** Place a coffee filter or piece of fine mesh fabric inside the neck of the cut bottle. Secure it with a rubber band or string around the outside of the neck to prevent larger materials from contaminating the filtered water.
3. **Add Activated Carbon:** Carefully pour a 1-inch layer of activated carbon over the coffee filter or mesh fabric, ensuring even distribution for maximum contact with the water. This layer is crucial for absorbing impurities, odors, and toxins.
4. **Incorporate Fine Sand:** Add a 2-inch layer of fine sand on top of the activated carbon. This sand captures smaller particles and further purifies the water. Ensure this layer is uniform to prevent preferential channels where water might bypass the filtering media.
5. **Include Coarse Sand:** Add another 2-inch layer of coarse sand over the fine sand. This layer captures larger particles and prevents fine sand from mixing with the gravel, maintaining the effectiveness of each filtering layer.
6. **Incorporate Small Gravel:** Pour a 2-inch layer of small gravel on top of the coarse sand. This gravel provides structural support for the sand layers and helps filter out larger debris. Evenly distribute the gravel to stabilize the filter media.
7. **Add Large Gravel:** Finally, place a 2-inch layer of large gravel at the top of the bottle. This gravel acts as a pre-filter to capture larger debris and prevents finer layers from being disturbed when water is poured into the filter.
8. **Assemble the Filter:** Position the filter bottle (cut end facing up) inside the second intact bottle. Ensure that the neck of the filter bottle is firmly inserted into the opening of the collection bottle, allowing filtered water to drip into the collection container while preventing unfiltered water from bypassing the system.
9. **Water Filtration:** Gradually pour the contaminated water into the top of the filter. The water will flow through each layer (large gravel, small gravel, coarse sand, fine sand, and activated carbon), trapping particles and impurities.
10. **Collection and Storage:** Once the water has passed through all the layers, carefully remove the collection bottle. The filtered water should appear clearer and free of visible debris.

Chemical Water Disinfection

Estimated Cost: $10 - $25
Difficulty Level: Easy
Time Required: 30-60 minutes (excluding storage time)

Chemical disinfection is a rapid and effective method for purifying water using substances such as chlorine or iodine. This approach efficiently eliminates bacteria, viruses, and protozoa, making it particularly useful during emergencies or when other filtration methods are unavailable. Understanding the correct dosages and application techniques is crucial for ensuring water safety.

Necessary Materials:
- **Chlorine or Iodine:** Available in tablet or liquid form for disinfection.
- **Clean Container:** For mixing and storing disinfected water.
- **Measuring Cup:** To accurately measure chlorine or iodine.
- **Agitator:** A spoon or stick for stirring the water after adding the disinfectant.

Instructions for Using Chlorine Bleach:
1. **Gather Materials:** Ensure you have unscented household bleach containing sodium hypochlorite in a concentration between 5% and 8.25%. Check the label for concentration. Use clean, food-safe containers to mix and store disinfected water.
2. **Calculate Dosage:**
   - **For Clean Water:** Use 8 drops (about 1/8 teaspoon) of bleach per gallon of water.
   - **For Cloudy or Contaminated Water:** Use 16 drops (about 1/4 teaspoon) of bleach per gallon of water.
3. **Add the Bleach:** Measure the appropriate amount using a dropper or measuring cup, then carefully add it to the water. For a 5-gallon container of clean water, add 40 drops (8 drops per gallon x 5 gallons) or about 5/8 teaspoon of bleach.
4. **Mix Thoroughly:** Use the stir stick to ensure the bleach is evenly distributed throughout the water. Proper mixing is essential for effective disinfection.
5. **Wait:** Allow the water to sit for at least 30 minutes. A slight chlorine smell indicates disinfection. If no chlorine smell is detected, add the same amount of bleach and wait another 15 minutes.
6. **Store:** Pour the disinfected water into clean, covered containers. Keep these containers sealed to prevent recontamination and label them with the disinfection date for reference.

Using Iodine:
1. **Gather Materials:** Choose 2% iodine tincture or commercial iodine tablets, using clean, food-safe containers for mixing and storing disinfected water.
2. **Calculate Dosage:**
   - **For Clear Water:** Use 5 drops of 2% iodine tincture per liter of water.
   - **For Cloudy Water:** Use 10 drops of 2% iodine per liter of water.
3. **Add Iodine:** Measure the appropriate amount with a dropper or add the specified number of tablets directly to the water. For instance, for a 1-gallon container of clean water, add 20 drops (5 drops per quart x 4 quarts) of iodine solution.
4. **Mix Thoroughly:** Stir the water well with the stir stick to ensure the iodine is evenly distributed.
5. **Wait:** Let the water sit for at least 30 minutes. If the water is cold (below 5°C), extend the waiting time to 60 minutes, as iodine's effectiveness decreases at lower temperatures.
6. **Store:** Transfer disinfected water to clean, covered containers to protect it from contaminants, storing it in a cool, dark place to maintain quality.

Maintenance Tips:
- **Regular Inspection:** Check the expiration dates of bleach and iodine to ensure they remain effective, as their strength may diminish over time.
- **Safe Handling:** Store disinfectant chemicals in a safe, cool, dry location, out of reach of children and pets. Clearly label containers to avoid accidental ingestion.
- **Reserve Supply:** Keep a backup supply of bleach or iodine in your emergency kit to ensure continuous access to purification methods during prolonged emergencies.
- **Water Analysis:** If possible, periodically test your water with a home testing kit to confirm that your disinfection methods are effective and that the water is safe for consumption.

These homemade filters and chemical purification techniques provide affordable and practical solutions to enhance water quality, ensuring a safe and reliable water supply.

Water Filtration

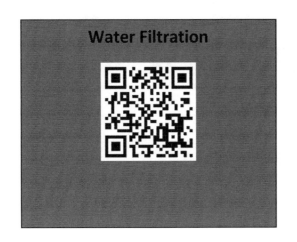

Water purification for bugging in

CHAPTER 4:

ENERGY GENERATION AND CONSERVATION AT HOME

Let's explore a crucial element of off-grid living: energy. As we've previously discussed regarding other vital resources, energy is not readily accessible outside the modern infrastructure we often rely on. Living off-grid means we can no longer depend on grid electricity, necessitating the pursuit of sustainable alternatives to fulfill our energy requirements. Energy underpins many daily activities, including cooking, charging devices, providing lighting, and temperature control. Without a dependable energy source, maintaining even basic comforts can turn into a formidable challenge. In this chapter, I will help you navigate alternative energy sources and demonstrate how to effectively utilize them to satisfy your needs. These alternative solutions not only foster independence and resilience during natural disasters or emergencies but also promote an eco-friendly lifestyle by minimizing your environmental footprint. While some of these concepts might appear daunting if you're inexperienced with energy management, with patience and commitment, you can master them and attain genuine energy independence. The key is to tackle each challenge gradually, step by step, building your knowledge and skills progressively.

Generate Your Own Energy

Securing your home is not solely about safeguarding against external threats; it also entails establishing a self-sustaining environment that supports you and your family under all circumstances. A vital aspect of this self-sufficiency is the management of your own energy supply. Given the potential for energy disruptions due to natural disasters, social unrest, or other emergencies, maintaining control over your energy becomes critical. Generating your own energy is not merely a convenience; it is essential for safety and survival. Recognizing that energy is a fundamental need is the first step. It powers everything from cooking and lighting to heating and communication. Without a stable energy source, even routine tasks can become challenging. Therefore, devising a strategy to ensure energy independence in the event of prolonged outages or emergencies is essential.

One effective method is to install a solar panel system. Solar energy is a renewable and plentiful resource capable of fulfilling various household needs. By harnessing solar energy, you can decrease your reliance on the electricity grid while maintaining a clean and consistent energy source, even during power failures or emergencies. To maximize the advantages of solar energy, it is vital to not only focus on the installation of solar panels but also to ensure that you have the capability to store the generated energy. Solar batteries are crucial for storing energy for use during the night or on cloudy days, thereby guaranteeing a dependable energy supply at all times.

Remember, the journey to self-sufficiency doesn't stop here. I encourage you to keep learning, stay updated, and expand your knowledge. The more you understand, the better equipped you will be to handle any situation with confidence and creativity. Whether through books, online resources, or hands-on experiences, never cease your pursuit of new information and techniques to enhance your skills.

Diversifying your energy sources is equally vital. Relying on a single type of energy source can leave you vulnerable. Incorporating a backup generator powered by fossil fuels can offer an additional energy supply during times of low sunlight or inclement weather. Even a small portable generator can be an invaluable asset, providing power for essential needs until conditions improve. It is crucial to use generators safely, ensuring proper ventilation and an adequate fuel supply to mitigate risks associated with harmful emissions.

Energy efficiency plays a critical role in enhancing your home's energy independence. Generating energy is only one part of the equation; using it efficiently is equally essential. Upgrading your home's insulation, utilizing energy-efficient appliances, and adopting practices that minimize waste can significantly bolster your energy autonomy. The more efficiently you utilize energy, the less you will require, thereby reducing your reliance on external sources and extending the longevity of your energy reserves.

Investing in energy self-sufficiency is not merely a precaution; it is a strategic approach for the future. Not only does it provide peace of mind, knowing that you are prepared for any situation, but it also results in long-term financial savings. By reducing your dependence on traditional energy suppliers and fossil fuels, you protect yourself from price volatility and service interruptions, while also contributing to a more sustainable environment. Effective energy management necessitates planning and foresight regarding potential challenges. By implementing the right technologies and strategies, you can ensure that your home remains functional and secure, regardless of external conditions. Energy self-sufficiency forms a fundamental pillar of your home's security and resilience.

Energy Requirements During Emergencies

In the face of natural disasters, power outages, or unforeseen emergencies, maintaining a stable and dependable energy supply is critical to successfully navigating the crisis. Planning for your home's energy needs is not just a matter of convenience; it is a fundamental survival aspect. During emergencies, access to energy becomes vital for heating, food preservation, operating medical devices, and staying connected. Proper preparation involves assessing your energy needs and strategizing to meet them.

Begin by identifying your essential energy requirements. These might encompass maintaining indoor temperatures, powering communication devices, storing food and water, and providing basic lighting. Understanding these priorities necessitates a thorough analysis of your home's energy consumption to determine how much energy is needed to sustain essential functions during a crisis. With a clear grasp of your needs, you can formulate a plan to meet them, which may involve installing solar panels to harness renewable energy, acquiring an emergency generator for backup power, and stockpiling sufficient fuel to operate the generator.

Efficiency is a crucial aspect of energy management during emergencies. Merely having an energy source is inadequate; it must be utilized efficiently to maximize its lifespan and efficacy. This includes adequately insulating your home to reduce heat loss or gain, selecting energy-efficient appliances, and timing energy-intensive tasks to lessen your overall consumption.

Another critical factor is the resilience of your energy system. Emergencies often disrupt traditional infrastructure, necessitating that your system operates independently of the main power grid. This could involve having a battery system charged by solar panels or a standalone generator. Regular maintenance is vital to ensure that these systems function optimally when needed. Avoid discovering issues with your generator or solar batteries only in times of crisis.

Develop a plan for the potential duration of emergencies, which could extend for days, weeks, or even months. Ensure you have adequate fuel, backup batteries, and a strategy for rotating food supplies and other resources to sustain your family over an extended period. Flexibility and adaptability are essential, as situations may shift unexpectedly. Effective energy management during emergencies is an integral part of maintaining a safe home amid external challenges. By planning ahead, comprehending your needs, optimizing efficiency, and ensuring your energy system's resilience, you can create a sanctuary where you and your loved ones are ready to confront any crisis.

Understanding Off-Grid Energy Solutions

Achieving off-grid energy independence begins with familiarizing yourself with the renewable energy sources available to you. The most common and effective options include solar, wind, and hydroelectric energy. Each of these sources offers unique benefits, making them suitable for different environmental conditions and requirements. Selecting the right combination of these resources is vital for ensuring a reliable and sustainable energy supply for your off-grid lifestyle.

- **Solar Energy**: Solar energy is harnessed through photovoltaic (PV) panels, which convert sunlight into electricity. This energy source is among the most accessible and scalable, suitable for a variety of applications, ranging from small portable systems to extensive installations. Solar energy is particularly effective in regions that receive ample sunlight throughout the year. However, it is crucial to consider factors such as the angle of your roof, shading, and local weather patterns when planning your solar system. Advances in solar technology have significantly increased efficiency, and integrating battery storage systems can ensure a consistent energy supply even on cloudy days.
- **Wind Energy**: Wind turbines convert the kinetic energy of wind into electricity. This renewable source is particularly effective in areas with consistent, strong winds, such as coastal regions or open plains. Wind energy can serve as a valuable complement to solar energy, especially during periods with diminished sunlight. When designing a wind energy system, it is important to assess the average wind speed in your area and any obstacles, such as buildings or trees, that could hinder the turbines' performance. Small-scale wind turbines are suitable for individual homes, while larger systems can power entire communities.

- **Hydroelectric Energy**: Micro-hydroelectric systems generate electricity from flowing water, making them ideal for properties near rivers, streams, or other moving water sources. Hydroelectricity offers a steady and reliable energy source, particularly in regions with consistent water flows year-round. Unlike solar and wind energy, which can be intermittent, hydropower can provide a continuous electricity supply, both day and night. However, establishing a hydroelectric system requires careful planning and an understanding of local water rights and environmental regulations. Additionally, micro-hydroelectric systems can be combined with other renewable sources to create a hybrid system that maximizes energy production.

In this section, we will explore various projects designed to help you access these essential energy sources. Given the complexity of the topic, I will provide detailed information on the materials needed and the steps to follow. As always, the best project or combination of projects will depend on your specific circumstances and energy requirements. Factors such as your geographic location, available resources, budget, and energy consumption patterns should guide your decision-making.

DIY Solar Panel Installation

Estimated Cost: $500 - $2,000
Difficulty Level: Medium
Time Required: 3-4 days

Harnessing solar energy is an effective and sustainable method to generate electricity for your off-grid home. This project will provide a step-by-step guide to installing solar panels, delivering a renewable energy source to power your essential appliances and devices.

Required Materials:
- **Solar Panels** (2 to 6 units, based on energy requirements)
  Capacity: Typically ranges from 250 to 400 watts per panel.
  Note: The precise number of panels required will depend on your energy consumption, geographical location, and available installation space.
- **Charge Controller** (1 unit)
  Capacity: Must align with the total amperage of your solar panels (e.g., a 30 amp regulator for smaller systems or a 60 amp regulator for larger systems).
  Type: An MPPT (Maximum Power Point Tracking) controller is advised for enhanced efficiency.
- **Inverter** (1 unit)
  Capacity: Should match your maximum load, typically between 1000 to 5000 watts.
  Type: A pure sine wave inverter is preferred for sensitive electronic devices.
- **Batteries** (2 to 4 units)
  Type: Deep cycle batteries, available in 12V or 24V, either lead-acid or lithium-ion.
  Capacity: Ranges from 100Ah to 200Ah per battery, depending on your storage needs.
- **Mounting Hardware**: This includes brackets, bolts, screws, and rails.
  Quantity: Should equal the number of panels; typically, you'll need 4 brackets and 8-12 bolts per panel, depending on size and mounting method.
- **Electrical Cables and Connectors**: These include solar panel cables, battery cables, MC4 connectors, and fuses/switches.

Detailed Instructions:
1. **Assess Your Energy Needs**: Calculate the total wattage for the appliances and devices you intend to power. For example, if you aim to power a refrigerator, lighting, and some electronic devices, you may need a system capable of generating 3 to 4 kWh daily. Consider the average sunlight hours in your location to establish the total number of panels required.
2. **Select Suitable Solar Panels**: Choose panels that strike a good balance between efficiency, durability, and cost. Monocrystalline panels typically offer higher efficiency but come at a higher price, while polycrystalline panels provide a more affordable option with slightly reduced efficiency.
3. **Prepare the Mounting Site**: Identify a location that receives unobstructed sunlight for a minimum of 5-6 hours daily. Roof installations are common, but if your roof is unsuitable, consider a ground mount. Set the mounting brackets at an angle appropriate for your latitude (usually between 30 and 45 degrees), ensuring they are level for optimal installation.
4. **Install the Solar Panels**: Secure the panels to the mounting hardware, ensuring they are firmly bolted. Double-check that the panels are angled correctly to maximize sunlight exposure.

5. **Connect the Charge Controller**: Position the charge controller in a sheltered area, preferably close to the battery bank. Attach the positive and negative wires from the solar panels to the input terminals of the controller.
6. **Install the Batteries**: Place the batteries in a safe, ventilated area, away from direct sunlight and moisture. Use appropriate gauge wire to connect the batteries in series or parallel (depending on your voltage requirements) to the charge controller.
7. **Configure the Inverter**: Connect the inverter's input terminals to the battery bank using heavy-duty battery cables, ensuring the positive and negative poles are connected correctly. Position the inverter in a cool, ventilated area near the batteries.
8. **Connect the Electrical System**: Run electrical cables from the AC output of the inverter to your home's electrical panel or directly to appliances. Use suitable fuses and circuit breakers to safeguard the circuit.
9. **Test the System**: Activate the system and check the voltage and current in each phase (solar panels, charge controller, batteries, and inverter) using a multimeter. Ensure your appliances are receiving power correctly and that the system operates smoothly.
10. **Monitor and Maintain the System**: Regularly monitor system performance via the charge controller display or an alternative monitoring system, if available. Clean solar panels periodically, particularly if they are exposed to dust, leaves, or bird droppings, to sustain optimal efficiency. Inspect all electrical connections for signs of corrosion or wear, and promptly address any issues.

Maintenance Tips:
- **Solar Panels**: Clean your panels at least twice a year, or more frequently if you reside in dust-prone areas. Regularly check for physical damage.
- **Batteries**: Frequently monitor electrolyte levels (for lead-acid batteries) and charge status. Ensure terminals are clean and free from corrosion.
- **Connections**: Regularly inspect all connections for tightness and signs of wear. Replace any damaged cables or connectors.

Following this step-by-step process will enable you to effectively harness solar energy, ensuring a consistent and reliable power supply for your off-grid home.

Building a Wind Turbine

Creating a wind turbine is an excellent way to generate electricity, especially in regions with consistent winds. This project will guide you through constructing and installing a small wind turbine to harness wind energy for your off-grid home.

Required Materials:
- **Wind Turbine Kit or Components** (1 kit or set):
  Includes: blades, hub, and motor (permanent magnet alternator or DC motor).
  Capacity: A small turbine typically produces between 400 and 1000 watts, depending on wind conditions.
  Note: Kits are budget-friendly; if purchasing individual parts, ensure they are compatible.
- **Tower or Pole** (1 unit):
  Height: Between 20 and 30 feet (the taller the tower, the better for capturing steady winds).
  Material: Steel or aluminum is recommended for durability.
  Anchoring: Includes guy wires, anchor bolts, and a concrete base for stability.
- **Charge Regulator** (1 unit):
  Capacity: Should correspond to the turbine's maximum power, typically between 30 and 60 amps.
  Type: Either PWM or MPPT, with the latter being more efficient.
- **Inverter** (1 unit):
  Capacity: Should be based on your maximum load, such as 1000W-5000W.
  Type: A pure sine wave inverter is recommended for sensitive electronics.
- **Batteries** (2-4 units):
  Type: Deep cycle, 12V or 24V, lead-acid or lithium-ion batteries.
  Capacity: Ranges from 100Ah to 200Ah per battery, depending on storage needs.
- **Electrical Cables and Connectors**:
  - **Turbine Wires**: 50 to 100 feet of 10 AWG wire to connect the turbine to the charge controller.
  - **Battery Wires**: AWG 4 or AWG 6, with appropriate connectors.
  - **Ground Wire**: 6 AWG copper wire, at least 25 feet long.
  - **MC4 Connectors**: Typically 2-4 pairs (depending on system configuration).
  - **Fuse/Breaker**: Rated according to your system, usually between 30 and 60 amps.

- **Basic Tools**: Drill, wrench set, screwdriver set, wire stripper/crimping pliers, multimeter, level.

Detailed Instructions:
1. **Evaluate Wind Resources**: Utilize an anemometer to gauge the average wind speed in your area. Small turbines perform best in winds of at least 10-15 mph. Position the anemometer at the height where you plan to install the turbine for accurate measurements.
2. **Select the Appropriate Wind Turbine**: Choose a turbine that aligns with your area's wind conditions and your energy needs. For instance, if you aim to generate 2 to 3 kWh daily, a turbine with a capacity of 500-1000 watts may be suitable. Consider the material durability, especially in harsh climates.
3. **Prepare the Site**: Select a location free from obstructions such as trees, buildings, or hills that could interfere with wind flow. The site should be as elevated as possible—rooftops, open fields, or hills are ideal. Mark the installation area, ensuring enough space for guy wires if necessary.
4. **Install the Tower**: Excavate a hole and create a concrete base for the tower, allowing the concrete to cure fully before erecting the tower. Secure the tower with guy wires to ensure stability, especially in high winds. Use a level to confirm that the tower is perfectly vertical before tightening all bolts and anchors.
5. **Mount the Wind Turbine**: Assemble the wind turbine per the manufacturer's guidelines, attaching the blades to the hub and then the hub to the motor. Carefully elevate the turbine and secure it atop the tower, ensuring all components are fastened. Tighten all bolts and verify that the blades can spin freely.
6. **Connect the Charge Controller**: Position the charge controller in a weather-resistant location, ideally near the battery bank. Connect the positive and negative wires from the turbine to the input terminals of the regulator. Ensure all connections are secure and well-insulated.
7. **Install the Batteries**: Position the batteries in a cool, dry, and ventilated area. Utilize the appropriate gauge wires to connect batteries in series or parallel, depending on your voltage requirements. Connect the batteries to the charge controller following the manufacturer's instructions for proper wiring.
8. **Configure the Inverter**: Link the inverter to the battery bank using heavy-duty battery cables. Double-check the polarity before making connections. Install the inverter in a cool, well-ventilated area to prevent overheating.
9. **Connect the Electrical System**: Run electrical wires from the inverter to your home's electrical distribution box or directly to your appliances. Install fuses or circuit breakers for system protection. Ensure all connections are properly insulated and that the system is adequately grounded to mitigate electrical hazards.
10. **Test the System**: Activate the wind turbine system and use a multimeter to assess the voltage and current across each component (turbine, charge controller, batteries, and inverter). Confirm that the turbine is generating power, charging the batteries, and supplying energy to your home or devices.

Maintenance Tips:
- **Wind Turbine**: Regularly inspect your turbine, especially after storms, for signs of wear, corrosion, or damage. Verify that the blades are balanced and can rotate freely.
- **Tower Stability**: Periodically check the guy lines and anchors of the tower to ensure stability. Tighten any loose connections.
- **Batteries**: Maintain proper charge levels and monitor electrolyte levels (for lead-acid batteries). Keep terminals clean and free from corrosion.
- **Electrical Connections**: Regularly inspect all electrical connections for signs of wear or corrosion and replace any damaged components.

By diligently following these instructions and prioritizing maintenance, you can construct a wind turbine that provides clean, sustainable energy for your off-grid home.

Wind-Powered Lighting

Utilizing wind energy to illuminate off-grid areas offers a sustainable and cost-effective solution for lighting needs. Wind-powered lighting systems employ small-scale wind turbines to convert the wind's kinetic energy into electrical power, which can be used to illuminate LED lights and other energy-efficient lighting solutions. This section discusses the components required to establish a wind-powered lighting system, including selecting a wind turbine, battery storage for energy, and integrating solar systems for a more consistent lighting solution.

Choosing the appropriate wind turbine is vital for an efficient lighting setup. The turbine's size and production capacity should align with the lighting system's energy requirements. Small wind turbines, typically producing between 400 watts and 1 kilowatt, are ideal for most off-grid lighting applications. The site selection for the turbine is crucial for its performance; locations with an average wind speed of at least 10 miles per hour are optimal. The turbine should be positioned on a tower high enough to capture steadier winds, while also adhering to local regulations and height restrictions.

Energy storage through batteries is a critical element of wind-powered lighting, ensuring that lights remain functional even in the absence of wind. Deep cycle batteries are recommended due to their capacity to endure repeated charging and discharging cycles. The battery bank's capacity should be adequate to store energy sufficient to power the lighting system for several days, factoring in periods of low wind.

Combining wind and solar systems can provide a more reliable energy supply for off-grid lighting. Solar panels can generate electricity on sunny days with little wind, while wind turbines can produce power at night or during cloudy, windy conditions. This hybrid approach optimizes the availability of renewable energy, lessening reliance on a single source. Charge controllers with dual inputs for wind and solar can manage battery charging from both sources, preventing overcharging and extending battery life.

DIY Project: Construct a Wind-Powered Streetlight

This project involves building a standalone streetlight powered by a small wind turbine. It encompasses selecting an appropriate turbine, creating a mounting tower, connecting the turbine to a battery bank, and installing LED lights designed for low energy consumption. Safety considerations, such as securing the tower and ensuring safe electrical connections, are highlighted to guarantee a reliable and secure installation.

Wind-powered lighting presents a sustainable method for illuminating off-grid areas, capitalizing on the abundant and renewable resource of wind. With careful selection of components and integration with solar energy, it is possible to create efficient and dependable lighting systems that minimize environmental impact and provide illumination without relying on grid electricity.

Utilizing Wind Turbines for Illumination

Harnessing wind energy for lighting requires a solid understanding of the principles behind wind energy generation and its application in lighting solutions. Wind turbines transform the kinetic energy from the wind into electrical power, which can either be stored in batteries or directly used to illuminate fixtures. The effectiveness of wind turbines for lighting relies primarily on the wind speed and consistency in your area, as well as the energy demands of your lighting system. LED lights are especially suitable for use with wind turbines due to their low energy consumption and long lifespan, making them an ideal option for off-grid lighting solutions.

When planning to utilize wind turbines for lighting, it's vital to assess the total energy consumption of your lighting setup and align it with the turbine's output to ensure adequate energy generation. Furthermore, incorporating an appropriately sized battery bank is essential for storing excess energy for use during calm periods, thus guaranteeing a continuous power supply for your lights.

The installation of wind turbines for lighting also necessitates consideration of the turbine tower's height; taller towers can capture more consistent wind flows. However, local regulations and practical constraints, such as available space and safety, must also be taken into account. The electrical wiring design connecting the turbine to the lights and battery bank requires careful planning to minimize energy losses and ensure safety, particularly in outdoor or exposed installations.

For those interested in DIY projects, creating a wind-powered lighting system can be a fulfilling endeavor. This process involves selecting the right turbine, constructing a mounting tower, establishing the battery storage system, and wiring the entire setup. Implementing safety measures, including proper grounding and secure attachment of the turbine, is crucial to prevent accidents and enhance the system's longevity. Overall, utilizing wind turbines for illumination represents a sustainable and cost-effective approach to off-grid lighting, providing an eco-friendly alternative to conventional energy sources. With thoughtful planning and consideration of the specific lighting system requirements, wind energy can serve as a dependable power source for off-grid lighting solutions.

Battery Storage for Wind-Powered Lighting

Battery storage is essential to ensure that wind-powered lighting remains functional during periods of low or no wind. Deep cycle batteries, known for their resilience and ability to be repeatedly discharged and recharged, are ideal for this application. These batteries store the electrical energy generated by wind turbines, making it available for use when needed. The capacity of the battery bank is crucial and should be determined based on the power consumption of the lighting system and the desired runtime, typically measured in days. This ensures that there is sufficient energy to maintain lighting during extended periods of insufficient wind.

Choosing the appropriate type and size of batteries involves understanding the overall energy requirements of the lighting system and the average wind conditions in the area. While lead-acid batteries provide a cost-effective solution, they require regular maintenance to ensure longevity. In contrast, lithium-ion batteries, though initially more expensive, offer higher energy density, longer lifespan, and virtually maintenance-free operation, making them an increasingly favored choice for off-grid applications.

Integrating the battery storage system with the wind turbine necessitates a charge controller to manage the charging process and prevent battery damage due to overcharging. Modern charge controllers can accommodate inputs from both wind turbines and solar panels, providing flexibility for hybrid systems that enhance reliability and reduce the risk of energy shortages. Properly sizing and configuring the battery bank guarantees that the lighting system has a constant and dependable power source, maximizing the advantages of wind energy for off-grid lighting. It is also vital to consider the placement of the battery bank, protecting it from environmental factors to ensure safety and durability. Adequate ventilation is crucial for lead-acid batteries to safely release gases during charging, while lithium-ion batteries, with their higher energy density and reduced weight, provide more flexibility in placement but require monitoring systems for operational safety. By thoughtfully planning and implementing battery storage solutions, off-grid wind lighting systems can deliver sustainable and reliable illumination, enhancing the autonomy and resilience of off-grid environments.

Integrating Wind and Solar Systems

Combining wind and solar systems for off-grid lighting solutions leverages the strengths of both renewable resources, ensuring a more stable and reliable energy supply. This hybrid approach mitigates the variability associated with wind and solar energy availability, guaranteeing that lighting needs are fulfilled regardless of weather conditions. Charge controllers with dual inputs are crucial for effectively managing energy harvested from both wind turbines and solar panels, efficiently directing this energy to the battery bank for storage. These regulators are essential for preventing overcharging and deep discharges, both of which can significantly shorten battery lifespan.

Designing a hybrid system entails calculating energy production from both sources based on historical weather data, ensuring that the combined output meets or exceeds the lighting system's requirements. Solar panels typically reach maximum output on sunny days, while wind turbines can generate energy both day and night, especially during storms or winter months when solar production may drop. This synergistic relationship between wind and solar energy creates a robust off-grid lighting system capable of providing dependable illumination without relying on grid electricity.

For optimal performance, the system should include a battery bank large enough to store energy sufficient to cover periods of low wind or solar production. This necessitates careful consideration of battery capacity, depth of discharge, and the lighting system's power consumption patterns. Furthermore, integrating wind and solar systems requires attention to the electrical compatibility of components, including the voltage ratings of the turbines, panels, charge controller, and batteries. Establishing a hybrid wind-solar system for lighting not only enhances energy reliability but also contributes to environmental sustainability by reducing dependence on fossil fuels. The initial investment in a hybrid system can be compensated by long-term savings on energy costs and minimal maintenance needs of wind and solar components. By taking advantage of the complementary nature of wind and solar energy, off-grid lighting systems can achieve unprecedented levels of autonomy and resilience, efficiently illuminating off-grid areas.

DIY Project: Construct a Wind-Powered Streetlight

Creating a wind-powered streetlight involves using a small wind turbine, a mounting tower, a battery bank, LED lights, and the necessary wiring. Begin by selecting a turbine capable of producing sufficient power for your lighting needs; typically, a model with a capacity between 400 watts and 1 kilowatt will suffice for a streetlight. The turbine should be mounted on a tower tall enough to capture steady winds, usually recommended at a height of 6 to 9 meters. Ensure that the tower is securely anchored to withstand strong winds.

For the battery bank, deep cycle batteries are ideal due to their capacity to endure repeated charging and discharging. Calculate the required capacity based on the wattage of your LED lights and the expected number of hours they will need to run without wind. A charge controller is essential for regulating the electrical flow from the turbine to the batteries, preventing overcharging.

Select LED lights for their low power consumption and longevity. Determine the total energy consumption of the lights to confirm that the turbine and battery bank can adequately support their operation throughout the night. Connect the turbine to the battery bank, then wire the battery bank to the LED lights using outdoor-rated electrical cables and waterproof connectors to ensure safety and durability.

Mount the LED lights to the streetlamp structure, which can be constructed from metal or treated wood, ensuring it is tall enough to provide sufficient illumination and positioned for optimal lighting coverage. The streetlamp itself must be firmly anchored to the ground to avoid falling in strong winds.

Finally, test the system by allowing the wind turbine to charge the battery bank and power the LED lights. Adjustments may be necessary to optimize the system for efficiency and reliability. Regular inspections of the turbine, battery bank, and wiring will ensure that your wind-powered streetlight continues to function effectively for years to come. This project not only provides a sustainable lighting solution but also demonstrates a practical application of renewable energy for off-grid living.

Constructing a Pedal Generator

A pedal generator offers a practical solution for converting human energy into electricity, utilizing the mechanical energy generated from pedaling. While solar, wind, and hydroelectric power are key resources for off-grid living, human energy can also serve as a valuable asset. This type of generator is particularly beneficial for charging batteries, powering small devices, and acting as a sustainable backup source, especially when other renewable energy options are limited. In this project, I will guide you through building a pedal generator, an essential addition to your off-grid energy toolkit.

Required Materials:
- **Bicycle**: Can be a stationary bike or a standard one, provided it has sturdy support. For a regular bicycle, you will need a stand that elevates the rear wheel off the ground.
- **Permanent Magnet DC Motor**: 1 unit, capable of generating electricity. Look for a motor with a voltage range that is compatible with your battery, usually 12V or 24V, with a rating of around 100-200 watts for general usage.
- **Belt or Chain**: 1 unit to connect the rear wheel of the bicycle to the motor. The type of connection depends on the configuration of the bike and motor; a standard bicycle chain is typically used.
- **Charge Regulator**: 1 unit, to manage the voltage and current entering the battery. This prevents overcharging and prolongs battery life.
- **Battery**: 1 unit, preferably a deep cycle battery for better long-term energy storage. A lead-acid or lithium-ion battery with a capacity of at least 50Ah is recommended.
- **Inverter (Optional)**: 1 unit, to convert direct current (DC) to alternating current (AC) if you need to power AC devices. Choose an inverter with a wattage capacity greater than your expected maximum load.
- **Cables and Connectors**: 10 to 20 feet of wire of various thicknesses, suitable for transmitting current from the motor to the charge controller and battery.
- **Basic Tools**: Wrenches, screwdrivers, pliers, a drill with bits, wire strippers, and electrical tape for installation and connections.

Detailed Instructions:
1. **Prepare Your Bicycle**: Place the bike on a sturdy stand or roller to stabilize it. Ensure the rear wheel is elevated and can rotate freely. For a regular bicycle, securely attach the stand to prevent tipping or movement during pedaling.
2. **Connect the Motor**: Position the DC motor near the rear wheel, aligning the motor's drive shaft with the wheel. You may need to create a custom mounting bracket or use an existing one to secure the motor. Drill holes and use bolts to firmly attach the bracket and motor to a stable platform or directly to the bike stand.
3. **Link the Motor to the Wheel**: Wrap the belt or chain around the rear wheel of the bicycle and the motor's drive shaft. Adjust the tension to ensure the belt or chain is tight enough for effective power transfer without excessive friction. Use a belt tensioner or adjust the motor's position to achieve the correct tension.
4. **Install the Charge Controller**: Secure the charge controller in a convenient location near the motor and battery. Connect the motor's output wires to the controller's input terminals, following the wiring diagram provided by the manufacturer. Use appropriate gauge wires to handle the current, typically 12 gauge or larger.
5. **Connect the Battery**: Position the battery on a stable, well-ventilated surface. Connect the charge controller's output terminals to the battery terminals, ensuring the polarity is correct (positive to positive, negative to negative). Use ring connectors on the ends of the wires, securing them with nuts on the battery terminals. Ensure all connections are tight and insulated.
6. **Configure the Inverter (Optional)**: If you need to power AC devices, connect the inverter to the battery. Attach the positive and negative input cables of the inverter to the corresponding terminals on the battery. The inverter should be placed in a well-ventilated area to avoid overheating. Connect your AC devices to the inverter outlets as necessary.
7. **Test the System**: Begin pedaling and observe the system's functionality. The motor should spin as the wheel turns, generating electricity. Check the charge controller for any indicators or displays showing the charging status. Use a multimeter to measure the battery voltage, which should gradually rise if charging is successful.
8. **Monitor and Maintain the System**: Periodically inspect the entire setup. Check the tension of the belt or chain and adjust it if it becomes loose. Keep both the bike and motor clean, lubricate moving parts, and ensure electrical connections are secure. Monitor the battery's charge and discharge cycles to maintain efficiency, ensuring that the charge controller operates within the specified parameters.

Maintenance Tips:

- **Cleaning and Lubrication**: Regularly clean your bicycle and motor components. Apply lubricant to the chain, wheel bearings, and motor shaft to minimize friction and wear.
- **Voltage Control**: Inspect the belt or chain for signs of wear or looseness. Replace as needed and adjust the tension to ensure smooth operation.
- **Battery Care**: Keep battery terminals clean and free of corrosion. If the system is not used regularly, utilize a battery maintenance charger to keep it in good condition.
- **Electrical Safety**: Always disconnect the battery before performing maintenance on electrical components to prevent accidental shocks or short circuits.
- **Storage of Equipment**: Store your bicycle, battery, and other components in a dry, cool place to protect them from humidity and extreme temperatures that could damage your equipment.

Constructing a pedal generator can significantly enhance your off-grid energy system, providing a sustainable and reliable backup option for generating power when other resources may be limited.

Conclusion

Now that we understand how to access abundant and sustainable renewable energy sources, it's essential to focus on how to store and utilize that energy effectively to meet our needs. Without a proper storage system, the electricity generated by renewable energy solutions could be wasted, leaving us powerless at the times we need it most. This section will guide you through the fundamentals of energy storage and management, helping you optimize the use of renewable energy resources.

Core Concepts of Energy Storage

Energy storage is a vital aspect of any off-grid energy system. It enables the capture of energy produced by solar panels, wind turbines, hydroelectric systems, or other sources, storing it for use during times when direct generation isn't available. Grasping the basic principles of energy storage is essential for maintaining a reliable and consistent electricity supply in an off-grid setting.

1. **Importance of Energy Storage** In off-grid systems, energy production can be inconsistent. Solar panels generate power only during daylight hours, wind turbines are contingent on wind conditions, and micro-hydroelectric systems can fluctuate based on seasonal water flow. Energy storage allows you to utilize energy even when production sources are inactive, such as at night, during calm weather, or in dry seasons. It acts as a buffer, helping to smooth out fluctuations and ensure a stable electricity supply.
2. **Types of Energy Storage Solutions** There are various methods for storing energy, each with unique benefits and limitations. The most commonly used types in off-grid systems include:
    - **Batteries**: The most prevalent storage method in off-grid configurations. Batteries store electrical energy chemically and release it when needed. Different types of batteries include:
        - **Lead-Acid Batteries**: These are the most common, offering a good balance of cost and reliability. They come in two main varieties: flooded and sealed (AGM and Gel).
        - **Lithium-Ion Batteries**: While more expensive than lead-acid, they provide a longer lifespan, higher efficiency, and increased energy density, making them ideal for long-term storage requirements.
        - **Nickel-Iron Batteries**: Known for their durability and long life, these batteries resist overcharging and deep discharging but are less efficient and more costly than lead-acid batteries.
        - **Saltwater Batteries**: An emerging technology offering a safe and eco-friendly alternative to traditional batteries. They are non-toxic, have a long lifespan, and require minimal maintenance, but are currently pricier and less common.
    - **Pumped Hydroelectric Storage**: This method employs surplus electricity to pump water to a higher reservoir. When energy is required, the water is released to flow downstream through a turbine, generating electricity. While highly efficient, this system is typically used in larger setups and needs specific geographic features.
    - **Flywheels**: These devices store energy mechanically by spinning a rotor at high speeds. While less common in small-scale off-grid systems, flywheels can provide quick bursts of energy and have a long lifespan with minimal maintenance.
3. **Key Considerations for Energy Storage** When selecting and designing an energy storage system, several factors must be taken into account:
    - **Capacity**: The total energy that can be stored, measured in kilowatt-hours (kWh). This should be sized according to your energy needs during periods of low or no production.

- **Depth of Discharge (DoD)**: This indicates the percentage of a battery's capacity that can be utilized without significantly shortening its lifespan. For example, a battery with a 50% DoD can safely use half of its stored energy before recharging.
- **Efficiency**: This measures the energy lost during the storage and retrieval processes. Higher efficiency indicates more stored energy is available for use. Lithium-ion batteries typically have better efficiency compared to lead-acid batteries.
- **Lifespan**: The number of charge and discharge cycles a battery can handle before its capacity significantly decreases. Lifespan is a critical factor for determining the cost-effectiveness and reliability of a long-term storage solution.
- **Cost**: It's important to consider not just initial costs but also long-term maintenance and replacement expenses. Although lithium-ion batteries have higher upfront costs, their longevity and efficiency may offer better value over time.

4. **Management and Monitoring of Energy Storage** Proper management and monitoring of the storage system are essential to ensure its longevity and performance. This includes routinely checking battery health, ensuring adequate ventilation to control heat, and utilizing a battery management system (BMS) to prevent overcharging and deep discharging while balancing the cells.

Integrating the storage system with a charge controller and an inverter is crucial for effective energy conversion and utilization. The charge controller ensures batteries are charged safely from your energy sources, while the inverter converts stored DC energy into AC energy for your appliances.

Setting Up a Battery Bank

$: $500-$3,000
🔧: Medium difficulty
🕒: 1-2 days

Creating a battery bank is essential for storing the electricity generated by your renewable energy systems. A well-structured battery bank ensures a reliable power supply, even when solar or wind resources are unavailable. This project will guide you through the process of establishing a battery bank for your off-grid home.

Required Materials:
- **Batteries**: 4 to 8 batteries, depending on your energy storage requirements.
  Type: Deep cycle lead-acid (flooded, AGM, or Gel) or lithium-ion batteries.
  Capacity: 100Ah to 200Ah per battery (common for most off-grid systems).
  Note: Lithium-ion batteries provide greater efficiency and longevity, but they come at a higher cost.
- **Battery Cables and Connectors**: 50 to 100 feet of cable, depending on configuration.
  Gauge: AWG 4 or AWG 6 for interconnecting the batteries and linking them to the charge controller/inverter.
  Connectors: Suitable terminals (e.g., ring connectors) to ensure secure connections.
- **Battery Management System (BMS)**: 1 unit (only necessary for lithium-ion batteries).
  Purpose: Protects lithium batteries by balancing charge and preventing overcharging or deep discharging.
- **Battery Container or Rack**: 1 unit.
  Type: Metal or plastic enclosure, or a custom-built wooden rack with ventilation.
  Size: Large enough to securely hold all batteries while allowing for airflow.
- **Charge Regulator**: 1 unit.
  Capacity: Sized to accommodate the total amperage of your solar array or other power sources (e.g., 30A-60A).
  Type: MPPT (Maximum Power Point Tracking) controller is recommended for enhanced efficiency.
- **Inverter**: 1 unit.
  Capacity: Sized according to your maximum power requirements (e.g., 1000W-5000W).
  Type: Pure sine wave inverters are preferred for sensitive electronic devices.
- **Isolated Tools**: Wrenches, screwdrivers.
- **Safety Equipment**: Gloves (rubber or insulating to protect against electric shock), protective glasses.

Detailed Instructions:

1. **Assess Your Energy Needs**: Calculate your daily energy consumption in watt-hours (Wh) to determine the total capacity required for your battery bank. This should encompass the total wattage of your essential appliances and the expected usage duration.
2. **Select the Appropriate Batteries**: Choose the type and quantity of batteries that fit your energy needs and budget. Lead-acid batteries are economical and widely used, striking a good balance between cost and performance. Although lithium-ion batteries are pricier, they offer superior efficiency, deep discharge capabilities, and extended lifespans.
3. **Prepare the Battery Container**: Designate a safe, well-ventilated space for your battery bank. Utilize a battery container or rack to organize and safeguard your batteries. Ensure the area is dry and adequately ventilated to prevent overheating, particularly crucial for lead-acid batteries, which can off-gas.
4. **Install the Batteries**: Position the batteries in the container or rack. Ensure lead-acid batteries are placed vertically to prevent electrolyte spills. Secure lithium-ion batteries appropriately and connect them to the BMS to guarantee balanced charging and discharging.
5. **Connect Batteries in Series or Parallel**:
    - **Series Connection**: Increases voltage (e.g., 12V + 12V = 24V) while maintaining capacity. Connect the positive terminal of one battery to the negative terminal of the next.
    - **Parallel Connection**: Increases capacity (e.g., 100Ah + 100Ah = 200Ah) while keeping the same voltage. Connect all positive terminals together and all negative terminals together. Use appropriate gauge wires and connectors. Always utilize insulated tools and wear safety gear to prevent electric shocks.
6. **Connect the Battery Bank to the Charge Controller**: Use correctly sized cables to link the battery bank to the charge controller. The regulator manages the voltage and current from your renewable energy sources, preventing overcharging and ensuring safe operation.
7. **Configure the Inverter**: Attach the inverter to the battery bank using heavy-duty battery cables. The inverter converts DC electricity stored in the batteries into AC electricity, suitable for powering household devices. Ensure all connections are secure and well-insulated.
8. **Test the System**: After all connections are made, test the battery bank to ensure proper functionality. Monitor the charge controller and inverter outputs, checking battery voltage and charge levels with a multimeter.
9. **Monitor and Maintain the System**: Regularly inspect the battery bank for signs of wear, corrosion, or damage. Maintain appropriate charge levels and perform routine maintenance to guarantee optimal performance and longevity of the system.

Maintenance Tips:
- **Lead-Acid Batteries**: Regularly check electrolyte levels and add distilled water as needed. Clean battery terminals and connections to prevent corrosion.
- **Lithium-Ion Batteries**: Ensure your BMS is functioning correctly to balance the cells and protect against overcharging and deep discharging.
- **General Maintenance**: Monitor battery voltage and state of charge to prevent deep discharge and overcharging, which can drastically reduce battery lifespan.

Constructing a Solar Charger

A solar charger is an effective and sustainable approach to harnessing solar energy, providing a dependable power source for numerous off-grid applications. By converting sunlight into electricity, it enables the charging of batteries that can power essential devices and appliances. This system is particularly beneficial for charging small electronic devices such as phones and tablets, powering LED lights, and serving as a vital backup power source during emergencies. In this project, you will learn how to build a solar charger to ensure a sustainable and reliable energy supply, enhancing your off-grid living experience.

Required Materials:
- **Solar Panel (1 unit)**:
    - **Power**: Between 20W and 100W, depending on your charging requirements.
    - **Type**: Monocrystalline or polycrystalline.
    - **Note**: Select the panel size based on battery capacity and available sunlight. A 20W panel is sufficient for charging small devices, while a 100W panel is better for larger batteries or applications that need more power.
- **Charge Regulator (1 unit)**:

- o **Capacity**: Should match the solar panel output, typically between 10A and 20A for small to medium-sized systems.
- o **Type**: PWM (Pulse Width Modulation) or MPPT (Maximum Power Point Tracking) for enhanced efficiency.
- **Battery (1 unit)**:
  - o **Type**: Deep cycle, lead-acid (AGM or Gel) or lithium-ion battery.
  - o **Capacity**: Between 12V, 20Ah, and 100Ah, based on energy needs.
  - o **Note**: Lithium-ion batteries provide greater efficiency and longevity, while lead-acid batteries are more affordable.
- **Battery Holder or Container (1 unit)**:
  - o **Type**: Plastic or metal box designed to safely hold the battery.
  - o **Dimensions**: Must accommodate the chosen battery while allowing for ventilation.
- **Diode (1 unit)**:
  - o **Type**: Schottky diode, rated for at least the maximum output current of the solar panel (e.g., 10A).
  - o **Function**: Prevents current from flowing back from the battery to the solar panel during nighttime.
- **Cables and Connectors**:
  - o **Gauge**: 12 AWG for connections between the solar panel and charge controller, and 10 AWG for connections to the battery.
  - o **Connectors**: MC4 for solar panel connections, ring terminals for battery connections.
  - o **Length**: Between 10 and 20 feet of cable.
- **Fuse/Breaker**: Suitable for your system, generally rated between 30 and 60A.
- **Basic Tools**: Screwdrivers, wire cutters, soldering iron.
- **Safety Gear**: Gloves, protective eyewear.

Detailed Instructions:
1. **Select the Right Solar Panel**: Choose a solar panel according to your energy needs. For charging small devices or a single battery, a 20W-50W panel may be sufficient. For more extensive use, such as powering lights or small appliances, choose a 100W panel. Ensure the solar panel specifications can handle your expected load and are compatible with your system.
2. **Install the Solar Panel**: Position the solar panel in a location with optimal sun exposure, ideally facing south at an angle equal to your latitude. Secure the panel with mounting brackets or a stand, ensuring it is stable and oriented to maximize sunlight capture throughout the day. Adjust the angle seasonally to optimize solar energy collection.
3. **Set Up the Charge Controller**: Mount the charge controller in a shaded, weather-protected area close to the battery. Connect the positive and negative wires from the solar panel to the charge controller's input terminals, ensuring correct polarity. The charge controller manages the voltage and current from the solar panel, protecting the battery from overcharging.
4. **Connect the Battery**: Place the battery in an appropriate holder or container to shield it from physical damage and exposure to the elements. Connect the battery to the charge controller using suitable cables, making sure to respect the polarity (positive to positive, negative to negative). Verify that all connections are secure and that the battery is on a non-conductive surface.
5. **Add a Diode**: Install a Schottky diode in series with the positive wire between the solar panel and charge controller. This prevents current from flowing back to the solar panel at night, safeguarding the panel and ensuring efficient charging. The diode's stripe should face the battery, indicating the current flow direction.
6. **Complete System Wiring**: Finish all electrical connections among the solar panel, charge controller, and battery. Utilize MC4 connectors for the solar panel connections and ring terminals for battery connections. Ensure all connections are tight and secure. If needed, use a soldering iron to reinforce connections and cover exposed wires with electrical tape to avoid short circuits.
7. **Test the System**: Once all connections are finalized, test the solar charger by exposing the solar panel to direct sunlight. Monitor the charge controller for indicators showing charging status and check the battery voltage with a multimeter to confirm it is receiving a charge. Ensure the charge controller displays the correct charging indicators (e.g., LED lights or digital readouts).
8. **Monitor and Maintain the System**: Regularly check the system to ensure it operates efficiently. Clean the solar panel periodically to remove dust or debris that could diminish efficiency. Monitor battery charge status and inspect connections for wear or corrosion. Replace any damaged components to maintain the system in excellent condition.

Maintenance Tips:
- **Keep the Solar Panel Clean**: Regularly clean the panel with a soft cloth and water to optimize sun exposure and efficiency. Avoid abrasive cleaners that might scratch the panel surface.

- **Monitor Battery Health**: Periodically examine the battery for wear, leaks, or corrosion. Replace batteries as necessary to ensure a dependable power supply. For lead-acid batteries, check and maintain electrolyte levels as recommended.
- **Inspect Connections**: Frequently check that all electrical connections are tight and free of corrosion. Clean and tighten connections as needed to ensure good electrical contact. Use an anti-corrosion gel on battery terminals to prevent oxidation.

By constructing a solar charger, you'll create a reliable and sustainable energy source essential for powering your key devices, allowing your home to run off-grid even during emergencies.

Long-Term Solutions for Lighting

During extended emergencies, such as blackouts, there may be times when resources become scarce. If your home visibly possesses valuable resources, like fuel for lighting, it could attract unwanted attention, making it a target for theft. While I don't intend to cause unnecessary alarm, it's important to note that if you plan to keep your home brightly lit, like during the holiday season, consider installing blackout curtains. This approach not only offers discretion but also helps conserve heat.

With an independent energy system, you can keep the lights on even if the main power grid fails. However, if you rely entirely on the grid or wish to conserve energy, you need emergency solutions for total blackout situations. We will explore several options shortly, but first, let's address some security considerations for particularly severe scenarios.

Emergency Lighting Options

Oil Lamps and Lanterns

While I previously touched on garden lanterns, they may not be the best choice if the power grid fails due to severe weather conditions. Instead, consider hurricane lanterns, designed to remain lit even in high winds. Although yard lanterns can be useful, I strongly recommend acquiring at least one hurricane lantern.

One of my favorites is the Feuerhand Storm Lantern, which I can confidently endorse. Its tank holds over half a liter of fuel, allowing for approximately 20 hours of burn time. This lantern can be easily hung from a hook or branch and withstands harsh weather. I have tried using paraffin, which is likely the most economical fuel for these lanterns, but the odor is overwhelming for me, so I opt for clear lamp oil instead. Although it's pricier, I believe it's worth it. In the event of a blackout caused by an earthquake or hurricane, which may lead to gas leaks or ground instability, it's wise to avoid flammable lighting options. While a hurricane lantern is suitable during such storms, always assess environmental conditions before selecting your lighting source.

Oil lamps and lanterns have the added benefit of generating heat while providing light. To enhance this feature, you can place tin foil on a wall behind the lamp to reflect heat back into the room. However, if you reside in a warm climate, alternative lighting solutions may be preferable, as you wouldn't want to increase indoor temperatures when you're already trying to stay cool.

When considering oil lamps and lanterns, remember that size matters. Smaller lamps may be convenient for transport, but larger models have broader wicks, producing more light. Personally, I prefer larger lamps and save portable flashlights for travel, as they also offer a safer option. Don't forget to stock up on fuel and wicks. Most lamps operate on paraffin, clear lamp oil, or kerosene, and you can also use citronella, which serves the dual purpose of repelling insects during summer. Regardless of whether they use candles or oil, lamps and lanterns pose a fire hazard, so keep them away from clothing, soft fabrics, and other flammable materials. I also recommend having a fire extinguisher at home; while it's hoped it will never be needed, it's better to be cautious.

Propane Lanterns

Propane lanterns represent another viable alternative. These run on one-pound propane tanks and, similar to oil lamps, generate heat. However, they should be kept away from flammable items and only used in well-ventilated spaces. There's a risk of carbon monoxide poisoning, so having a carbon monoxide detector in your home is essential. It's also important to maintain an adequate propane supply, which has the advantage of being non-perishable, allowing you to stock up without worry.

Candles

Certain garden lanterns are designed to accommodate candles, and you can also use actual candles to light your home during emergencies. While I wouldn't rely solely on them, anyone preparing for emergencies should keep some on hand. Moreover, in the event of a blackout caused by an electromagnetic pulse (EMP), candles might be the most effective solution, as they don't contain electrical components.

I recommend thick candles, like church candles, or those housed in jars, as they tend to burn longer and are less likely to tip over. However, the best option might be an emergency candle such as the SDS Liquid Oil Candle. Unlike traditional candles, this one burns liquid paraffin instead of solid wax and boasts a burn time of around 115 hours—much longer than regular candles. If you opt for traditional solid candles, look for emergency varieties with a burn time of at least 36 hours; however, keep in mind that many cannot be reused. Traditional candles do have the advantage of being reusable despite their shorter lifespan. If you keep fresh wicks available, you can melt leftover wax to create new candles. Keep jars handy to contain them; the more you protect the flame, the safer your household will be. Once again, having a fire extinguisher on hand is advisable.

LED Lanterns

Shifting to more contemporary options, LED lanterns are an excellent choice. They can illuminate entire rooms, are energy-efficient, and have a good runtime. If you live in a warm area, this may be a preferable option compared to oil or propane lanterns, as they produce less heat. Additionally, they do not pose fire hazards and eliminate the need for storing oil or propane. However, you will need to ensure a supply of batteries or a way to recharge rechargeable models, though some lanterns feature built-in solar panels to address this issue.

Solar Lights

Solar lights are an outstanding choice for outdoor illumination and have significantly improved in recent years. I have a set of solar lights that illuminate the pathway to our front door. While they don't provide intense light, they are perfect for lighting driveways. If you choose motion-activated solar lights, like those mounted on your garage, you'll enhance safety even during a blackout. Additionally, you can use solar lights indoors. In emergency situations, they can serve well to light corridors and staircases, allowing you to navigate safely without needing bright lights. A practical tip: place them in the sun during the day and bring them inside at night, stabilizing them in polystyrene blocks for convenience. You can position them wherever you desire.

Battery-Powered Lighting Solutions

When it comes to battery-powered lighting, the most common choice is the flashlight, but there are numerous alternatives to consider. Stick-on lights can be particularly handy if you need portable options. They work well in hallways or similar spaces where intense illumination isn't necessary. Many of these lights feature Velcro attachments, allowing you to position them almost anywhere. Be sure to check the battery requirements and stock up on an adequate supply. Relying solely on battery-powered lights may not be wise, as they will eventually run out of power. Instead, prioritizing rechargeable or fuel-powered devices would be a smarter decision. Nonetheless, flashlights and headlamps remain essential tools, and you can find additional recommendations on this in Chapter Two.

Moreover, we haven't yet discussed the everyday carry (EDC) flashlight, which is crucial to have on hand. I highly suggest that each family member keep one in their pocket or bag. This ensures that everyone has immediate access to light during a power outage. While premium models are available, I opted for a more budget-friendly choice for my family, selecting the Maglite XL50, which is durable and dependable, even if it isn't the brightest option. Don't forget to stock up on AAA batteries for these flashlights.

Chemical Glow Sticks

In today's world, glow sticks are often associated with festivals, but having some at home for emergencies is a smart idea. Similar to solar lights, they can provide illumination in high-traffic areas like hallways. One of the aspects I appreciate most about glow sticks is that they can make emergency situations feel more enjoyable and less frightening for children. Some of these sticks can glow for approximately 12 hours. While they may not be the most environmentally friendly option, they are fun, reliable for short durations, and easy to store.

Adequate lighting is always crucial, especially during shorter days. The great news is that all these lighting options can be easily prepared in advance. I recommend maintaining several alternatives to address both short-term and long-term emergencies. This way, regardless of the cause of the blackout, you'll have effective solutions ready to light up your home.

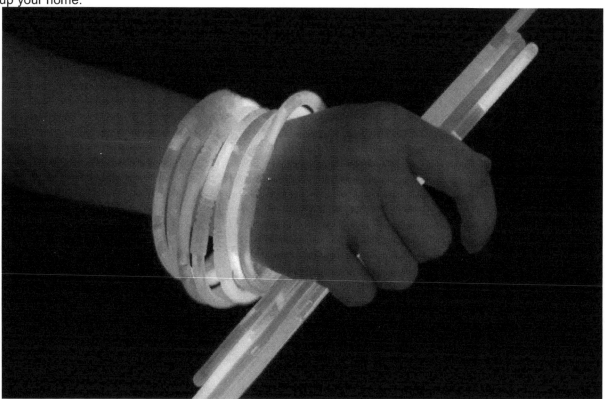

Creating Emergency Lighting Solutions

DIY Emergency Light Project

While there are numerous lighting options available, I can't help but appreciate a good DIY project—especially one that involves food! Every well-stocked pantry should have a supply of canned fish, and if it includes sardines in oil, you have the perfect materials for a creative project. This idea works specifically with sardines preserved in oil. After enjoying the contents, save both the oil and the can to craft your own DIY oil lamp. Just insert a natural fiber wick into the oil-filled can, and once the wick absorbs enough oil, light it. You might be amazed at how long this little lamp can burn!

If you're seeking a project with a more pleasant aroma, collect excess bacon grease in a jar until you have enough to make a candle. Coat a natural fiber wick with the grease, pushing it down to the bottom of the jar, and voilà: a

DIY candle with a delightful bacon scent! However, be warned—after making this, your family might demand bacon sandwiches too!

Solar-Powered Lighting
Solar-powered lighting captures energy from the sun and converts it into electricity to illuminate your space after dark. This technology is particularly beneficial for those living off the grid, where traditional energy sources may not be available or desirable. Solar lights consist of photovoltaic cells that collect sunlight during the day, a battery for storing the converted energy, and LED bulbs that use this stored energy at night. The efficiency of solar lighting systems has seen significant improvements, making them suitable for various applications, from pathway lighting to security systems for off-grid properties.

Installing solar lights is straightforward, usually requiring only the placement of solar panels in a sun-exposed area and the mounting of light fixtures as needed. Maintenance is minimal, primarily involving keeping the solar panels clean and ensuring the batteries are in good condition. For those looking to enhance their off-grid lighting solutions, solar-powered lighting is a sustainable, cost-effective, and eco-friendly option that aligns perfectly with the broader goal of self-sufficiency. By harnessing the abundant and renewable resource of sunlight, off-grid residents can illuminate their surroundings without relying on the conventional electricity grid, further bolstering their autonomy and resilience against external interruptions.

Installing Solar Lights
Setting up solar floodlights is a simple yet effective process that greatly enhances safety and functionality for off-grid properties. These lights are designed to illuminate large areas brightly, making them ideal for deterring potential intruders, lighting pathways, or providing visibility for outdoor tasks after dark. The first step involves selecting the optimal location for the floodlights, focusing on areas that require extensive coverage, such as entry points, walkways, and open spaces.

It's crucial to position the solar panel where it will receive maximum sunlight during the day, ensuring the batteries are fully charged by night. After determining the ideal location, mount the solar panel using the provided hardware and instructions. The panel should be tilted to capture the most sunlight, which can vary depending on your geographic location. In the Northern Hemisphere, orienting the panel to face south provides the best exposure to the sun.

Once the solar panel is secured, install the floodlight, directing the light to cover the desired area effectively and adjusting the angle as necessary. The connection between the solar panel and the floodlight is typically made via cables included in the kit. Ensure these cables are positioned to minimize exposure to the elements and prevent damage. Waterproofing the connectors and cables is vital to avoid moisture infiltration that could impair the system's functionality.

A critical final step is testing the floodlight system. Most solar lights operate automatically, turning on at dusk and off at dawn. Testing the lights for a few nights will confirm proper operation and adequate illumination. You may need to adjust the positioning of the lights or the angle of the solar panel based on your test results. Regular maintenance includes cleaning the solar panels to remove dust, dirt, and debris that can block sunlight and decrease charging efficiency. Checking the lights and their components for signs of wear should be part of your routine maintenance to ensure the longevity and optimal performance of your solar lighting systems. This straightforward addition to your off-grid lighting options provides peace of mind while enhancing safety and visibility around your property.

DIY Project: Constructing Solar Lights for Your Driveway

Overview
This project involves the creation of solar lights to illuminate your driveway, garden, or path using renewable energy. These lights automatically charge during the day and activate at night, offering an eco-friendly, low-maintenance outdoor lighting solution.

Difficulty Level:
Easy to Moderate | Estimated Time: 3-5 hours

Benefits
Solar lights for driveways reduce energy costs, require minimal upkeep, and contribute to a sustainable lifestyle by utilizing clean energy from the sun. They are ideal for enhancing the safety and visual appeal of outdoor spaces.

Required Materials:
- **Small Solar Panels**: One for each light, generally between 2V to 5V.
- **Rechargeable Batteries**: NiMH or Li-ion, one for each light.

- **LED Lights**: One for each light.
- **Photoresistor or Light-Dependent Resistor (LDR)**: For automatic on/off functionality.
- **Diode**: 1N5819 or similar, to prevent reverse current.
- **Resistors**: Appropriate values for the circuit.
- **PVC Pipes or Wooden Posts**: For mounting lights.
- **Clear Plastic or Glass Jars**: To contain LED lights.
- **Wiring and Connectors**.
- **Soldering Components**: Soldering iron, tin.
- **Hot Glue or Waterproof Sealant**: To secure components.

Tools Required:
- **Soldering Iron and Tin**.
- **Wire Cutters and Strippers**.
- **Multimeter**: For testing connections.
- **Electric Drill with Bits**: For assembly.
- **Pliers**.
- **Safety Equipment**: Gloves and glasses.

Alternative Materials:
- **Recycled Items**: Such as old solar garden lights for components.
- **Bamboo Stakes**: Instead of PVC pipes for a natural look.

Step-by-Step Instructions:
1. **Prepare the Solar Panels**: Choose small solar panels capable of generating sufficient energy to charge batteries and power LED lights. Panels rated between 2V and 5V are suitable for driveway lights. Ensure the panels are clean and functional. If repurposing old solar panels, use a multimeter to verify their output voltage and current.
    - **Time**: 30 minutes
2. **Build the Lighting Circuit**: Create a straightforward circuit incorporating the solar panel, rechargeable battery, diode, LED light, and photoresistor. The photoresistor will automatically activate the LED light when it gets dark. Connect the solar panel's positive terminal to the diode's anode, with the cathode linked to the battery's positive terminal. Connect the panel's negative terminal to the battery's negative terminal. The LED light should be connected parallel to the photoresistor to ensure it activates only when low light levels are detected.
    - **Time**: 1-2 hours
3. **Test the Circuit**: Before assembling the light, test the circuit with a multimeter and the LED light to confirm proper functionality. Position the solar panel in sunlight to check that the battery is charging. Then cover the photoresistor or place it in a dark area to verify that the LED light illuminates. Make any necessary adjustments to the circuit.
    - **Time**: 30 minutes
4. **Prepare the Light Housing**: Use clear plastic or glass jars to house the LED lights. Drill a small hole in the lid of each jar to allow the wires to pass through. Secure the LED light inside the jar with hot glue or sealant. The jar will safeguard the light from moisture while providing a diffused lighting effect.
    - **Time**: 30 minutes
5. **Mount the Solar Panel**: Attach the solar panel to the top of the jar lid or a separate mounting structure like PVC pipe or a wooden stake. The panel should be angled to capture maximum sunlight during the day. Use waterproof sealant to protect connections and ensure the panel is firmly secured.
    - **Time**: 30 minutes
6. **Install Driveway Lights**: Decide on the arrangement of lights along the driveway, pathway, or garden. Drive the PVC pipes, wooden stakes, or bamboo poles into the ground at regular intervals, ensuring they are stable and at the desired height. Secure the light housing to the top of each stake or tube, positioning the solar panel to receive sunlight during the day.
    - **Time**: 1-2 hours
7. **Test the Installation**: After installing all the driveway lights, wait until evening to test them. Ensure that each light activates automatically when it gets dark and provides adequate illumination. Adjust the positioning of solar panels or lights as needed.
    - **Time**: 30 minutes

Care and Maintenance:
Regularly clean the solar panels to remove dust and debris that could diminish their efficiency. Check the lights for any signs of wear or damage, especially after adverse weather conditions. Replace rechargeable batteries every 1-2 years to maintain optimal performance.

Creating Candles and Oil Lamps

Making candles and oil lamps is a vital skill for those living off the grid, providing a dependable, sustainable, and comforting light source. These traditional lighting methods have been utilized for centuries and can be easily adapted for modern off-grid living with minimal tools and materials. Crafting your own candles and oil lamps not only reduces reliance on industrial products but also fosters a rewarding sense of self-sufficiency.

Candle Making
The process of candle making begins with selecting the appropriate wax. Paraffin wax is readily available and easy to work with, but for those seeking more natural alternatives, beeswax and soy wax are excellent choices, providing a cleaner burn without emitting potentially harmful chemicals. The wax is melted using a double boiler, ensuring even heating and preventing overheating. While the wax melts, prepare the wick by securing it to a wick holder or pencil placed over the mold or container, allowing it to remain centered and vertical.
Once the wax is fully melted, you can add optional fragrances or colorants to customize your candles. When pouring wax into molds or containers, proceed carefully to avoid trapping air bubbles, which can affect the burn quality. Allow the wax to cool and solidify completely before trimming the wick to the appropriate length. The beauty of candle making lies in the ability to experiment with different shapes, colors, and scents to create unique lighting solutions for any occasion.

Oil Lamps
Conversely, oil lamps provide a more continuous light source and can be fueled by a variety of oils, including vegetable oil, olive oil, or specially formulated lamp oils. The basic components of an oil lamp consist of a container, a wick, and a fuel source. Glass jars, metal cans, and ceramic vases can be repurposed to create functional oil lamps. The wick, typically made of cotton or fiberglass, absorbs the oil and draws it to the flame, where it vaporizes and burns. Adjusting the wick length allows you to control the flame size, brightness, and fuel consumption rate.
DIY oil lamps can be as simple as filling a container with oil and inserting a wick, but for those looking for aesthetic appeal, decorative elements such as pebbles, glass beads, or small metal charms can be added. Safety is paramount when creating and using oil lamps; they should always be placed on stable, heat-resistant surfaces, away from flammable materials, and never left unattended while lit. The ability to craft candles and oil lamps allows for customized off-grid lighting solutions, illuminating physical spaces while also adding warmth and ambiance to the home. Acquiring these skills ensures a reliable, functional, and visually appealing light source, enhancing the off-grid living experience.

Crafting Oil Lamps from Everyday Items
Creating oil lamps using common materials is a practical and clever way to ensure a consistent light source in off-grid settings. Begin by selecting a suitable container; this can be anything from a glass jar to a tin can or even a ceramic dish. It's crucial to choose non-flammable and sturdy materials to safely hold the oil. For the wick, cotton twine or strips of cotton fabric are effective options, but make sure they are clean and dry. If you opt for fabric, twist it tightly to form a makeshift wick that can absorb the oil efficiently.

Fill the chosen container with an appropriate oil. Vegetable oils like olive or canola are easily accessible options that burn cleanly and are often found in off-grid homes. Insert the wick into the oil, ensuring that one end touches the bottom of the container to absorb the oil, while leaving enough wick exposed above the oil to be ignited. If the container has a wide opening, consider using a metal washer or a small piece of foil to thread the wick, keeping it upright and preventing it from sinking into the oil.

For enhanced stability and flame control, you can create a wick holder from a piece of wire or a small metal clip. This holder should rest on the container's edge, securing the wick in place and allowing for easy adjustments to its length as needed. Before lighting the lamp for the first time, let the wick absorb the oil for several minutes to ensure it is thoroughly saturated, promoting more efficient and consistent burning.

Safety is critical when using oil lamps. Always position them on stable, heat-resistant surfaces, away from drafts and flammable materials. Never leave an oil lamp unattended while lit, and ensure it is extinguished before sleeping or leaving the area. By adhering to these safety guidelines, creating and utilizing oil lamps from everyday materials becomes an effective method for illuminating off-grid spaces, providing a dependable light source that embodies ingenuity and sustainability.

Fire-Based Lighting Solutions
Fire-based lighting, a practice as ancient as humanity itself, is a vital component of off-grid living, offering not only illumination but also warmth and a communal gathering space. Creating focused lighting systems involves various techniques and materials, each with its own advantages and considerations. The simplest form of fire-based lighting includes open flames, such as campfires and torches, which can be fueled by wood, animal fats, or vegetable oils. These lighting sources are relatively easy to establish, requiring minimal equipment and resources readily available in natural environments.

For more controlled and long-lasting illumination, oil lamps and candles made from beeswax or tallow provide a reliable solution. These methods yield a more stable light source, suitable for indoor use where an open flame may pose a risk. Understanding the properties of different fuels and their burning rates is essential for effective fire-based lighting, ensuring a consistent and safe light source. For instance, the burning duration and intensity of wood vary based on type and moisture content. Hardwoods like oak and maple offer longer burn times, while softer woods such as pine burn faster and are ideal for kindling.

Building a fire-based lighting system also requires constructing structures to contain and manage the flame. For portable lighting, a handle and a fuel-filled material at the end can effectively project light outdoors. When constructing a hearth or fireplace for both light and heat, incorporating stone or metal to reflect light and retain heat enhances efficiency and safety. The design of these structures must prioritize ventilation, ensuring a steady supply of oxygen for the flame while directing smoke away from living areas or gathering spaces.

Maintenance and safety are paramount when using fire-based lighting. Regular cleaning and removal of ash and soot from lamps, candles, and hearths prevent unwanted smoke and ensure a brighter flame. It is also essential to keep fire extinguishing tools on hand and establish clear safety protocols to avert accidental fires, especially in densely wooded or dry regions where fire risks are heightened.

Beyond their practical utility, fire-based lighting offers aesthetic and psychological benefits. The flickering glow and warmth of a fire create a sense of comfort and security, fostering social interaction and relaxation. This atmosphere is challenging to replicate with modern lighting solutions and is highly valued in off-grid environments. Mastering the techniques of fire-based lighting can significantly enhance the off-grid living experience, providing not only functional illumination but also enriching the quality of life in remote or self-sufficient settings. Whether through simple candles, oil lamps, or gatherings around a campfire, fire-based lighting remains a cornerstone of off-grid living, connecting us to our ancestral roots and to one another.

Constructing Reflectors for Fire-Based Lighting

Creating reflectors for fire-based lighting greatly enhances the efficiency of light emitted from open flames, torches, or oil lamps in off-grid settings. Reflectors work by directing and amplifying light, making fire sources more effective for illuminating larger areas or focusing light in specific directions for activities such as cooking or reading. The simplest form of a reflector can be made from materials easily found in natural or off-grid environments, such as aluminum foil, polished metal sheets, or even surfaces painted white.

For a more permanent setup, a reflector made from curved sheet metal placed behind the light source can double the light output by reflecting rays that would otherwise scatter. To construct a basic reflector, start with aluminum foil or a flat metal sheet. If using aluminum, attach it to a more rigid support like a piece of wood or cardboard to maintain its shape. Position the reflective surface at an angle behind the flame, ensuring it is far enough away to prevent fire hazards. Adjust the angle and distance from the flame to optimize light reflection and direction.

For those desiring a more durable solution, polishing a sheet of metal and shaping it into a parabolic design can create a concentrated beam of light, ideal for precision tasks or reading. When utilizing reflectors, safety and fire risk must be considered. Ensure that the reflector is securely mounted or positioned to prevent tipping or direct contact with the flame. Additionally, reflective surfaces can become hot; therefore, they should be placed to minimize the risk of accidental contact. Regular maintenance, including cleaning the reflective surface to remove soot and debris, will ensure continued optimal reflection. By effectively employing reflectors alongside fire-based lighting, off-grid areas can achieve enhanced illumination without requiring additional fuel or energy sources, making this method an efficient and sustainable way to maximize the utility of firelight.

Building a Rustic Fireplace

To create a rustic fire pit that serves as both a light source and a cooking area, start by choosing a safe, open location free from overhanging branches, structures, or flammable materials. The ground should be level to ensure stability and safety. Begin by outlining a circle for the desired size of the fire pit, typically about 3 to 4 feet in diameter for a medium-sized fire. Using a shovel, excavate the marked area to a depth of about 12 inches. This excavation will create a containment for the fire, minimizing the risk of accidental spread.

For drainage and to enhance fire pit safety, add a 6-inch layer of gravel to the bottom of the excavated area. This layer helps manage water accumulation and provides a stable base for the fire. For the walls of the fire pit, natural stones or fire-resistant bricks are ideal choices. These materials blend well with the natural surroundings and can withstand high temperatures. Starting from the gravel base, arrange the stones or bricks in a circular pattern, stacking them to a height of about 12 to 18 inches. Mortar is unnecessary, as the rustic design benefits from the natural arrangement of the stones, allowing for adequate airflow to sustain the fire. However, ensure that the structure is stable and that each layer of stone or brick is securely fastened to the one below.

To enhance the functionality of the fire pit for cooking, consider incorporating a flat grate over the opening. Select a grate that fits snugly within the opening and rests securely on the stone or brick edges. This grate can be utilized for grilling food or supporting pots and pans, offering versatile cooking options. The open flames of the fire pit will naturally provide light, illuminating the surrounding area. To maximize this illumination, arrange seating or activity areas around the fire pit where the light will be most beneficial. Additionally, for specific tasks like cooking or reading by the fire, portable stands or hooks can be employed to hang lanterns or place other additional light sources.

Safety is paramount when utilizing a rustic fire pit. Always keep a bucket of water, sand, or a fire extinguisher on hand for emergencies. Before igniting the fire, check the wind direction to ensure smoke doesn't cause issues for you or your neighbors. Never leave a fire unattended, and ensure it is completely extinguished with water, stirring the ashes to confirm that no burning embers remain before departing the fire pit area. This rustic fire pit not only provides warmth and a cooking area but also serves as a gathering point for sharing meals and stories under the stars, enriching the off-grid living experience with a touch of simplicity and tradition.

Off-Grid Energy Solutions: Generators, Wind Power, and Solar Energy

To ensure your home is genuinely secure, it is essential to have a reliable and independent energy source. Embracing an off-grid lifestyle provides complete control over your energy requirements, particularly vital during emergencies, natural disasters, or for individuals aiming for enhanced self-sufficiency. Off-grid energy options, such as generators, wind turbines, and solar panels, offer various ways to fulfill your energy needs, each presenting unique benefits and challenges.

Generators are among the most immediate and dependable off-grid solutions. They operate using fuels like diesel, gasoline, or propane to produce electricity, making them perfect for quickly powering essential appliances, medical devices, or heating systems. However, generators come with limitations: they rely on fuel availability, which must be stored safely due to its hazardous nature. Moreover, generators can be noisy and emit pollutants, making them more suitable for short-term rather than long-term use.

Wind energy provides a sustainable, long-term strategy for achieving energy independence. Installing wind turbines allows for electricity generation to meet daily needs, especially in regions characterized by consistent, strong winds. Wind energy is both clean and renewable, with low operating costs after the turbines are set up. However, the effectiveness of wind energy is contingent upon weather conditions, so a backup power source or storage system is essential during periods of low wind.

Solar energy is arguably the most versatile and accessible off-grid option. Solar panels, which can be installed on any sunlit surface, offer a silent and emissions-free energy source. They can power home systems during daylight and, with the addition of battery storage, retain electricity for nighttime use or cloudy days. While solar energy does depend on environmental factors, a well-designed system with adequate storage can cover a significant portion of a home's energy needs.

Selecting the right off-grid solution requires careful consideration of long-term reliability and the ability to maintain a continuous energy supply. Often, a combination of these technologies yields the best results: utilizing solar energy during the day, a generator for emergencies or high-demand periods, and wind energy for supplemental support in breezy areas. This integrated approach enhances your home's energy autonomy and resilience against fluctuations and interruptions.

Regular maintenance is vital for any off-grid system to ensure it functions effectively when needed. This includes checking and replacing batteries, periodically running generators, and inspecting wind turbines or solar panels for damage or obstructions. By preparing for various scenarios and maintaining a reliable power source, you will ensure that your home remains safe and functional, with light, hot water, and stored food, regardless of external conditions. True confidence stems from thorough preparation and the ability to be self-sufficient in any situation.

Fuel Safety and Management

Fuel is a vital resource for powering generators, vehicles, and other critical equipment during emergencies. However, managing fuel safely involves addressing several challenges and risks with diligence. Proper fuel management is crucial not only for convenience but also for the safety of you, your family, and your home.

First, it's essential to understand the nature of the fuel. Fuels like gasoline, diesel, and propane are highly combustible and can pose dangers if mishandled. They should be stored in approved containers specifically designed for this purpose, in well-ventilated areas away from heat sources, sparks, or open flames. Additionally, fuel supplies should be kept in a safe location, ideally separate from the main house and out of reach of children and pets to minimize fire hazards.

Another important consideration is the shelf life of fuel. Different types of fuel have varying shelf lives and can degrade over time. For instance, gasoline can start to break down within three to six months without stabilizers, while diesel has a longer lifespan but may become contaminated with algae or sediment. Using expired or contaminated fuel can harm engines, leaving you powerless in critical situations. Regularly rotating your fuel supplies is essential, utilizing the oldest fuel first and replenishing with fresh supplies to maintain optimal condition.

Safety also extends to transporting fuel. When moving fuel, use approved, sealed containers, avoid overfilling to allow for expansion, and always keep containers upright. Any spills should be promptly cleaned up using suitable absorbent materials, and the area should be well-ventilated to prevent flammable vapors from accumulating.

Prepare for emergency scenarios where access to fuel might be limited or unavailable. Your energy strategy should not only focus on conserving fuel but also on optimizing energy use through practices such as operating generators only when necessary and exploring alternative energy sources like solar panels. These actions can prolong the life of your fuel reserves and enhance your self-sufficiency during crises.

Educating your family about fuel safety is equally important. Everyone should know how to handle and store fuel properly, respond to spills, and take action in the event of a fire. Establishing a clear emergency plan and conducting regular drills related to fuel incidents can mean the difference between a minor issue and a major disaster.

Fuel storage and management are integral components of a comprehensive safety plan. By understanding the risks, implementing the appropriate precautions, and maintaining a proactive approach, you can ensure your home and loved ones are well-protected. Fuel is a precious resource that, when managed with care and respect, contributes to your safety and preparedness in any situation.

CHAPTER 5:

SECURITY MEASURES AND ALARM SYSTEMS FOR HOMES

Perimeter Protection

Establishing fences and barriers forms the foundational level of defense for safeguarding the perimeter of an off-grid property. These physical barriers not only deter unauthorized access but also clearly mark property boundaries. The selection of materials—ranging from wood and metal to natural fences made of thick hedges—depends on local environmental features, resource availability, and the desired security level. When constructing a fence, it's vital to consider its height and depth, as these aspects significantly affect the barrier's effectiveness. A fence that is too low may fail to deter intruders, while a shallow one could be easily overcome.

Integrating natural defense strategies, such as planting thorny plants along the perimeter, can enhance security without detracting from the aesthetic appeal of the landscape. Plants like hawthorn, bramble, and roses create formidable obstacles due to their thorns. This method of perimeter protection is especially beneficial in rural settings, where blending security with the natural environment is preferred.

Adding motion detectors provides an extra technological layer on top of physical barriers. These devices can be set to activate lights, alarms, or send notifications to a mobile device when movement is detected in a designated area. Their placement should be strategic, covering potential entry points and blind spots along the property perimeter. Adjusting the sensitivity of these detectors is essential to minimize false alarms caused by wildlife or environmental conditions.

A DIY project for constructing a defensive fence requires thorough planning and careful implementation. Begin by surveying the property to determine the best location for the fence, taking into account topographical features and potential threats. Gather durable materials that are appropriate for the climate. Treated wood, galvanized steel, and reinforced concrete are common choices due to their durability and resistance to weather conditions. Depending on the complexity of the project and the materials selected, tools such as posthole diggers, hammers, saws, and welding equipment may be necessary.

During the construction process, continually assess the stability and integrity of the fence, making any necessary adjustments to maintain its security. Additionally, consider the fence's impact on local wildlife and aim to minimize adverse effects, such as obstructing migration routes or access to water sources.

By combining physical barriers, natural defenses, and technological solutions, off-grid inhabitants can develop a comprehensive perimeter protection system that prevents unauthorized access while harmonizing with the surrounding environment. This integrated security approach emphasizes the importance of preparedness and resilience in off-grid living, ensuring the property remains a safe refuge for its residents.

Erecting Fences and Barriers

Constructing fences and barriers is a crucial element in establishing a secure off-grid property. These structures not only define property lines but also guard against wildlife intrusion and unauthorized entry. The choice of materials and fence design should align with the property's specific needs, taking into account factors such as local wildlife, climate, and available resources. For instance, a fence intended to keep out deer will need to be significantly taller than one designed to deter smaller animals.

Common material options include wood, metal, and recycled resources, each offering varying benefits concerning durability, cost, and ease of installation. Wooden fences blend seamlessly with the natural landscape but may require treatments to resist decay. Metal options, particularly chicken wire or barbed wire, provide greater strength but can be pricier and less visually appealing. Recycled materials, like pallets or repurposed construction supplies, can serve as an environmentally friendly and economical solution, though they may require more maintenance over time.

The construction process involves planning the layout, securely placing posts in the ground (using concrete or driving them directly into the earth), and attaching the selected material to the posts. Gates are a vital component, facilitating easy access while maintaining security, and should be strategically positioned for convenience.

Natural barriers, such as hedges or living fences, can serve as alternatives, offering privacy and reducing wind impact, though they may take longer to establish. In regions with high wildlife activity or heightened security concerns, the installation of barbed wire or spikes might be necessary; however, it's crucial to consult local regulations to ensure compliance.

Natural Barriers with Thorny Vegetation

Incorporating thorny plants as a natural barrier significantly enhances perimeter security in off-grid environments. These plants serve as effective deterrents against both wildlife and human intruders, providing an environmentally friendly and sustainable method of protection. When selecting thorny species, it's crucial to choose those that grow densely and possess robust thorns, such as blackberries, hawthorn, barberry, and pyracantha shrubs. These plants can be strategically positioned along property lines or around vulnerable areas like windows and easily accessible entry points.

Beyond their protective role, thorny plants offer ecological advantages, such as providing habitats for wildlife, supporting bee pollination, and bearing fruit in certain species. This multifunctionality makes them an essential component of a comprehensive off-grid security plan.

Implementation of Motion Sensors

The installation of motion sensors is a proactive step towards enhancing the security of an off-grid property. When placed appropriately, these devices can alert residents to unexpected movements around the perimeter or within specific zones of the property, serving as an early warning system against potential intrusions. Selecting sensors should be guided by the area needing coverage, the desired detection range, and the preferred type of alert—be it visual, audible, or a notification to a mobile device.

The installation process begins with identifying critical areas where sensors will be most effective. Ideal locations include entrances, walkways, and vulnerable spots near windows or outbuildings. It's vital to mount the sensors at the recommended height, typically between 1.8 and 3 meters off the ground, to maximize the sensor's field of vision and minimize false alarms triggered by small animals or environmental conditions.

To ensure uninterrupted protection, it's essential to select sensors that are powered by solar panels or batteries, guaranteeing functionality even when the electricity grid is unavailable.

Defense Tools and Strategies

Tools and Techniques for Home Defense

Securing your home necessitates a continuous commitment and a proactive mindset that keeps you ahead of any potential threats. Home security comprises a complex array of tools and techniques that must function in unison to ensure your residence remains safe and secure. It is imperative that no detail is overlooked; every aspect must be addressed with care, and every choice should contribute to an environment where safety is guaranteed rather than merely hoped for.

The arsenal for defending your home is extensive and diverse, but possession alone is insufficient. Mastery of how to use these tools and their integration into a comprehensive security strategy is vital. For instance, an alarm system is not merely a device that sounds an alert when someone attempts to break in; it must be meticulously configured to cover all possible entry points and linked to a monitoring system that provides immediate notifications. Ideally, it should remain operational even during power outages or tampering attempts. An effective alarm system not only warns you of danger but does so in a timely manner, allowing for a prompt response.

Surveillance cameras are another critical component of home defense. Their function goes beyond recording events; they serve as a visible deterrent to those with ill intentions. The mere presence of a camera can significantly discourage potential intruders. These cameras should be strategically placed to monitor blind spots and should connect to a system that allows real-time observation, even remotely. Importantly, not all cameras need to be overtly visible; a mix of both visible and concealed cameras can complicate matters for anyone trying to breach your security.

Beyond technology, there are various techniques to enhance the safety of your home. One highly effective method is to establish an unpredictable routine. Avoid allowing a potential intruder to study your patterns or letting your home appear unoccupied for extended periods. Timed lighting systems, as well as programmable devices to turn on televisions or radios, can simulate activity even in your absence. Such simple measures can be crucial in transforming your home from an easy target into a less appealing one.

In terms of physical security, never underestimate the importance of mechanical barriers. Doors and windows should be robustly reinforced, and locks should be of high quality, resistant to break-in attempts. If your property features a garden or outdoor area, ensure it is secured with adequate fencing and controlled access. While these physical barriers need not transform your home into a fortress, they should be sufficiently strong to delay or deter an intrusion, providing you valuable time to react.

Possessing the right tools is just one part of the equation; knowing how to use them and how to respond during a crisis is equally important. Mental preparedness is as vital as physical readiness. Every family member must be clear about their role in an emergency, including where to seek shelter, how to communicate, and how to act cohesively. Security is a collective effort, and each individual must be equipped to fulfill their responsibilities. Drills are not reserved for professionals; they are an effective way to ensure that, in the event of a real emergency, everyone knows precisely what actions to take without hesitation.

Defending your home demands discipline, focus, and ongoing threat assessment. It is not a one-time setup but a continual priority. Each time you introduce a new tool or technique, assess how it complements your overall strategy and enhances your home's security.

With a systematic approach rooted in prevention and preparedness, you can ensure that your residence remains a secure sanctuary—a place where you can relax, confident that you have taken all necessary steps to protect yourself and your loved ones.

Techniques for Sustainable Construction

Natural construction methods emphasize the utilization of local, sustainable, and minimally processed materials to create buildings that harmonize with their environment. These time-honored techniques have evolved to suit various climates and ecological conditions, offering functional and sustainable housing solutions. Central to these methods is the use of materials like earth, straw, wood, and stone, which enable the creation of ecological, visually appealing, and healthy living spaces.

Earth, one of the most abundant resources, can be utilized in various forms, such as compressed earth, cob, adobe, and earth bags. For instance, compressed earth is produced by compacting a mixture of soil, clay, and aggregates to create solid, durable walls, often stabilized with a small amount of cement or lime. Cob is made from clay soil, straw, and water, crafted by hand into organic shapes that naturally control humidity and temperature. Adobe, which is similar to cob but molded into sun-dried bricks, has been used for thousands of years in arid regions. Earthbag construction involves stacking filled bags of soil, reinforced with barbed wire, providing a flexible and strong solution suitable for varying climates.

Another effective technique is straw bale construction, which leverages the insulating properties of straw to create walls with significant thermal resistance, keeping interiors warm in winter and cool in summer. The bales are stacked and plastered with clay or lime, creating a breathable system that also provides excellent soundproofing. This method is appreciated for its simplicity and speed, making it accessible even for those with minimal construction experience.

Wood, a classic building material, is valued in sustainable construction for its versatility, aesthetic appeal, and carbon-storing properties. Techniques like timber framing, log construction, and firewood construction harness the natural qualities of wood, showcasing its structural and visual advantages. Timber framing creates a skeletal structure with large beams, connected by mortise and tenon joints, combining strength with the beauty of exposed wood. Firewood construction employs short logs arranged crosswise in a mortar mix to form naturally insulated, uniquely designed walls. Log construction, one of the oldest methods, utilizes whole logs to create robust structures that maintain a deep connection with nature.

Stone, known for its durability, is commonly used for foundations, walls, and decorative features. The dry stone construction method, which requires skill and patience, involves interlocking stones without mortar, utilizing gravity and careful stone selection to produce lasting structures.

Sustainable building also emphasizes passive solar design, positioning buildings to optimize sunlight exposure, enhancing winter warmth while reducing overheating in summer. Key features include large south-facing windows, thermal mass for heat storage, and adequate insulation, all crucial for minimizing reliance on external energy sources for temperature control.

Incorporating green roofs and living walls extends these sustainable techniques, creating structures that blend seamlessly with their surroundings while supporting local ecosystems. Green roofs, covered with vegetation, provide insulation, absorb rainwater, and serve as habitats, while living walls improve air quality and mitigate heat absorption.

Sustainable building transcends mere materials and techniques; it embodies a lifestyle philosophy that fosters a deeper connection with the environment. It challenges conventional construction practices to rethink sustainability, advocating for a holistic perspective that considers the entire lifecycle of a structure, from material selection to occupant well-being, and even to dismantling or repurposing materials. By adopting these methods, individuals and communities can create resilient, sustainable homes tailored to their climate and landscape, reflecting a profound respect for the natural world.

Selecting Suitable Natural Materials

Choosing appropriate natural materials for your off-grid dwelling is crucial for ensuring durability, sustainability, and comfort. The materials selected significantly affect the building's thermal efficiency, ecological impact, and overall aesthetic. When opting for earth as your primary building material, it's essential to evaluate its composition and suitability for techniques such as compressed earth or cob. Soil with an appropriate clay content is vital for structural integrity and ease of handling. When utilizing straw bales, ensure they are dry, well-compacted, and free from mold to maintain optimal thermal insulation and structural stability.

When selecting wood, consider its source, durability, and resistance to pests and decay. Local timber not only minimizes transportation emissions but also supports the regional economy. Prioritize wood species that exhibit natural resistance to rot and insects to avoid the need for chemical treatments. For stone construction, the locally available stone type can dictate the construction technique, whether dry or mortared masonry. The density, workability, and aesthetic qualities of the stone should align with the project's requirements.

Insulation and Thermal Mass

Insulation and thermal mass are essential elements in creating an off-grid home that maintains comfort while minimizing energy consumption. Insulation acts as a barrier to heat transfer, keeping warm air inside during winter and outside during summer. Materials like straw bales, cellulose, and wool are effective natural insulators, boasting high thermal resistance (R-value) while remaining breathable to enhance indoor air quality and moisture regulation. Conversely, thermal mass pertains to a material's capacity to absorb and store heat energy. Stone, compressed earth, and adobe are excellent high-thermal-mass materials that can capture sunlight during the day and gradually release it as temperatures fall, naturally regulating indoor climates without reliance on mechanical heating or cooling systems.

The strategic application of insulation and thermal mass is critical in natural building practices, particularly in passive solar design. By positioning high-thermal-mass materials in areas where they can absorb direct sunlight—such as floors or south-facing walls—and combining them with effective insulation, remarkable energy efficiency can be achieved. This synergy stabilizes internal temperatures, reducing dependency on external energy for heating and cooling.

Building an Off-Grid Cabin

Crafting a Sustainable Cabin

Constructing an off-grid cabin embodies the essence of self-reliance and adaptability, creating a lifestyle that coexists harmoniously with nature. The journey begins with a meticulous selection of the site, prioritizing southern exposure to maximize passive solar gain while assessing crucial factors like water accessibility, land drainage, and proximity to essential resources. The choice of materials is vital for ensuring the cabin's sustainability and efficiency, favoring local and natural options that minimize environmental impact and blend seamlessly with the surroundings. Employing techniques such as timber framing, log construction, and utilizing reclaimed materials can significantly reduce the carbon footprint, enhancing the character and durability of the structure.

During the design phase, integrating principles of energy efficiency is essential, leading to compact layouts that lower heating and cooling demands while incorporating thermal mass and insulation for a comfortable indoor environment. Windows should be strategically positioned to optimize natural light and airflow, thus decreasing reliance on artificial lighting and mechanical systems. Furthermore, the incorporation of rainwater harvesting systems and solar panels ensures a consistent supply of clean water and renewable energy. The construction process emphasizes manual skills and community participation, turning the building experience into a shared opportunity for learning and connection.

Attention to detail is paramount in the interior design, where space-saving solutions and multifunctional furniture enhance the usability of smaller spaces. Wood stoves serve as a sustainable heating source, complemented by passive solar designs and insulation methods that maintain warmth during winter while keeping the cabin cool in summer. Implementing off-grid waste management systems, such as composting toilets and gray water recycling, reduces the cabin's environmental impact.

The final touches on the cabin reflect a dedication to sustainability and self-sufficiency, featuring a greenhouse or garden for food production, outdoor cooking facilities, and areas for relaxation amidst nature. The outcome is a resilient, efficient, and cozy off-grid cabin that showcases the potential of sustainable living and the fulfillment that comes from building a home with your own hands. This approach not only provides practical solutions for off-grid life but also fosters a deeper connection with the environment and a sense of achievement in aligning your home with principles of ecological stewardship.

Selecting the Ideal Site and Layout

Choosing the right location for your off-grid cabin involves analyzing several critical factors to ensure sustainability, safety, and comfort. The land's orientation is paramount; south-facing slopes receive maximum sunlight, making them perfect for passive solar heating and efficient solar panel performance. However, it's equally important to assess the risks of natural hazards such as flooding, landslides, or heavy snowfall that could jeopardize the cabin's safety and viability. Accessibility year-round is crucial; the site must be reachable in all seasons, especially if you plan to reside there permanently or need regular access for maintenance and supplies.

Water availability is a key consideration; being near a clean, reliable water source is vital for off-grid living. However, balance this with the need for proper drainage to prevent water accumulation and structural damage. Also, evaluate the soil type and its stability for the foundation; rocky or unstable terrain may necessitate special construction methods or additional site preparation costs.

When planning your cabin layout, consider not just the building itself but also how to utilize the surrounding land. Identify optimal locations for solar panels, wind turbines, or water collection systems and how these will interact with the natural landscape and sunlight paths. Account for potential future expansions, such as gardens, greenhouses, or additional structures, ensuring enough space and suitable conditions for these projects.

Finally, familiarize yourself with local zoning laws and building codes to understand any restrictions or requirements related to off-grid construction in your chosen area. These may include minimum distances from water bodies, maximum building dimensions, or specific environmental protections. Engaging with the local community and authorities early in the planning process can help facilitate the realization of your project, ensuring compliance with all legal and community standards for sustainable living.

Foundation Options for Off-Grid Cabins

Selecting an appropriate foundation for your off-grid cabin is essential to guarantee the structure's longevity and stability. The type of foundation is often determined by factors such as terrain, soil conditions, climate, and cabin design. Common foundation options include pier, slab, crawl space, and basement foundations. Pier foundations, consisting of buried concrete posts, are economical and suitable for uneven terrain or flood-prone areas, allowing airflow beneath the cabin to prevent moisture issues. Slab foundations entail pouring concrete directly onto the ground, creating a solid base ideal for stable soils and warmer climates where frost heave is not a concern. This type requires minimal upkeep but can be challenging to repair in case of plumbing issues.

Crawl space foundations elevate the cabin off the ground, allowing access to plumbing and electrical systems while offering pest protection; however, they require adequate ventilation to avoid moisture buildup. Basement foundations, although more costly, provide extra living or storage space and are advantageous in colder climates, as they sit below the frost line, offering natural insulation.

When selecting a foundation, consider the environmental impact and sustainability of the materials used. For instance, utilizing local stone or recycled concrete can lower the cabin's carbon footprint. Additionally, aligning the foundation design with the cabin's energy efficiency, such as incorporating thermal mass into slab foundations for passive solar heating, further supports off-grid living principles. Always consult a structural engineer or a professional experienced in off-grid construction to ensure the chosen foundation meets the cabin's requirements and adheres to local building codes.

Thoughtful foundation planning and selection will ensure not only the safety of the structure but also help create a sustainable and resilient off-grid living environment.

Enhancing Home Defense

To achieve optimal home defense, each entry point and potential vulnerability must be thoroughly examined. Envision how an intruder could exploit your home's weaknesses and proactively address these vulnerabilities. The goal is to adopt a proactive mindset, focused on fortifying defenses.

Begin by bolstering physical barriers. Ensure that doors and windows are sturdy and reinforced; relying on a basic padlock is insufficient. Invest in high-security locks designed to withstand break-in attempts. Consider additional reinforcements, such as security bars or window protection films, to enhance impact resistance. For further protection, install security doors at primary entrances to reinforce security.

Effective defense extends beyond the physical structure to encompass a comprehensive alarm system. Install a dependable alarm system that monitors all critical areas, including less visible spots. Complement this setup with motion detectors and surveillance cameras to add extra layers of security. Regularly check and maintain these systems to ensure they are always functioning optimally.

Preparation and planning are equally important. Develop a detailed emergency response plan that includes every family member. Ensure that everyone is aware of their roles and knows the actions to take during an emergency or intrusion. Establish clear meeting points and procedures for contacting authorities. Regular drills and open communication can significantly enhance response efficiency.

Engaging with your neighbors strengthens community awareness. Building positive relationships within your neighborhood can serve as a deterrent against potential threats. Attend local safety meetings and share relevant information with residents. Collective vigilance and mutual awareness will enhance the security of the entire area.

Lastly, cultivate a mindset of ongoing vigilance. Maintaining the safety of your home is an evolving process, not a one-time task. Periodically review and adjust your security measures based on emerging threats and developments. Every effort made to bolster safety contributes to a secure environment for you and your loved ones.

Strengthening the Home's Structural Integrity

Every structure has its own vulnerabilities, and recognizing these is key to enhancing overall security. Begin with an assessment of the foundation, the cornerstone of the home's protection. Ensure it is solid and free from significant cracks. If necessary, reinforce the foundation using techniques like resin injection or steel reinforcement. A stable foundation not only provides structural integrity but also acts as a deterrent against intrusion.

Next, focus on the exterior walls. They must be robust enough to withstand impacts. Enhance them with high-quality materials and advanced construction methods that boost their resistance to external forces. Remember that walls serve not only as physical barriers but also as crucial components in defending against intruders.

The roof also plays a vital role. Ensure it is well-maintained and free from leaks or damage. Upgrade the roof with durable materials and schedule regular inspections. A well-kept roof prevents water damage and supports the building's overall stability.

Do not overlook windows and doors. Strengthen these entry points with high-security locks and additional protections such as security bars or reinforced glass. Windows should be designed to resist impacts and deter unauthorized access. Investing in sturdy door and window systems enhances security and provides peace of mind.

Ultimately, the overall safety of your home hinges on the quality of materials used. Select durable and reliable materials for every aspect of your home. The strength and longevity of these materials contribute significantly to the stability and overall protection of the property.

Bulletproof and Blast-Resistant Protections

Implementing bulletproof and blast-resistant features can significantly enhance your home's safety. View your residence as a stronghold designed to withstand extraordinary threats, necessitating a detailed and thorough fortification approach.

Start with ballistic protection. These systems are designed to defend against gunfire and shrapnel, utilizing advanced materials like bullet-resistant glass and high-tech fibers such as Kevlar or carbon fiber. Installing bulletproof, multi-layered, reinforced windows can be a critical step in high-risk areas. These windows not only provide substantial protection but also enhance the overall security of your home against external hazards. For doors, consider armored models specifically designed to resist break-ins and assaults. Constructed with materials that absorb and disperse impact energy, these doors make unauthorized access extremely difficult. Additionally, applying bullet-resistant materials around vulnerable points, such as primary entrances and high-risk windows, can provide further defense.

For explosion protection, which guards against blasts and intense fires, it's essential to use specialized fire-retardant materials and insulation. Reinforce walls and ceilings with materials capable of withstanding high temperatures and treating external surfaces to resist explosions and flames. Fireproof materials such as drywall or ceramic siding can protect your home from extreme heat and shockwaves. Installing an early detection system for fires and explosions is equally important. Fit smoke and gas detectors linked to an alarm system that immediately alerts emergency services, ensuring a swift response during critical situations.

While these measures represent a substantial investment, the value of enhanced security is immeasurable. Each component of bulletproof and blast protection must be meticulously integrated, tailored to your specific needs and potential threats. A strategic, comprehensive approach to planning and preparedness is crucial not only for addressing immediate dangers but also for ensuring long-term safety. With thoughtful preparation and tactical implementation, you can transform your home into a formidable fortress, ready to withstand even the most extreme scenarios.

Creating a Covered Safety Area

Designing a secure haven within your home begins with selecting the ideal location. This area should ideally be situated centrally, away from windows and doors, to minimize exposure to external threats. Accessibility is crucial; ensure all family members can reach this space quickly and without confusion during an emergency.

Once you've chosen the location, the next step is to fortify the space. Reinforce the walls and ceiling with robust materials like reinforced concrete or steel beams to enhance their ability to withstand impacts and stress. If your budget permits, incorporating bulletproof elements can provide extra protection.

Equipping this shelter with essential supplies is vital. Stock non-perishable food, clean water, and basic medical kits. Ensure you have a reliable light source and a functioning communication system, such as a battery-operated radio, to stay informed about external conditions and contact emergency services when necessary. A ventilation system is also critical for maintaining air quality, especially during emergencies that may compromise air safety, such as fires or contamination. This system should filter harmful particles and ensure a continuous airflow.

Additionally, designate this safety area as a family gathering spot. Develop a clear emergency response plan, ensuring that everyone knows how to access and utilize the space effectively. Familiarizing each family member with the location and resources of the shelter can be crucial in high-stress scenarios.

Creating a safe haven is not merely about constructing a shelter; it's about providing a reliable sanctuary for you and your loved ones during critical times. With careful planning and meticulous execution, you can transform this space into a sturdy bastion of security and peace of mind.

CHAPTER 6:

COMMUNICATION

Effective Communication and Navigation Techniques

This chapter delves into various projects and methods that enable effective communication and navigation, even when conventional infrastructure is unavailable. Mastering these skills will equip you to stay connected, orient yourself, and handle emergencies, regardless of your location. Proficient communication and navigation are vital for survival in offline contexts, as well as online, particularly when energy sources for standard electronic devices like phones, radios, and computers are absent. Whether navigating unfamiliar landscapes or your home, coordinating with others, or seeking assistance, having reliable tools and methods is essential. In emergency situations, where modern conveniences such as smartphones and GPS may be rendered useless, it becomes imperative to understand and utilize alternative communication and navigation strategies.

The Importance of Communication During Emergencies

When traditional communication methods like phones or internet messaging are unavailable, staying in touch demands alternative solutions. Effective communication in emergency situations requires technologies that operate independently of electrical grids or standard internet services. It's crucial to have a mix of short- and long-range communication tools to address diverse needs. Short-range tools can help you connect with family or neighbors, facilitating quick information sharing and coordination. Conversely, long-range communication devices allow you to tap into a broader network for gathering information, seeking assistance during crises, or staying informed about regional developments.

Preparation is the cornerstone of successful offline communication. This involves understanding the necessary equipment, ensuring reliable power sources, and knowing how to operate and maintain your devices. Alternative energy sources such as solar panels, hand-crank generators, and backup batteries are essential to keep communication tools functional when traditional power sources are unavailable. By effectively learning to use these tools and practicing regularly, you will be ready to communicate when it matters most. This section introduces three practical projects for effective off-grid communication: constructing a HAM radio, setting up walkie-talkies, and establishing a solar-powered radio.

Constructing a HAM Radio

Cost: $200-$500
Difficulty: High
Estimated Time: 3-5 days

A HAM radio serves as an excellent tool for long-distance communication, enabling connections with other radio operators locally and globally. This reliability is invaluable in emergencies or for coordinating activities. Constructing and configuring a HAM radio system ensures you have a robust tool for your off-grid communication needs.

Materials Required:

- **HAM Radio Transmitter-Receiver:** 1 unit. Choose a model that covers HF, VHF, or UHF bands based on your requirements. Brands like Icom, Yaesu, and Kenwood are highly regarded. Ensure the transmitter has sufficient output power (typically between 5 and 100 watts) for your desired communication range.
- **Antenna:**
    - **Dipole Antenna:** Consists of two wires of equal length, generally between 33 and 66 feet for the HF band, along with insulators and a center connector.
    - **Vertical Antenna:** 1 pre-assembled vertical antenna suitable for the required frequency range.
    - **Yagi Antenna:** 1 Yagi antenna meeting manufacturer specifications, ideal for directional communication.
- **Coaxial Cable:** 50-100 feet of RG-8 or RG-58 coaxial cable, depending on the distance between the antenna and the transmitter. Ensure the cable has PL-259 connectors for easy connection.
- **Power Supply:** A solar panel with battery storage or a hand-crank generator. The power supply must deliver a constant voltage (typically 12V DC) and adequate current for the transmitter.
- **Grounding Rod and Cable:** 1 grounding rod (8-foot copper or galvanized steel) and 10-20 feet of ground wire. Use heavy-gauge wire (10 AWG or greater) for effective grounding.
- **SWR Meter (Standing Wave Ratio):** 1 unit, essential for tuning the antenna and ensuring minimal signal loss.
- **Basic Tools:** Screwdrivers, pliers, wrenches, wire cutters, and a soldering iron for secure connections.

Instructions:
1. **Obtain a HAM Radio License:** Before operating a HAM radio, you must secure a license. Study for the exam, which covers basic electronics, operating procedures, and regulations. Online study guides and practice tests are available. Passing the exam grants you a license and a call sign, necessary for legal operation.
2. **Select a HAM Transmitter:** Choose a transmitter that meets your communication needs, considering factors like range (local or long-distance), frequency bands (HF for long distances, VHF/UHF for local communications), and output power. Reliable brands include Icom, Yaesu, and Kenwood, which offer transmitters with various features. Ensure your transmitter supports SSB (Single Side Band) mode for long-distance communication.
3. **Install the Antenna:**
    - **Dipole Antenna:** Cut two equal-length wires using the formula: 468 / frequency (in MHz) = length in feet. Connect the wires to a central insulator and suspend them horizontally between two support points (like trees or poles) using non-conductive string. Adjust height and angle for optimal signal reception.
    - **Vertical Antenna:** Mount a pre-assembled vertical antenna on a pole, raising it at least 10-20 feet above ground to enhance signal reception. Ensure the antenna base is properly grounded.
4. **Connect Coaxial Cable:** Attach the coaxial cable from the antenna to the transmitter, securing it along the pole or mast with cable ties or clips. Ensure connectors are tightly screwed and insulate external connections with rubber sheaths or electrical tape to protect against the elements.
5. **Set Up the Grounding System:** Insert the grounding rod into the ground near the radio system and attach the ground wire to the rod using clamps. Connect the other end to the transmitter and antenna. This system protects equipment from electrical surges and lightning, which could cause damage.
6. **Power Supply:** Establish a reliable power source for your HAM radio. Connect a solar panel to a deep cycle battery for sustainable energy or use a hand-crank generator as a backup. Ensure your power supply consistently provides 12V DC output. If necessary, incorporate a voltage regulator for stable voltage.
7. **Connect the SWR Meter:** Install the SWR meter between the transmitter and antenna. This tool measures the standing wave ratio, indicating the antenna's power transmission efficiency. Adjust the antenna's length and position for the lowest possible SWR reading (ideally under 1.5:1).
8. **System Testing:** Activate the transmitter and select a frequency. Use the SWR meter to test your setup and make necessary antenna adjustments for optimal performance. Familiarize yourself with the transmitter controls, including tuning, frequency selection, and power adjustment. Practice contacting other operators to evaluate signal range and clarity.
9. **Establish Communication Protocols:** Define communication protocols with your family or group. Assign specific frequencies or channels for various purposes, like emergencies and general discussions. Agree on regular check-in times to ensure everyone's safety and maintain contact.
10. **Routine Maintenance:** Periodically inspect and maintain your HAM radio system. Check the antenna for signs of corrosion or damage. Examine the coaxial cable for wear and replace it as necessary. Ensure the grounding system remains effective. Keep the transmitter clean and dust-free.

Maintenance Tips:
- Regularly renew your HAM radio license and stay informed about regulations and best practices.
- Engage with amateur radio communities and networks to enhance your skills and knowledge.
- Store the transmitter and accessories in a dry, dust-free area when not in use.
- Conduct monthly tests to ensure all components function correctly and to practice your communication skills

Installation of Two-Way Radios

Cost: $50 - $200
Difficulty Level: Easy
Estimated Time: 1-2 hours

Two-way radios, commonly referred to as walkie-talkies, are efficient and user-friendly devices for short to medium-range communication in off-grid scenarios. They are particularly useful for staying connected within a group, coordinating activities, or requesting assistance. This guide will help you select, set up, and effectively utilize walkie-talkies for reliable communication.

Required Materials:
- **Walkie-Talkies:** Choose between GMRS (General Mobile Radio Service) or FRS (Family Radio Service).
    - **FRS:** Typically has a range of 1-5 miles and does not require a license.
    - **GMRS:** Offers a range of up to 20 miles under ideal conditions, but a US license is necessary.
- **Rechargeable Batteries:** 4-8 AA or AAA batteries depending on your chosen model. Opt for NiMH or lithium-ion batteries for extended life.
- **Charger:** 1 compatible charger for the selected battery type.
- **Protective Cases:** 1 for each walkie-talkie to safeguard them during transport.
- **External Antennas (Optional):** 1 for each walkie-talkie. These antennas can enhance range and signal clarity, especially in challenging terrains.

Instructions:
1. **Select the Appropriate Walkie-Talkie:** Choose walkie-talkies based on your communication needs. For general usage, FRS models suffice and require no licensing. If a greater range is necessary, opt for GMRS models, but remember that they require a license for legal operation in the US.

2. **Battery Setup:** Insert rechargeable batteries into the walkie-talkies. Using rechargeable batteries is more sustainable and convenient for the long term. Keep a solar charger handy for recharging when off-grid. Ensure the batteries are fully charged before the initial use of the walkie-talkies.
3. **Understand Basic Functions:** Familiarize yourself with the core features of the walkie-talkies. Most models include:
    - **Power Button:** To turn the device on and off.
    - **Push-to-Talk (PTT) Button:** Hold this button while speaking to transmit your message.
    - **Volume Control:** To adjust the speaker volume.
    - **Channel Selector:** To navigate different communication channels. Refer to the user manual for specific instructions for your model.
4. **Select and Set Channels:** Choose a clear channel for communication. Walkie-talkies operate on specific frequencies, so it's important to select a channel with minimal interference. Experiment with different channels to find the best option. GMRS radios provide access to additional channels, including repeater channels to extend your range.
5. **Conduct a Range Test:** Perform a range test to determine the communication limits of your walkie-talkies. Start with a short distance and gradually increase it to assess clarity. Be mindful of obstacles like buildings or trees that may interfere with signal strength.
6. **Using External Antennas (Optional):** If you need to improve communication range or clarity, consider attaching external antennas. Connect them to the walkie-talkies according to the manufacturer's instructions. External antennas are especially beneficial in mountainous or heavily wooded areas where signals may be obstructed.
7. **Establish Communication Protocols:** Create straightforward communication protocols within your group. Use clear and concise language, and agree on standard phrases or codes for common messages. For instance, say "Over" to indicate you have finished speaking and expect a reply, or "End" to signal the conclusion of the conversation.
8. **Store and Transport Walkie-Talkies:** When not in use, keep walkie-talkies in protective cases or holsters. This will safeguard them from damage and facilitate easy transport. Ensure they are always within reach, particularly during activities like hiking or traveling.
9. **Routine Maintenance:** Regularly check walkie-talkies for signs of wear or damage. Clean the exterior to eliminate dust and debris. Test the batteries frequently and recharge as needed. Ensure that the antennas are firmly connected.

Maintenance Tips:
- **Battery Management:** Keep batteries charged and replace them when they show diminished capacity. Avoid leaving batteries in the walkie-talkies for extended periods when not in use to prevent drainage or corrosion.
- **Antenna Inspection:** Ensure the antennas are securely attached and free from damage, as a compromised antenna can significantly hinder communication range.
- **Proper Storage:** Store walkie-talkies in a cool, dry place when not in use to prevent moisture damage. Use protective cases to avoid impact damage during storage or transport.
- **Regular Practice:** Use the walkie-talkies frequently to stay familiar with their functionality and ensure they remain in good working condition.

Installation of a Solar-Powered Radio

Cost: $30 - $100
Difficulty Level: Moderate
Estimated Time: 1-2 days

A solar-powered radio is an invaluable tool for staying updated and connected during emergencies. It enables you to receive news, weather updates, and alerts without relying on traditional grid power. This guide will assist you in assembling a solar radio system.

Required Materials:
- **Solar-Powered Radio:** Choose a model equipped with an integrated solar panel and a hand crank. Popular options include the Kaito KA500 and the Eton Scorpion II.
- **Rechargeable Batteries:** 4-8 AA or AAA batteries, depending on your radio model. Refer to the manual for specifications and recommendations on replacements.
- **External Solar Panel (Optional):** For enhanced charging capacity. Ensure compatibility with your radio model.
- **USB Charging Cable (Optional):** If your radio supports USB charging, use a suitable cable for additional charging options.
- **Basic Tools:** Screwdrivers and pliers for any necessary adjustments or repairs.

Instructions:
1. **Select the Right Solar-Powered Radio:** Choose a radio based on your specific needs. Look for features such as AM/FM/NOAA band reception for weather forecasts, an integrated solar panel, a hand crank, and USB charging capability. Ensure the radio is robust and intended for outdoor use or emergencies. Reading user reviews can help inform your decision.
2. **Installation and Initial Testing:** Carefully unpack the radio and read the manual to familiarize yourself with its features and functions. Charge the radio using the integrated solar panel by placing it in direct sunlight. Charging may take several hours depending on light intensity. Turn on the radio to test reception for AM, FM, and NOAA channels, and try tuning into various stations to check signal clarity.
3. **Utilizing the Hand Crank Generator:** In the absence of sufficient sunlight, use the hand crank to charge the radio. Turn the crank steadily for a few minutes; generally, one minute of cranking yields about 10-15 minutes of radio playtime, although this can vary by model. Check the battery indicator (if available) to

ensure the radio is sufficiently charged for operation, and use the hand crank periodically to maintain battery levels, especially during prolonged use.
4. **External Solar Panel (Optional):** For additional charging capacity, consider connecting an external solar panel. Ensure it is compatible with your radio and follow the manufacturer's instructions for setup. Position the external panel in a sunny area and connect it to the radio using the appropriate cable. This can enhance charging speed, especially in low-light conditions or when the integrated panel is insufficient.
5. **USB Charging (Optional):** If your radio allows for USB charging, connect it to other solar chargers, power banks, or USB outlets using a USB cable. This adds another reliable method for charging, useful for integrating the radio into a larger off-grid power setup.
6. **Emergency Usage:** During emergencies, tune in to NOAA weather channels for real-time updates and alerts. These channels provide vital information regarding severe weather, natural disasters, and other emergencies. Utilize the hand crank or external solar panel to keep the radio powered during extended use, and maintain a moderate volume to conserve energy and ensure continuous operation.
7. **Routine Use and Upkeep:** Regularly use the radio to stay informed about local news, weather, and events. This helps you become familiar with its functions and keeps the device in good working order. Periodically clean the solar panel with a soft cloth to remove dust and debris, enhancing its sunlight absorption. Routinely check rechargeable batteries and replace them if they show signs of wear. Keep spare batteries on hand for uninterrupted usage.

Maintenance Tips:
- **Proper Storage:** Store your radio in a dry, cool environment when not in use to shield it from moisture and extreme temperatures. Use a protective case, if available, to prevent damage.
- **Regular Testing:** Frequently test all charging methods (solar, hand crank, USB) to ensure they are functioning properly. Regular checks can help identify issues early on.
- **Reception Optimization:** Extend the radio antenna and position it correctly to enhance reception quality. Adjust the angle or position of the antenna to improve signal clarity.
- **Stay Informed:** Keep abreast of any firmware updates or recalls for your specific radio model, as manufacturers may release updates to enhance performance or resolve issues.

Shortwave radios and HAM radios are essential tools for off-grid communication, providing a reliable way to connect with the outside world even without traditional communication infrastructure. Shortwave radios operate on frequencies between 1.6 and 30 MHz, allowing you to access international news, emergency broadcasts, and information from around the globe. This capability is especially valuable in remote locations, ensuring access to critical information during natural disasters or emergencies when standard media may be unavailable.

HAM radios, or amateur radios, take this further by enabling two-way communication. Operators can send and receive messages over considerable distances, leveraging the reflection of radio waves on the ionosphere to connect with other continents. This form of communication is beneficial not only for casual conversations but also plays a vital role in emergency response, relief efforts, and community networking. HAM operators often engage in networks that provide emergency communication services when other systems fail.

To begin using shortwave and HAM radios, it's essential to grasp the basic equipment required. For shortwave listening, the main tool is a shortwave receiver, which can vary from simple portable units to more sophisticated desktop models. In contrast, setting up a HAM radio involves more complexity, requiring a transceiver for sending and receiving signals, an antenna for transmission, and a power source such as a battery or solar panel. Furthermore, obtaining a license for HAM operators is a crucial step, ensuring users comprehend the technical aspects and regulations surrounding radio communications. In the United States, the Federal Communications Commission (FCC) manages this licensing process, offering various levels of licenses that permit operation on different frequency bands. Preparing for and passing the examination not only legitimizes HAM radio use but also educates the operator on best practices and operational ethics.

Antenna construction and placement are critical to the success of shortwave and HAM radio setups. For shortwave radios, a straightforward long-wire antenna is often sufficient, while HAM radios may require more advanced antennas for effective transmission. Numerous DIY projects exist that enable operators to build antennas customized to their specific needs and environmental conditions. Proper antenna placement can significantly enhance signal strength and clarity, making it an essential consideration for off-grid configurations.

Integrating solar panels with battery storage systems provides a sustainable energy source for radio equipment, ensuring functionality even when conventional power sources are unavailable. This setup is especially beneficial in remote areas or during prolonged blackouts, highlighting the resilience and self-sufficiency of off-grid living.

Whether for everyday communication, emergency preparedness, or casual exploration of radio waves, these tools create a genuine link to the broader world. Engaging with the global community of shortwave listeners and HAM operators fosters a sense of connection, knowledge sharing, and camaraderie, reinforcing the importance of communication in promoting understanding and collaboration across distances. This system, particularly valuable for amateur radio operations, provides a dependable means to maintain contact with the outside world, whether for daily requirements or in emergencies. The combination of solar panels, charge controllers, batteries, and communication devices forms the backbone of a solar-powered communication setup, enabling continuous operation without reliance on traditional energy sources.

Selection of Solar Panels

When choosing the right solar panels, it is essential to assess the power requirements of your communication devices. A small to medium-sized panel setup generally suffices for powering a basic HAM radio configuration. The energy generated by the panels charges a battery bank, which in turn powers the radio equipment. It is crucial to calculate the total energy consumption of the devices and appropriately size the solar system, taking into account worst-case scenarios to ensure efficiency even under reduced sunlight. A charge controller is a vital component, protecting batteries from overcharging and deep discharge. Modern controllers equipped with MPPT (Maximum Power Point Tracking) technology optimize the energy produced by the panels, enhancing system efficiency, especially in areas with variable lighting conditions, thus maximizing energy collection and storage.

Battery Selection

Selecting the right batteries is another critical factor, with deep cycle batteries being the most suitable for solar-powered systems due to their durability during repeated charge and discharge cycles. The capacity of the battery bank must be adequate to store energy for periods when solar charging is not feasible. Lithium batteries, while pricier, offer greater energy density and longevity compared to traditional lead-acid batteries, making them a worthwhile investment for anyone looking to establish a long-term, resilient communication system for emergency scenarios.

Connecting Communication Devices

Connecting communication devices to the solar setup requires careful planning to ensure uninterrupted operation. Using the right cables and connectors is essential to minimize power losses and configure the system for easy switching between solar power and battery reserves when needed. For HAM radio operators, this setup not only allows for independence from the power grid but also adds an extra layer of resilience, crucial for disaster recovery situations or for coordinating with emergency services.

Advantages of Solar-Powered Communications

The advantages of solar-powered communication systems extend beyond mere emergency preparedness, providing off-grid individuals and communities with a sustainable means to stay connected. By harnessing solar energy, these systems demonstrate the potential of renewable resources to power vital services, aligning with self-sufficiency and environmental stewardship goals. As technology advances, the efficiency and accessibility of solar-powered communication systems will continue to improve, enabling remote communities to maintain dependable communication channels without sacrificing their commitment to sustainability.

Choosing Solar Panels for Communication Devices

When selecting solar panels for communication devices, such as HAM radio systems, the main considerations are the wattage and efficiency of the panels. Solar panels vary in size and power output, ranging from small 10-watt panels suitable for charging portable devices to larger 300-watt panels designed for greater energy demands. For devices requiring continuous power, it's vital to choose a panel or a set of panels capable of meeting your daily energy needs, even during periods of limited sunlight.

Another significant factor is the compatibility of the solar panels with the existing system, particularly regarding the charge controller and battery bank. Ensuring that the panel output voltage aligns with system requirements is critical to prevent battery damage or charging inefficiencies. In systems using MPPT charge controllers, employing panels with higher output voltage can optimize energy capture, as these controllers can convert surplus voltage into additional current, enhancing overall system efficiency.

Portability is also an important consideration for off-grid mobile setups or temporary installations. Lightweight, flexible solar panels can be easily transported and installed on uneven surfaces, making them ideal for portable HAM radio stations or emergency communication kits.

Ultimately, the selection of solar panels for communication devices hinges on a comprehensive understanding of the devices' energy requirements, the environmental conditions of the installation site, and a careful balance between cost and efficiency.

Battery Backup Solutions for Communication Devices

Battery backup systems for radios and telephones are vital for any communication setup, ensuring that these essential devices remain functional during power failures or when solar charging isn't feasible. At the core of a battery backup system are deep-cycle batteries, which are engineered to deliver a consistent power supply over extended periods and can be repeatedly discharged and recharged. Since radios and telephones typically consume less energy compared to other household devices, a compact battery bank is often sufficient, making the system cost-effective and efficient in terms of space.

The capacity of the battery bank should be calculated based on the energy requirements of the radios and telephones, as well as the desired runtime. This involves determining the wattage used by your devices and estimating their daily usage in hours; multiplying these figures will give you the total watt-hours needed each day. It's wise to include a safety margin for days with higher consumption or reduced sunlight exposure to ensure dependable operation. Charge controllers are crucial in backup systems, as they manage the energy flow from solar panels to batteries and prevent overcharging, which can significantly shorten battery life. An MPPT (Maximum Power Point Tracking) charge controller is particularly beneficial, as it optimizes the energy harvested from the solar panels, leading to more effective charging.

To enhance reliability, integrating a battery management system (BMS) can provide additional advantages, such as monitoring the charge level and health of each battery, preventing excessive discharges, and balancing the charge among batteries to encourage uniform wear and extend their lifespan. Including an inverter in the setup allows the DC power stored in the batteries to be converted into AC power, making it compatible with many standard chargers for radios and phones. However, many modern communication devices can operate directly on DC power, which helps to eliminate energy losses that occur during conversion. Ensuring that radios and telephones are equipped with a dedicated backup system is crucial for maintaining effective communication, even in critical circumstances.

Constructing a Solar Device Charger

This project focuses on creating a solar charger for small electronic devices such as smartphones, tablets, or cameras. A solar charger captures the sun's energy to offer a portable and eco-friendly power source, making it ideal for outdoor activities and emergency situations.

Difficulty Level: Easy to Moderate
Estimated Time: 2-4 hours

Benefits:
A solar charger is a sustainable solution for keeping devices powered without relying on the electrical grid. It is perfect for camping, hiking, or serving as a backup during power outages. Building a custom solar charger can be more economical than purchasing a commercial model and allows you to tailor the system to your specific needs.

Materials Required:
- **Solar Panel:** 5W to 10W, based on charging requirements.
- **USB Charging Module:** (Boost converter or voltage regulator with a 5V output).
- **Rechargeable Battery Pack:** (Optional, for energy storage when sunlight is not available).
- **Diode:** (1N5819 or similar, to prevent reverse current).
- **Enclosure:** (To safeguard components).
- **USB Port or Cable:** (For connecting devices).
- **Wires and Connectors.**
- **Switch:** (Optional, to power the charger on and off).
- **Fasteners:** (Velcro, adhesive, or screws to secure components in the enclosure).

Tools Needed:
- **Soldering Iron and Solder.**
- **Wire Cutters and Strippers.**
- **Multimeter:** (To check connections and voltage).
- **Screwdriver.**
- **Drill:** (For creating holes in the enclosure).
- **Hot Glue Gun:** (Optional, for attaching components).

Alternative Materials:

- **Recycled Solar Panels:** From old garden lights or similar devices.
- **DIY Wooden or Metal Enclosure:** Instead of plastic.

Step-by-Step Instructions:
1. **Select and Prepare the Solar Panel:** Choose a solar panel with sufficient power to charge your devices, typically a 5W to 10W panel is adequate for smartphones. Ensure it has a voltage output of 5V for USB charging. Clean and inspect it for damage. **Time Required:** 30 minutes.
2. **Prepare the Enclosure:** Select a case that can hold the solar panel, USB module, and other components securely. Ensure the enclosure is sturdy and weather-resistant, especially for outdoor use. Create openings for the USB port, switch (if included), and wiring. Ensure the solar panel can be attached firmly to the outside of the case. **Time Required:** 30 minutes.
3. **Connect the Solar Panel to the USB Charging Module:** Solder the positive lead of the solar panel to the anode of the diode. Connect the cathode to the positive input of the USB module to prevent current from flowing back to the panel in low light. Connect the negative lead of the panel to the negative input of the USB module. If a battery pack is used, connect it to the solar panel first, then to the USB module to store energy for times without sunlight. **Time Required:** 1 hour.
4. **Install the USB Port or Cable:** If the USB module lacks a built-in port, you will need to attach one. Solder the output wires from the USB module to the corresponding pins on the USB port or directly to a USB cable. Ensure all connections are secure and that the USB port or cable is easily accessible from the enclosure. **Time Required:** 30 minutes.
5. **Optional: Incorporate a Switch:** If desired, solder a switch inline with the positive wire from the solar panel to the USB module. This allows you to control when the charger is active, helping conserve energy when not in use. **Time Required:** 30 minutes.
6. **Assemble the Charger:** Place all components inside the enclosure, securing them with screws, adhesive, or Velcro. Attach the solar panel to the outside of the case, ensuring it faces outward to collect sunlight. Neatly arrange the wires inside and close the case securely. **Time Required:** 30 minutes.
7. **Test the Solar Charger:** Position the charger outside in direct sunlight. Use a multimeter to measure the voltage output from the USB port, which should be around 5V. Connect a device to verify its charging capability. If functional, your device should begin charging. Test with various devices for compatibility. **Time Required:** 30 minutes.

Care and Maintenance:
- Regularly clean your solar panel to maintain efficiency.
- Inspect the connections within the enclosure for any signs of wear or corrosion, especially if exposed to outdoor conditions.
- Store the charger in a cool, dry location when not in use to extend its lifespan.

Constructing an Emergency Beacon

Project Overview: This project entails building an emergency beacon, a straightforward device that emits a bright light or radio signal to assist rescuers in locating you during emergencies. An emergency beacon is crucial in outdoor survival scenarios, particularly in remote locations where other communication methods may not function.

Difficulty Level: Moderate
Estimated Time: 3-5 hours

Benefits:
An emergency beacon enhances safety during outdoor activities like hiking, camping, or boating. By emitting a visible light or radio signal, it increases the chances of being detected by search and rescue teams. This project is ideal for creating a portable, customized beacon tailored to your specific requirements.

Required Materials:
- **High-Intensity LED:** For visual signaling.
- **Timer IC 555:** For creating a flashing circuit (if using a visual beacon).
- **Radio Frequency Transmitter Module:** For radio signaling.
- **Antenna:** Suitable for the transmitter frequency.
- **Battery Pack:** (AA, AAA, or lithium-ion batteries).
- **Switch:** To turn the light on and off.

- **Resistors and Capacitors:** For the LED flashing circuit.
- **Enclosure:** Waterproof container to protect components.
- **Wiring and Connectors.**
- **Soldering Supplies:** (Soldering iron, solder).

Tools Needed:
- **Soldering Iron and Solder.**
- **Wire Cutters and Strippers.**
- **Multimeter:** For testing circuits.
- **Screwdriver Set.**
- **Drill:** For creating holes in the container.
- **Hot Glue Gun:** (Optional, for component attachment).

Alternative Materials:
- **Pre-assembled Flashing LED Module:** To simplify the visual beacon.
- **Components Recycled from Old Electronics:** To reduce costs.

Step-by-Step Instructions:
1. **Determine the Type of Beacon:** Decide if you want to create a visual beacon (using LEDs) or a radio beacon (using a radio frequency transmitter). A visual beacon is simpler to construct and can be seen from far away, particularly at night. A radio beacon can transmit a signal over a wide area, but requires a more complex setup.
2. **Prepare the Container:** Select a container that will safeguard your components from the elements. Ensure it is waterproof and durable for outdoor use. Drill openings for the LED, antenna, switch, and wiring. Confirm that all components fit securely within the container. **Time Required:** 30 minutes.
3. **Build the Visual Beacon Circuit (if applicable):** For a visual beacon, connect the high-intensity LED to the 555 timer circuit to create a flashing effect. Use resistors and capacitors to configure the flashing interval (typically 1-2 flashes per second).
   - Pin 1: Ground
   - Pin 2: Trigger (connected to Pin 6)
   - Pin 3: Output (connected to LED)
   - Pin 4: Reset (connected to positive battery terminal)
   - Pin 5: Control Voltage (connected to capacitor to ground)
   - Pin 6: Threshold (connected to Pin 2)
   - Pin 7: Discharge (connected to resistor towards battery positive)
   - Pin 8: Power (connected to battery positive)

Test the circuit with a multimeter to ensure proper function, then solder the components and secure the LED and circuit within the container. **Time Required:** 1-2 hours.

4. **Construct the Radio Beacon Circuit (if applicable):** If creating a radio beacon, connect the radio frequency transmitter module to the antenna and battery pack. Ensure the transmitter is tuned to a frequency that is legal and appropriate for emergency use. You can add a simple oscillator to create a pulsating signal for easier detection. Solder the components and secure them within the container, extending the antenna outward for improved transmission. **Time Required:** 2-3 hours.
5. **Install Power Source:** Place the battery pack inside the container. For the visual beacon, connect the positive terminal to the 555 timer circuit and the negative terminal to ground. For the radio beacon, connect the battery pack directly to the transmitter module. Add a switch between the battery and circuit to control the beacon's activation. **Time Required:** 30 minutes.
6. **Test the Beacon:** Before sealing the container, test the beacon to ensure it functions correctly. For the visual beacon, take it to a dark area and verify that the LED is flashing prominently. For the radio beacon, use a radio receiver to confirm that the signal is being transmitted clearly. Make necessary adjustments to enhance performance. **Time Required:** 1 hour.
7. **Seal and Finalize the Beacon:** Once satisfied with the beacon's performance, secure all components inside the enclosure using hot glue or mounting brackets. Seal the container to shield it from moisture and dirt. If intended for outdoor use, consider adding a lanyard or clip for easy attachment to your gear. **Time Required:** 30 minutes.

Care and Maintenance:
Regularly check your beacon to ensure the battery is charged and all components are functioning properly. Replace the battery as needed, especially before extended trips. Inspect the enclosure for any cracks or damage if exposed to harsh conditions, and promptly make any necessary repairs.

Connectivity Solutions

Satellite Internet Alternatives

Satellite internet is an essential asset for individuals facing emergency situations, as it provides a dependable means of staying connected to the outside world, even in remote areas. Unlike conventional internet services that rely on cables or phone lines, satellite internet transmits and receives data through orbiting satellites. This technology ensures high-speed internet access in even the most isolated locations, making it invaluable for communities during crises. When assessing satellite internet options, it's crucial to examine the various providers available, as coverage, speeds, and data plans can vary significantly. Many providers offer packages tailored for activities ranging from basic web browsing and email to more intensive tasks like streaming and video conferencing. One of the critical factors to consider when selecting a provider is latency, which is the delay inherent in satellite communications. This latency can impact real-time online activities, such as gaming or video chatting, but is generally manageable for most applications, including web browsing and streaming. Another important consideration is the data cap policy set by the provider. Some satellite services impose monthly data limits, charging extra fees if these limits are exceeded. It is essential to understand your usage needs and select a plan that aligns with them to avoid unexpected costs.

Setting up satellite internet involves installing a dish and modem, typically supplied by the service provider. The dish must be positioned to have an unobstructed view of the sky to communicate effectively with the satellite, making the choice of installation location critical. In certain cases, professional installation may be necessary to ensure proper alignment and signal strength. Once installed, satellite internet delivers a stable connection, with speeds adequate to support a broad range of online activities.

For those living off-grid, satellite internet also provides avenues for remote work, online education, and access to digital resources related to health, entertainment, and communication. Additionally, it plays a crucial role in emergency preparedness, establishing a vital link during natural disasters or other crises when conventional communication networks may fail.

Considering the future of satellite internet technology is also beneficial. Advances in satellite communications, particularly low Earth orbit (LEO) networks, promise to deliver lower latency, faster speeds, and more reliable services.

Data Management and Bandwidth Optimization

Data management and bandwidth optimization are crucial for ensuring efficient internet access, especially when connectivity is limited or data plans impose usage constraints. To maximize available bandwidth and ensure that essential online activities can proceed smoothly, several strategies can be implemented. The first step is to prioritize data usage, focusing on essential tasks like communication and information retrieval while minimizing bandwidth-heavy activities such as high-definition video streaming, particularly during peak hours.

Utilizing data compression tools can significantly reduce the amount of data transmitted and received. For instance, employing compression software can cut down the data required for web browsing and emailing. Additionally, optimizing images and videos by lowering their resolution before uploading or sharing can conserve bandwidth.

Another effective approach is caching, which allows frequently accessed data to be stored locally, thereby reducing the need to download it repeatedly from the internet. Although most modern browsers automatically perform caching, adjusting your browser settings can further enhance efficiency.

Monitoring data consumption is essential for conserving bandwidth. Numerous tools are available to track the data usage of different applications. By identifying high-consumption apps, you can modify their settings to reduce usage, such as lowering video quality or disabling automatic updates and background tasks. Network management tools can also prioritize traffic, ensuring that critical applications—like VoIP calls or remote work sessions—receive the necessary bandwidth, preventing interruptions due to limited resources.

Ensuring Network Security

Network security is vital for safeguarding the privacy and integrity of communications and data. Relying on satellite internet or other forms of remote connectivity introduces specific vulnerabilities that must be addressed to protect against cyber threats. Implementing robust security measures not only defends against external risks but also ensures the reliability of communication systems.

The first step in securing your network is to employ strong encryption protocols for all data transmissions. Encryption serves as a protective shield, making it challenging for unauthorized entities to intercept and decode communications. Utilizing virtual private networks (VPNs) is an effective method for encrypting your internet traffic, adding another layer of security by masking your IP address and location.

Regularly updating all software and devices is another critical element of network security. Cyber threats are continually evolving, and keeping your software up to date ensures you have the latest security enhancements and fixes. This includes updating the operating systems of devices, installed applications, and the firmware of networking equipment such as routers and satellite modems.

Using strong and complex passwords is essential for network protection. Implement unique passwords that combine letters, numbers, and special characters, and change them periodically. Additionally, enabling two-factor authentication (MFA) adds another level of security, requiring a second verification method beyond just your password for network access.

Segmenting your network can significantly enhance security by dividing it into smaller, isolated sections. This limits the spread of any intrusions and makes it more difficult for attackers to access critical systems or sensitive information.

Regular monitoring and auditing of network activity help identify suspicious behavior or unauthorized access attempts early on. Installing firewalls and intrusion detection systems can automatically block known threats and alert you to potential breaches. Furthermore, maintaining logs of network activity allows for thorough investigations in the event of security incidents.

CHAPTER 7:

EMERGENCY MEDICAL SUPPLIES AND PERSONAL WELL-BEING

Medical Supplies and First Aid Essentials

In off-grid living, maintaining a comprehensive first aid kit along with necessary medical supplies is crucial for managing health issues and preventing them from escalating into critical situations. With limited access to healthcare facilities, it's vital to be equipped to address a range of medical concerns independently.

Consider the scenario where you or a family member sustains a serious cut while chopping firewood. Without proper first aid resources, this injury could become infected, leading to prolonged discomfort and potentially serious health complications. Conversely, having the right tools allows you to properly clean the wound, apply antiseptic, and secure a bandage, thus reducing the risk of complications and fostering quicker recovery.

It's equally important to prepare for common ailments like colds, fevers, or digestive issues. Stocking over-the-counter medications—such as pain relievers, antihistamines, and anti-diarrheal medicine—is essential for situations when accessing a pharmacy is not possible. Keeping a thermometer, disposable gloves, and disinfectants readily available ensures you can effectively monitor health and uphold hygiene, thereby minimizing the spread of illness within your household.

Key Elements of a First Aid Kit

A well-rounded first aid kit should be equipped to handle injuries such as cuts, burns, and sprains, as well as other typical medical emergencies. The following components are essential:

1. **Bandages and Dressings:**
    - Adhesive bandages (various sizes)
    - Sterile gauze pads
    - Medical tape
    - Elastic bandages (e.g., ACE wraps)

2. **Antiseptics and Ointments:**
    - Antiseptic wipes or solutions (e.g., hydrogen peroxide, iodine)
    - Antibiotic ointment
    - Burn relief cream or gel

3. **Tools and Equipment:**
    - Tweezers
    - Scissors
    - Safety pins
    - Digital thermometer
    - Disposable gloves

4. **Pain Relief and Medication:**
    - Analgesics (e.g., ibuprofen, acetaminophen)
    - Antihistamines

- Anti-inflammatory medications
- Any necessary prescription medications for family members

5. **Emergency Items:**
    - CPR mask
    - Emergency blanket
    - Instant cold packs
    - Splinting materials

6. **Additional Items:**
    - Eye wash solution
    - Oral rehydration salts
    - Safety pins
    - First aid handbook

Organize your medical supplies in a waterproof, durable container that is easily accessible to all family members. Clearly label the container and designate a specific location for it within the home. Regularly check and restock your kit, ensuring all items are within their expiration dates and remain in good condition.

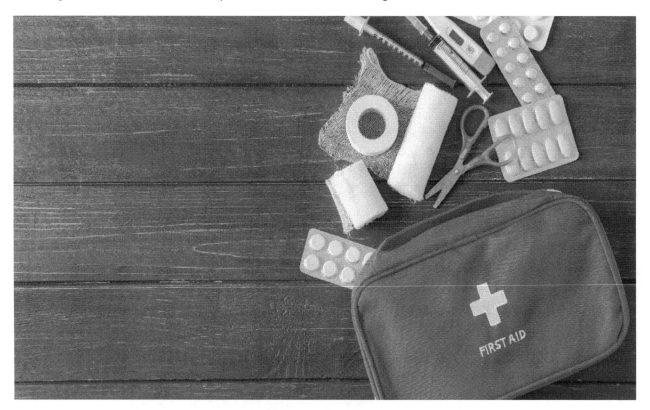

Essential First Aid Techniques

Acquiring fundamental first aid techniques is equally vital as possessing the appropriate medical supplies. Enroll in a first aid and CPR training program to gain skills in the following areas:
- Administering CPR and utilizing an automated external defibrillator (AED)
- Managing wounds, burns, and various typical injuries
- Identifying and reacting to signs of prevalent illnesses and medical issues
- Effectively utilizing the resources available in your first aid kit

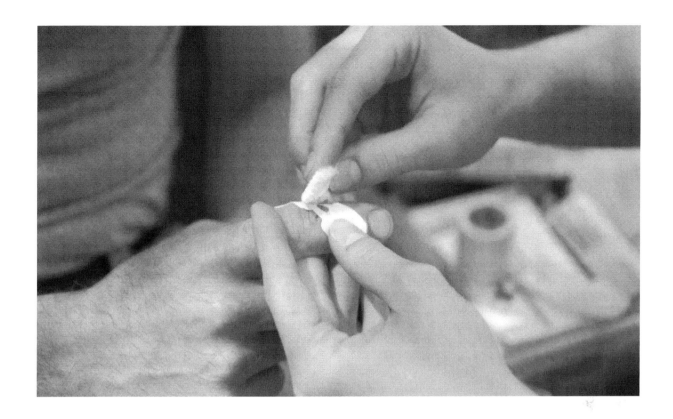

Building a Comprehensive First Aid Kit

Having a fully stocked first aid kit is vital for off-grid living, ensuring you are ready for any medical emergencies that may arise when professional healthcare is unavailable. Start by understanding the common injuries and health issues that could occur in an off-grid context, such as cuts, burns, sprains, and potential infections.

From this understanding, assemble a kit that addresses these issues while also catering to your family's specific medical requirements.

Begin with essentials: adhesive bandages of various sizes for minor cuts, sterile gauze, and tape for more serious wounds. Include antiseptic wipes and antibiotic ointment to clean and protect injuries from infections. For sprains or strains, elastic bandages can provide necessary support and reduce swelling. Scissors and tweezers are vital for cutting tape or gauze and for removing splinters or ticks.

Ensure that pain relief medications, such as acetaminophen and ibuprofen, are included to manage pain and reduce fevers. Antihistamines are important for allergic reactions, while hydrocortisone cream can soothe insect bites or rashes. For treating burns, aloe vera gel can be soothing. Additionally, include medications for gastrointestinal issues, such as antacids and anti-diarrheal medications.

Don't forget about personal medications or those required for chronic conditions. Maintain a sufficient supply of these prescriptions in your first aid kit, considering potential supply disruptions. Items like a thermometer, blood pressure monitor, and glucose meter may be necessary for specific health monitoring needs.

Besides physical components, include emergency contact numbers, such as local emergency services and poison control, as well as a list of personal emergency contacts. A first aid manual can provide invaluable guidance during medical emergencies, offering step-by-step instructions.

Regularly check and replenish your first aid kit to ensure all contents are in good condition and not expired. Familiarize yourself and your family members with the kit's contents and how to use them. Participating in a first aid course can enhance your knowledge and skills for handling emergencies, further ensuring your preparedness for medical situations.

By creating a complete first aid kit, you are not just gathering supplies; you are taking proactive steps to safeguard the health and safety of your loved ones, providing peace of mind in the face of unexpected challenges associated with off-grid living.

DIY First Aid Kit

- **Cost:** €50-150
- **Difficulty:** Easy
- **Time:** 2-4 hours

Creating a well-stocked first aid kit allows you to effectively manage minor injuries and common medical emergencies. This guide will help you assemble a comprehensive DIY first aid kit tailored for an off-grid lifestyle.

Materials Needed:
- **Durable, Waterproof Container:** 1 unit. Choose a strong container, such as a plastic toolbox or a dedicated first aid kit that is spacious enough for all items and allows easy access during emergencies.
- **Adhesive Bandages:** Various sizes, 50-100 pieces. Include a range of types, such as standard strips and butterfly bandages.
- **Sterile Gauze:** 4x4 inch, 20-30 pieces. Useful for covering larger wounds or providing additional padding to control bleeding.
- **Adhesive Tape:** 1 roll. Select a hypoallergenic medical tape that adheres well yet is gentle on the skin.
- **Elastic Bandages (ACE Bandages):** 2-3 rolls. Great for securing dressings and providing support for sprains.
- **Antiseptic Wipes:** 20-30 pieces. Individually packaged to clean wounds and help prevent infections.
- **Antibiotic Ointment:** 1 tube. A broad-spectrum ointment for application on cuts and abrasions.
- **Burn Cream or Gel:** 1 tube. Look for products with lidocaine or aloe for pain relief and healing support.
- **Tweezers:** 1 unit. For removing splinters, ticks, or debris from wounds; stainless steel tweezers are durable and easy to sanitize.
- **Scissors:** 1 pair. Medical-grade scissors for cutting bandages and tape, ensuring they are sharp and have blunt tips for safety.
- **Safety Pins:** 10-20 pieces. Useful for securing bandages.
- **Digital Thermometer:** 1 unit. To measure body temperature; choose a fast-responding model with an easy-to-read display.
- **Disposable Gloves:** 10 pairs. Nitrile gloves are preferred for their durability and lower likelihood of causing allergic reactions.
- **Pain Relievers:** 1 bottle each of ibuprofen and acetaminophen. Useful for pain management and fever reduction.
- **Antihistamines:** 1 bottle. Include a non-sedating formula for allergic reactions.
- **Anti-Inflammatory Medication:** 1 bottle. Over-the-counter options like ibuprofen help reduce inflammation and pain.
- **CPR Mask:** 1 unit. Provides a barrier for safe resuscitation during CPR.
- **Emergency Blanket:** 1 unit. Compact and reflective, to help retain heat and prevent shock.
- **Instant Cold Compresses:** 2-3 units. Useful for alleviating swelling and pain from sprains or injuries.
- **Immobilization Materials:** 1 SAM splint or similar item for immobilizing broken bones or sprains.
- **Eye Wash Solution:** 1 bottle. A sterile saline solution for rinsing eyes in case of contamination.
- **Oral Rehydration Salts:** 5-10 packets. Essential for treating dehydration from diarrhea or heat.
- **First Aid Manual:** 1 unit. A comprehensive guide covering a wide range of medical emergencies and their treatments.
- **Personal Medications:** Any specific prescriptions for family members. Include necessary medications labeled correctly and stored appropriately.

Instructions:
1. **Select a Container:** Choose a sturdy, waterproof container for first aid supplies. It should be easily transportable with a secure closure to protect contents, and clearly labeled as a first aid kit.
2. **Gather Bandages and Dressings:** Include a variety of adhesive bandages for minor cuts. Add sterile gauze for larger wounds or padding. Use tape to secure gauze and bandages.
3. **Add Antiseptics and Ointments:** Include antiseptic wipes or solutions for cleaning wounds. Add antibiotic ointment for preventing infections and burn cream for minor burns. Select easy-to-apply ointments with long-lasting effects.

4. **Include Tools and Equipment:** Add tweezers for removing splinters and ticks. Include medical scissors for cutting bandages and tape. Safety pins are handy for securing splints. Ensure all tools are durable and easily cleaned.
5. **Incorporate Pain Relief and Medicines:** Include pain relievers like ibuprofen and acetaminophen for discomfort. Add antihistamines for allergies and anti-inflammatory drugs for swelling. Keep any essential prescription medications on hand.
6. **Emergency Supplies:** Add a CPR mask for safe resuscitation, an emergency blanket for warmth, instant cold packs for swelling, and a SAM splint for injuries. These items are critical for handling emergencies like hypothermia or fractures.
7. **Include Additional Items:** Place eye wash solution for rinsing eyes, oral rehydration salts for dehydration, and disposable gloves for hygiene. These supplies ensure you can effectively manage a variety of situations.
8. **Incorporate a First Aid Manual:** Include a comprehensive manual with clear instructions. This guide will be essential in an emergency, offering step-by-step procedures for various medical scenarios.
9. **Organize the Kit:** Arrange all items neatly for easy access. Use compartments, small bags, or labeled sections to keep supplies organized. Clearly label each section for quick reference during emergencies.
10. **Maintain the Kit:** Regularly check your first aid kit to ensure all items are in good condition and not expired. Immediately replace any used or expired items to keep your kit ready for use. Store the kit in an easily accessible location known to all family members.

Maintenance Tips:
- **Periodic Review of the Manual:** Regularly reread your first aid manual to stay informed on emergency procedures.
- **Restocking Items:** Replenish supplies as needed, especially after using the kit for an injury or illness.
- **Cleaning and Drying the Kit:** Keep your kit clean and dry to ensure all supplies remain in optimal condition.
- **Family Training:** Educate family members on the location of the first aid kit and how to use it properly to ensure effective preparation in emergencies.

Managing Common Off-Grid Injuries

Living off-grid presents distinct challenges, particularly when dealing with common injuries with limited access to medical facilities. A prompt and effective response to cuts, burns, sprains, and other injuries can prevent complications and facilitate healing. For cuts, it is vital to clean the wound with fresh water and apply pressure to stop bleeding. Use antiseptic wipes or solutions to disinfect the area before covering it with a sterile bandage. Regularly changing the bandage and monitoring for signs of infection, such as redness, swelling, or pus, is crucial for proper wound care.

Burns need immediate cooling under running water for at least ten minutes to minimize skin damage and alleviate pain. Avoid direct ice application, as it can further harm the skin. Cover the burn with a sterile, non-adhesive bandage or clean cloth, ensuring it is loose enough to avoid pressure on the burned area. For minor burns, applying aloe vera can provide soothing relief; however, severe burns that blister or cover a significant area require prompt medical attention.

Sprains and strains are frequent in rugged off-grid environments where uneven terrain can lead to injury. To manage these injuries, rest the affected limb, apply ice to reduce swelling, compress with a bandage for support, and elevate the injury above heart level. Over-the-counter pain relief can help with discomfort, but it's crucial to avoid activities that may aggravate the injury until it has fully healed.

Insect stings or bites can be managed by removing any stinger if present, washing the area, and applying ice to minimize swelling. Over-the-counter antihistamines can relieve itching and swelling. However, be vigilant for signs of allergic reactions, such as difficulty breathing, swelling of the face or mouth, or rapid heartbeat, which necessitate immediate medical attention.

Preparation is vital for effectively managing off-grid injuries. A well-stocked first aid kit, knowledge of basic first aid techniques, and awareness of when to seek professional help are essential aspects of off-grid living. Regularly updating first aid skills through courses or self-study ensures readiness to handle common injuries efficiently, minimizing their impact on your off-grid lifestyle. Being prepared enables individuals and communities to respond confidently to health emergencies, securing safety and well-being even in remote settings.

Herbal Remedies and Natural Approaches

Integrating Herbal Solutions

In addition to conventional medical supplies, utilizing herbal remedies and natural solutions can enhance your health care practices. Numerous plants have medicinal properties that assist in addressing minor health issues and promoting overall wellness. For instance:
- **Aloe Vera:** Effective for soothing burns and skin irritations.
- **Echinacea:** Supports the immune system and may help combat colds.
- **Peppermint:** Aids in alleviating headaches and digestive concerns.

Combining traditional first aid supplies with these natural remedies can create a holistic approach to health care in off-grid settings.

Kit Maintenance
Ensure your first aid kit is always prepared for use by conducting regular checks and updates:
- Promptly replace any used or expired items.
- Periodically review and refresh your first aid manual.
- Replenish supplies as necessary to maintain a complete and effective kit.

Having a well-stocked first aid kit along with the knowledge to utilize it is a crucial aspect of living off-grid. This readiness allows you to handle medical emergencies confidently and safeguard your family's health, even when professional medical assistance is unavailable.

Cultivating a Medicinal Herb Garden

- **Cost:** €100-150
- **Ease:** Easy
- **Time:** 1-2 days

Establishing a medicinal herb garden is an effective and sustainable way to provide natural remedies for common ailments while enhancing overall health. Herbs have been utilized for centuries to treat a variety of health issues, and growing your own ensures a steady supply of fresh, potent ingredients. This guide will assist you in setting up and maintaining a medicinal herb garden.

Materials Needed:
- **Raised Garden Bed or Containers:** Depending on your available space, a 4'x8' raised bed or 10-15 medium-sized pots (12-18 inches in diameter) will suffice.
- **Quality Soil and Compost:** 4-6 bags of 18 kg each. A nutrient-rich, well-draining soil mix is essential for successful herb cultivation.
- **Medicinal Herb Seeds or Plants:**
  - **Aloe Vera:** 2-3 plants, known for its healing benefits for burns and skin issues.
  - **Echinacea:** 5-6 plants, popular for immune support and cold treatment.
  - **Lavender:** 5-6 plants, valued for its calming properties and ability to promote restful sleep.
  - **Peppermint:** 3-4 plants, beneficial for digestive issues and headaches.
  - **Chamomile:** 5-6 plants, recognized for its soothing and digestive properties.
  - **Thyme:** 5-6 plants, supports respiratory health and has antiseptic benefits.
  - **Calendula:** 5-6 plants, effective for skin healing and inflammation reduction.
  - **Yarrow:** 3-4 plants, useful for wound healing and fever reduction.
- **Mulch:** 1-2 bags of 18 kg each. Organic mulch helps retain moisture, suppress weeds, and maintain soil temperature.
- **Garden Tools:** Transplanter, hoe, watering can, pruning shears.
- **Labels or Markers:** 1 pack of 20-30 markers to identify different plants, aiding in their recognition during early growth stages.

Steps to Follow:
1. **Select a Location:** Find a sunny spot for your medicinal herb garden. Most herbs thrive in full sunlight, requiring at least 6-8 hours of sun daily. Ensure the area has good drainage to prevent water accumulation, avoiding low spots where water may gather.
2. **Prepare the Soil:** If using a raised bed, fill it with a mixture of quality potting soil and compost. For pots, ensure they have drainage holes and fill them with the appropriate soil mix.
3. **Plant the Herbs:** Evenly space the seeds or seedlings in the bed or pots, adhering to the specific planting instructions regarding depth and spacing for each herb.
4. **Apply Mulch:** Disperse a layer of organic mulch over the soil to retain moisture and curb weed growth.
5. **Watering and Maintenance:** Keep the soil consistently moist but not oversaturated. Regularly inspect the plants for any signs of disease or pest infestations and address issues promptly.
6. **Harvesting and Storage:** Gather herbs at the appropriate time, generally when they are in full bloom to maximize their medicinal properties. Store dried herbs in airtight containers in a cool, dry environment.

Ongoing Maintenance
To keep your medicinal herb garden healthy and productive, conduct regular checks and maintenance:
- **Pruning:** Regularly remove wilted flowers and damaged leaves to foster healthy growth.
- **Fertilization:** Add compost or organic fertilizers as needed to support the plants.
- **Weed Management:** Keep the area free from weeds to minimize competition for nutrients and water.
- **Crop Rotation:** If feasible, rotate plants periodically to prevent soil depletion and reduce disease risks.

Creating a medicinal herb garden not only provides easy access to natural remedies but also contributes to a sustainable, self-sufficient lifestyle. With careful planning and ongoing care, you can enjoy a diverse array of beneficial herbs for the entire family.

Preparing the Garden Bed
- **For Raised Beds:** Fill the bed with a combination of quality potting soil and compost. Use about 4-6 bags, ensuring it is well-draining and nutrient-rich, ideally a mix of 60% garden soil to 40% compost. Loosen the soil to a depth of 30-45 cm to promote healthy root growth.
- **For Pots:** Fill each pot with the same soil and compost blend, ensuring drainage holes are present to prevent water buildup. Before adding soil, place a layer of gravel or small rocks at the bottom of each pot to enhance drainage.

Selecting Medicinal Herbs
Choose herbs based on their therapeutic benefits and your specific needs. Consider the following popular medicinal herbs:
- **Aloe Vera:** Effective for burns, cuts, and skin irritations.
- **Echinacea:** Enhances immune function and assists in combating colds.
- **Lavender:** Alleviates stress and anxiety, improving sleep quality.
- **Peppermint:** Eases digestive issues, headaches, and muscle discomfort.
- **Chamomile:** Calms the nervous system and supports digestion.
- **Thyme:** Exhibits antiseptic properties and aids respiratory health.
- **Calendula:** Has anti-inflammatory effects and supports skin healing.
- **Yarrow:** Assists in stopping bleeding, reducing fever, and promoting wound recovery.

Planting the Herbs
Sow seeds or plant seedlings according to the recommended spacing for each herb:
- **Aloe Vera:** Space 30-45 cm apart. Requires well-drained soil and should not be overwatered.
- **Echinacea:** Space 30-45 cm apart. Thrives in full sun and well-drained soil.
- **Lavender:** Space 45-60 cm apart. Prefers well-drained, slightly alkaline soil.
- **Peppermint:** Space 30-45 cm apart. Can spread quickly, so using pots may help contain it.
- **Chamomile:** Space 20-30 cm apart. Grows well in light, sandy soil.
- **Thyme:** Space 30-45 cm apart. Enjoys well-drained, slightly alkaline soil.
- **Calendula:** Space 30 cm apart. Prefers sunny spots and well-drained soil.
- **Yarrow:** Space 30-45 cm apart. Adaptable to various soil types, it flourishes in full sun.

After planting, thoroughly water the plants to help them establish roots.

Watering and Mulching

Water your herbs regularly, maintaining consistent moisture without over-saturation. Most herbs prefer moderate watering. Apply a layer of mulch around the plants to retain moisture, suppress weeds, and help regulate soil temperatures. Organic mulch options, such as straw, grass clippings, or wood chips, are ideal.

Garden Upkeep
Monitor your plants frequently for any signs of pests or diseases. Common pests may include aphids, mites, and whiteflies. Remove any weeds that compete for resources, and utilize organic methods, such as neem oil or insecticidal soap, for pest control. Prune back herbs to encourage bushy growth and prevent legginess, and remove any dead or yellowing leaves to support overall plant health.

Harvesting Herbs
Collect herbs when they are at their most potent, typically in the morning after dew has dried. Use sharp scissors or pruning shears to cut the herbs, ensuring enough growth remains for the plant to continue thriving. Most herbs are best harvested just before flowering to maximize their medicinal properties. Handle herbs carefully to prevent bruising or damage.

Preserving and Using Herbs
After harvesting, preserve your herbs by drying, freezing, or making tinctures and salves. Dry herbs in a warm, well-ventilated area away from direct sunlight. Store dried herbs in airtight containers in a cool, dark space. Use these herbs to prepare teas, infusions, salves, and other remedies, labeling each container with the herb's name and harvest date.

Maintenance Suggestions
- **Crop Rotation:** Periodically rotate your herbs to prevent soil depletion and reduce pest buildup. This practice supports soil health and lowers the risk of infestations and diseases.
- **Soil Enrichment:** Maintain soil fertility by incorporating compost or organic fertilizers. Apply compost or well-rotted manure in spring and fall to enrich the soil.
- **Detailed Record-Keeping:** Accurately log your planting and harvesting activities to monitor growth and the effectiveness of your medicinal herb garden. Record planting dates, growth patterns, harvest times, and any encountered issues to enhance future gardening practices.

Herbal Medicine

Cultivating Medicinal Plants

Growing medicinal plants offers a sustainable approach to enhancing health and well-being, rooted in the ancient practices of herbal medicine. This time-honored tradition leverages the therapeutic properties of various plants to address common health issues, promote overall wellness, and supply vital nutrients. To start this rewarding journey, it's essential to grasp the fundamentals of identifying, cultivating, and harvesting these herbs. Selecting the right species requires considering the specific health benefits each herb provides alongside their optimal growing conditions. Popular choices include lavender for stress relief, chamomile for relaxation, and echinacea for boosting the immune system, all of which can be seamlessly integrated into a dedicated garden.

Preparing Herbal Remedies
Creating herbal remedies blends art and science. Techniques like drying, infusion, and decoction enable the extraction of beneficial compounds found in plants. Mastering the drying process is vital, as it helps retain the herbs' potency for future use. Infusions and decoctions, on the other hand, provide immediate therapeutic effects. An infusion—similar to brewing tea—involves steeping leaves or flowers in hot water, while a decoction entails simmering tougher plant materials such as roots or bark to draw out their active ingredients.

The storage and application of herbal medicines must be carefully managed to maintain their efficacy. Dried herbs should be kept in airtight containers, protected from light and moisture to preserve their quality. Understanding correct dosages and administration methods is crucial for ensuring safety and effectiveness. Additionally, incorporating these natural remedies into daily practices can foster a holistic approach to health, emphasizing prevention and the body's innate healing capabilities.

Establishing a Medicinal Herb Garden
Creating a medicinal herb garden serves as a practical project for off-grid living, providing a renewable resource for health care. This endeavor includes choosing a sunny location, enriching the soil with organic matter to ensure fertility, and selecting a diverse array of herbs that cater to various health needs. Employing intercropping techniques can enhance the growth and efficacy of medicinal plants, while organic gardening practices help safeguard their integrity and protect the surrounding environment.

By embracing herbal medicine in your off-grid lifestyle, you not only promote self-sufficiency but also strengthen your connection to nature and traditional healing methods. This approach empowers individuals to take charge of their health using readily available natural resources to nurture both body and mind. As with any health-related initiative, it is essential to complement herbal practices with professional medical advice, especially for serious or chronic conditions. Recognizing and honoring the power of plants can unlock the immense potential of herbal medicine, enriching your off-grid experience.

Cultivating Medicinal Herbs

Starting your herbal garden begins with selecting species that are well-suited to your local climate and soil conditions. For those living off-grid, focusing on perennial herbs such as mint, lavender, and lemon balm can provide a consistent supply of herbs with minimal replanting needs. Annuals like basil and cilantro add diversity and can be incorporated into crop rotation to promote soil health. Understanding each herb's requirements for sunlight, water, and soil is essential for successful cultivation. Most medicinal herbs thrive in well-drained soil and need at least six hours of sunlight daily, although some, such as ginseng and goldenseal, prefer shaded environments.

When planning your garden, consider the spatial requirements of each herb. Taller plants like fennel should be positioned at the back of garden beds to avoid shading shorter herbs. Utilizing companion planting can naturally deter pests and encourage growth; for example, planting chamomile alongside other herbs can enhance their flavor and vitality. Applying mulch around plants not only retains moisture but also suppresses weed growth, decreasing the reliance on chemical herbicides.

Harvesting and Utilizing Herbs
Timing is crucial when harvesting herbs to maximize their medicinal properties. Generally, leaves are most potent when picked before the plant flowers, while roots should be harvested in the fall when the plant has stored energy underground. After gathering, herbs can be dried by hanging them in bunches in a well-ventilated, dark space or by using a low-temperature dehydrator to preserve their essential oils.

Incorporating these herbs into your daily routine can range from brewing teas and infusions to crafting salves and tinctures. For instance, a simple tea can be prepared by steeping fresh or dried leaves in boiling water, while tinctures involve soaking herbs in alcohol to extract their active compounds. These preparations not only provide therapeutic benefits but also deepen the understanding of available natural resources for those living off-grid, fostering a sustainable, self-reliant lifestyle.

Crafting Herbal Remedies

Creating herbal remedies necessitates a blend of traditional knowledge and hands-on skills, focusing on maximizing the therapeutic benefits from plants. The process begins by selecting high-quality herbs, whether fresh or dried. Fresh herbs, harvested at their peak, have potent medicinal properties, while properly stored dried herbs can be equally effective. Success in remedy preparation hinges on understanding the unique qualities of each herb and the best methods for their use.

For tinctures, a widely used and potent form of herbal remedy, the process involves infusing herbs in alcohol or vinegar to extract active compounds. This method allows for extended storage, making tinctures a practical choice for off-grid living. To prepare a tincture, finely chop or grind the herbs, place them in a clean jar, and cover them with alcohol or vinegar, ensuring the herbs are fully submerged. Seal the jar tightly and store it in a cool, dark location, shaking it daily for four to six weeks. Afterward, strain the liquid through a fine mesh or cheesecloth, pressing out as much liquid as possible, and transfer the tincture into dark glass bottles. Clearly label each container with the herb's name, the date, and the solvent used.

Ointments and balms provide a soothing method for applying herbal remedies externally, ideal for skin issues, wounds, or muscle discomfort. To create an herbal ointment, infuse oils with herbs through a slow, low-temperature process on the stovetop or by leaving the mixture in a sunny spot for several weeks. Once the oil is infused, strain out the herbs, then gently heat the oil and mix it with beeswax until fully melted. The more beeswax used, the firmer the ointment will be. Pour the mixture into clean jars or tins and allow it to cool and solidify.

Herbal teas or infusions are among the simplest forms of herbal remedies, suitable for daily use to enhance overall health. To prepare, pour boiling water over fresh or dried herbs and let them steep, covered, for 5-15 minutes, depending on the desired strength. Filtering the herbal tea ensures a clear and enjoyable beverage. Some herbs, like chamomile, are particularly well-suited for infusions, offering gentle, calming effects.

Decoctions are used for tougher plant materials such as roots, bark, and seeds, requiring a longer simmering time to extract their active compounds. Place the plant material in a pot, cover it with cold water, and bring it to a boil slowly. Reduce the heat and let it simmer for 20-45 minutes, then strain. Decoctions are generally more concentrated than infusions and are typically used for more potent medicinal effects.

Understanding proper dosages is essential for the safety and effectiveness of herbal remedies. Factors such as herb potency, the condition being treated, and individual sensitivity influence the appropriate dosage. Begin with lower doses to gauge tolerance and gradually increase as needed. Integrating herbal remedies into daily life not only enhances health but also connects individuals to the natural rhythms of life and the tradition of herbal medicine. Through practice and respect for the power of plants, preparing herbal remedies becomes an integral aspect of off-grid living, facilitating self-sufficiency and a stronger bond with the natural world.

Storage and Utilization of Herbal Medicines

Proper storage of herbal medicines is crucial for preserving their potency and efficacy. Dried herbs should be stored in airtight glass or metal containers to shield them from moisture and light, which can diminish their quality. Labeling containers with the herb's name and storage date helps monitor freshness; most dried herbs retain their potency for up to a year when stored correctly. Tinctures, stored in dark glass containers, benefit from protection against light, while a well-sealed lid prevents alcohol evaporation. Under ideal conditions, tinctures can last several years, making them a reliable option for those living off-grid.

To use herbal medicines effectively, understanding dosage and timing is essential. The effectiveness of herbal remedies is often contingent upon consistent and appropriate usage. For herbal teas and infusions, a general guideline is to use one teaspoon of dried herbs or one tablespoon of fresh herbs per cup of boiling water, steeping for 5 to 15 minutes. This may vary based on the herb and desired strength. Tinctures, being more concentrated, typically require smaller doses, ranging from a few drops to a teaspoon, taken several times a day. Researching or consulting an herbalist about specific dosages for various herbs is advisable, particularly when addressing specific health concerns.

Integrating herbal medicines into daily routines can enhance well-being and provide targeted support for health challenges. For preventive care, including herbal teas in morning or evening rituals can be both therapeutic and enjoyable. For acute issues, more concentrated forms such as tinctures or capsules may deliver quicker relief. Always consider the cumulative effects of herbs and potential interactions with other medications or conditions. Starting with lower doses and gradually increasing based on individual responses can help determine the right balance for personal needs.

By adhering to these guidelines for storage and usage, herbal medicines can become a powerful and sustainable component of off-grid living, providing natural solutions for health maintenance and recovery.

DIY Project: Establishing an Herbal Medicine Garden

Creating an herbal medicine garden necessitates careful planning and selecting the right location. Choose a spot that receives a minimum of six hours of sunlight each day, as most medicinal herbs flourish in full sun. Ensure the soil is well-drained and rich in organic matter; you can enhance soil quality by adding compost or well-aged manure. Testing the soil pH can also help you make necessary adjustments since different herbs thrive at different pH levels.

After identifying the location, design your garden layout. Consider using raised beds to improve drainage and accessibility, or if space is limited, containers can provide a flexible alternative. Raised beds and pots also allow for better control over soil quality and can reduce the risk of soil-borne diseases affecting your herbs.

Selecting herbs for your garden should align with your health requirements and local climate compatibility. Start with easy-to-cultivate herbs like mint, chamomile, and lemon balm, which serve both medicinal and culinary purposes, making them a versatile addition to your garden. Research the specific needs of each herb regarding water, sunlight, and space to create a harmonious garden where plants can flourish without competing for resources.

When planting, ensure each herb has ample room to grow, and consider companion planting to naturally repel pests and foster growth. For example, planting garlic near roses can deter pests, while scattering marigolds throughout the garden can attract beneficial insects.

Watering your herbal garden requires attention to the needs of each plant; some herbs prefer drier conditions, while others require consistently moist soil. A drip irrigation system or soaker hoses can efficiently water plants while keeping leaves dry, reducing disease risk.

Applying mulch with organic materials like straw or wood chips can help retain soil moisture, suppress weeds, and add nutrients as it decomposes. Apply mulch after the soil warms in spring to avoid trapping cold moisture against the roots of the plants.

Regularly harvesting encourages new growth and prevents herbs from becoming woody or going to seed prematurely. Collect herbs in the morning after the dew has dried but before the sun is too hot to achieve the maximum concentration of essential oils. Dry or process harvested herbs immediately to retain their medicinal qualities.

Labeling each herb with its name and planting date aids in tracking growth and harvesting schedules. Consider maintaining a garden journal to document successful strategies and challenges for future reference.

As your garden develops, you may find that certain herbs can become perennials, yielding medicine year after year, while others may need replanting annually. Experimenting with different herbs and gardening methods will enhance your knowledge and expand your personal pharmacy straight from your garden.

By dedicating time and care to your herbal medicine garden, you are cultivating not just plants; you are establishing a sustainable, living pharmacy that empowers you to manage your health naturally. This endeavor offers immediate benefits in terms of fresh and potent medicinal herbs while contributing to long-term health, sustainability, and self-sufficiency in an off-grid lifestyle.

CHAPTER 8:

PERSONAL HYGIENE AND WASTE MANAGEMENT

Health and Hygiene

Let's now address another crucial aspect of daily living: health and personal cleanliness. Most individuals recognize the significance of maintaining proper hygiene, and our modern world offers numerous resources to assist with this. Our homes typically feature bathrooms equipped with showers and other sanitation facilities, we have easy access to various soaps and hygiene products, and every household possesses toothbrushes and toothpaste. Additionally, in the case of health issues, pharmacies provide remedies, and we can consult doctors, hospitals, and various health services. However, in off-grid scenarios, these conveniences might not be available. It then becomes our responsibility to find methods to uphold good hygiene and health without the support of modern infrastructure. In this chapter, we will delve into these two vital aspects and examine projects that enable you to stay clean and healthy, ensuring your well-being without relying on contemporary amenities.

Sustaining Health Off the Grid

Maintaining good health relies on a mix of proper nutrition, regular physical activity, and preventive care. A well-rounded diet and adequate hydration are essential for sustaining energy levels and ensuring optimal bodily function. Growing your own food, preserving it, and securing access to clean water are critical components of off-grid nutrition. Engaging in regular physical activity—whether through daily tasks or planned exercise—helps to strengthen your body and enhance resilience. Moreover, having a foundational understanding of first aid and keeping a well-stocked medical kit enables you to manage minor injuries and common ailments effectively, preventing complications and offering peace of mind.

1. **Preventive Care:** Regularly monitor your health and adopt proactive measures to stave off illness. This involves adhering to a balanced diet rich in vitamins and minerals, maintaining hydration, and getting sufficient rest. Preventive care also encompasses the use of natural remedies and medicinal plants to bolster immunity and address minor health issues.
2. **Physical Activity:** Incorporate physical exercises into your daily routine to keep your body robust and flexible. Living off the grid often entails manual labor, providing ample exercise opportunities. However, engaging in dedicated activities such as hiking, yoga, or simple stretching can enhance your overall physical and mental well-being.
3. **Mental Wellness:** Mental health is equally as vital as physical health. The challenges inherent in off-grid living can induce stress, making it essential to include practices that foster relaxation and mental clarity. Spending time in nature, practicing mindfulness, and engaging in hobbies can significantly boost your mental well-being.
4. **Clean Water Access:** Securing a source of clean drinking water is crucial for maintaining good health. Waterborne pathogens can lead to serious illnesses, making filtration and purification a priority. Simple techniques, such as boiling water, using portable filters, and setting up a rainwater harvesting system, can ensure a reliable supply of safe water.

Hygiene Strategies

Effective hygiene practices are paramount to preventing disease transmission and maintaining a healthy living environment. Proper waste management, consistent hygiene habits, and clean living spaces are essential components of off-grid hygiene strategies.

1. **Waste Management:** Proper disposal of human waste is vital to prevent the contamination of water sources and living areas. Composting toilets offer a sustainable solution, converting waste into usable compost while controlling odors and pathogens.
2. **Hygiene Practices:** Regular handwashing with soap and water, safe food handling, and maintaining personal cleanliness are crucial practices. In the absence of running water, utilizing hand sanitizers, homemade soap, and water storage systems can help maintain hygiene standards.
3. **Clean Living Spaces:** Keeping your home environment tidy and free from pests is essential. Regularly cleaning surfaces, storing food appropriately, and employing natural insect repellents can help sustain a hygienic environment. Additionally, ensuring proper ventilation in your shelter can help prevent mold and dampness.

By incorporating these hygiene practices and solutions into your off-grid lifestyle, you can ensure that you and your family remain healthy and resilient.

Composting Toilet

Composting toilets are a pivotal aspect of sustainable sanitation, processing human waste through natural decomposition and evaporation. This method not only conserves water but also prevents pollution of water resources, making it particularly suitable for off-grid settings where water is limited and traditional sewage systems are absent. The functionality of a composting toilet involves separating liquids from solids to enhance the composting process and minimize odors. Solid waste accumulates in a composting chamber, where it is mixed with carbon-rich materials like sawdust or straw, balancing nitrogen levels and facilitating aerobic decomposition. These materials also help absorb excess liquids, further reducing odors. Ventilation systems, whether passive or powered by low-voltage fans, ensure a steady airflow in the composting chamber, promoting liquid evaporation. Maintaining composting toilets is relatively straightforward, requiring periodic rotation of the compost to ensure uniform decomposition and the addition of carbon-rich materials. The frequency of maintenance will depend on the chamber's capacity, user count, and the specific design of the system. Once composting is complete, the resulting material should be extracted and allowed to mature for use as a natural soil enhancer in your garden. Selecting the appropriate composting toilet depends on the number of users, location, and the level of maintenance you are prepared to undertake. Options range from self-contained models for a few users to centralized systems for larger groups, some equipped with advanced features like urine-separating seats or built-in heaters to expedite composting.

Cost: $50-$150
Time: 1-2 days

A composting toilet presents an excellent solution for managing human waste in off-grid environments. It converts waste into valuable compost to enrich soil, conserves water, and produces organic material beneficial for gardening.

Materials Required:
- **Large Plastic Drum or Bin:** 1 unit (55-gallon capacity). This will serve as the main composting chamber. Ensure it is made from UV-resistant plastic to guarantee durability.
- **Toilet Seat with Lid:** 1 unit. Choose a robust, full-sized seat with a lid to contain odors.
- **Ventilation Hose:** 1 unit (4-inch diameter, 6-8 feet long). This aids in ventilating the system and minimizing odors.
- **Wood Chips or Sawdust:** 1 large bag. These will cover waste, absorb moisture, and assist in the composting process.
- **Hinges and Latch:** 1 set. Used to secure the seat to the drum and ensure the lid is tightly closed.
- **Drill and Saw:** 1 set. Necessary for creating holes in the drum and assembling various components.
- **Screws and Screwdriver:** 1 set. For attaching the toilet seat and other parts to the drum.
- **Silicone Sealant:** 1 tube. Used to seal any gaps to prevent odors and liquids from leaking.

Instructions:
1. **Select the Location:** Choose a well-ventilated site, away from living and kitchen areas, on a stable, level surface. Place it near the garden or the area where compost will be used, but keep it distant from water sources to avoid contamination.
2. **Prepare the Drum:** Use the saw to cut a hole in the top of the drum, slightly smaller than the seat's base for a snug fit. Use the seat as a template for tracing.
3. **Install the Toilet Seat:** Attach the toilet seat to the drum's top using hinges, ensuring it can be lifted for comfortable use and maintenance. Use screws to secure the hinges to both the drum and the seat, adding a latch if desired for a tighter closure. Seal the edges with silicone to prevent odors from escaping.
4. **Add Ventilation:** Drill a hole near the top of the drum for the ventilation tube. Insert the hose and ensure it extends at least 3-4 feet above the drum to assist with airflow. Secure the tube with screws and seal it with silicone to prevent air leaks.
5. **Prepare the Base Layer:** Add a 6-inch layer of wood chips or sawdust to the drum's bottom. This aids in liquid absorption, odor reduction, and kickstarts the composting process.
6. **Using the Toilet:** After each use, cover waste with a scoop of sawdust or wood chips to manage odors and promote composting. Ensure all waste is well-covered.
7. **Toilet Maintenance:** Regularly check the waste level in the drum. When it reaches two-thirds full, let the composting process continue. Swap the full drum for an empty one, sealing the former and allowing it to decompose for 6-12 months in a designated area.
8. **Compost Collection:** After the composting period, open the drum to inspect the compost. It should be dark, crumbly, and devoid of unpleasant odors. Use the compost in non-food gardening areas, such as flower beds or for ornamental plants.

Maintenance Tips:
- **Regularly Add Sawdust or Wood Chips:** This helps control odors.
- **Keep the Ventilation Tube Clear:** Ensure it is free of blockages.
- **Clean the Toilet Seat Periodically:** Use natural solutions to maintain hygiene.
- **Inspect the Drum for Cracks or Leaks:** Repair or replace as necessary.

Construction of an Off-Grid Shower System

Cost: $20-$100
Time: 2-4 hours

Creating an off-grid shower system allows you to maintain personal cleanliness without relying on conventional plumbing. This setup is perfect for off-grid living, camping, or emergency situations, offering a straightforward and effective method to stay clean and comfortable. Regular upkeep will ensure your system remains dependable and efficient.

Materials Needed:
- **5-Gallon Solar Shower Bag or Camping Shower Bag:** 1 unit. This portable bag will act as your main water reservoir and heating system. Opt for a bag made of heat-resistant materials, typically equipped with a shower head and hose.
- **Sturdy Rope or Hook:** 1 unit. This is used to suspend the shower bag above head height. Choose a rope that can support at least 10 pounds, or a metal hook if you have a solid mounting point available.
- **PVC Pipe (Optional for Shower Structure):** 20 feet of 1-inch diameter PVC pipe. This can be utilized to construct a simple frame for hanging the shower bag.
- **Hand Shower (Optional, if not included with the bag):** 1 unit. If your bag does not come with a shower head, select a small, low-water-use model.
- **Water Source:** This can be collected from rain, a well, or a stream. Ensure that the water is clean and suitable for bathing.
- **Water Heating Method:** Use solar, propane, or a wood stove, depending on what is available. Solar heating is the most straightforward and sustainable option.
- **Basic Tools:** Screwdriver, drill, and saw (if constructing a frame).

Instructions:
1. **Select the Location:** Find a private area with good drainage to prevent standing water. You could construct a simple walk-in shower for privacy. Ensure the location is near a water source and receives ample sunlight if using a solar shower bag.
2. **Install the Shower Bag:** Fill the bag with clean water to its 5-gallon capacity and position it in a sunny spot to warm up. On a clear day, the bag can heat water to a comfortable temperature (between 100°F and 120°F) in 3-4 hours. If needed, heat the water using a propane or wood stove and carefully pour it into the shower bag. Hang it from a sturdy branch using rope or a hook, ensuring it is at a height that allows the tube to be above your head.
3. **Construct a Shower Structure (Optional):** For a more stable solution, build a simple frame with PVC pipes. Cut four 6-foot pieces for the legs and two 3-foot pieces for the top horizontal bars. Assemble the frame by connecting the pipes with PVC elbows and T-joints to form a stable rectangle. Attach the hand shower to the top bar and connect the shower bag hose with adapters if necessary. Secure the frame to the ground by inserting the legs into the soil or using stakes.
4. **Prepare the Water Source:** Ensure access to a clean water source. Use a rainwater collection system, a well, or transport water from a nearby stream. If the water is untreated, filter or purify it to guarantee its safety for use.
5. **Heat the Water:** If utilizing a solar bag, allow the sun to naturally warm the water. On cloudy or chilly days, supplement heating with a wood or propane stove. Use a thermometer to check the water temperature before pouring it into the bag, aiming for a comfortable range (100°F-120°F).
6. **Shower Operation:** Open the valve on the bag or shower head to allow water flow. Adjust the flow to conserve water. Many solar bags feature a small lever or valve for flow control. Use biodegradable soap to lessen environmental impact, particularly if wastewater drains directly into the ground. Turn off the water while lathering to save water.
7. **Drainage and Cleaning:** Ensure the shower area has adequate drainage. Dig a small trench or create a well filled with gravel to facilitate water drainage. After showering, allow the bag to dry completely before storing it to prevent mold. Store the bag in a cool, shaded area.

Maintenance Tips:
- Clean the shower bag and shower head regularly to prevent algae or bacteria growth, using a vinegar and water solution.
- Regularly inspect the integrity of the hanging system (rope or hook) to ensure it remains secure.
- Store the bag in a dry, shaded location when not in use to extend its lifespan and prevent damage.
- If you have built a PVC structure, routinely check it for stability and any signs of wear. Replace or repair any damaged components to ensure system safety and functionality.

Homemade Soap and Detergent

Cost: $30-$100
Time: 1-2 days

Creating your own soap and detergent is a sustainable and cost-effective method to maintain cleanliness in an off-grid environment. You can tailor the products to your needs, using natural ingredients that are gentle on both the skin and the environment. This guide will walk you through the process of crafting soap and detergent from scratch.

Materials for Soap:
- **Lye (Sodium Hydroxide):** 10 oz. Handle with care, as it is corrosive.
- **Distilled Water:** 24 ounces, preferred to avoid impurities.
- **Olive Oil:** 24 oz, known for its gentle and hydrating qualities.
- **Coconut Oil:** 24 ounces, which adds lathering and cleansing properties.
- **Palm Oil:** 24 ounces, which gives hardness to the soap.
- **Essential Oils (optional, for fragrance):** 1-2 ounces, such as lavender or peppermint.
- **Safety Gear:** Gloves and goggles to protect against lye.
- **Mixing Containers:** Heat-resistant, preferably stainless steel or durable plastic.
- **Stainless Steel or Wooden Spoon:** For mixing the lye solution and oils.
- **Immersion Blender:** To speed up the saponification process.
- **Soap Mold:** Must hold at least 4 pounds of soap mixture.
- **Waxed or Baking Paper:** To line the mold and prevent soap from sticking.

Materials for Detergent:
- **Washing Soda:** 2 cups, a natural cleaner that eliminates dirt and odors.
- **Borax:** 2 cups, enhances cleaning power and softens water.
- **Soap (homemade or natural):** 1 bar.
- **Grater or Food Processor:** To create soap flakes.
- **Large Bowl:** For mixing all ingredients.
- **Airtight Container:** For storing detergent.

Soap Instructions:
1. **Safety Precautions:** Wear gloves and goggles before handling lye, which can cause chemical burns. Work in a well-ventilated area or outdoors to avoid inhaling fumes.
2. **Prepare the Lye Solution:** Carefully measure 10 ounces of lye and 24 ounces of distilled water. Slowly add the lye to the water (never the reverse), stirring gently. Allow the solution to cool to around 100°F.
3. **Prepare the Oils:** Measure out 24 ounces each of olive, coconut, and palm oil, and gently heat until fully melted. Let the oils cool to approximately 100°F.
4. **Combine Lye and Oils:** Once the lye and oils are at the same temperature, gradually pour the lye into the oils while stirring continuously. Then use an immersion blender until it reaches a creamy consistency, known as "trace."
5. **Add Essential Oils (optional):** If desired, add 1-2 ounces of essential oils for fragrance and mix well.
6. **Pour into the Mold:** Line the mold with waxed paper and pour in the soap mixture, smoothing it with a spatula. Be careful to eliminate any air bubbles.
7. **Let the Soap Harden:** Cover the mold with a towel and let it rest for 24-48 hours. Once hardened, cut the soap into bars and allow it to cure in a well-ventilated area for 4 to 6 weeks before use.

Detergent Instructions:
1. **Grate the Soap:** Use a grater or food processor to shred a bar of soap into fine flakes.
2. **Mix the Ingredients:** In a large bowl, combine 2 cups of washing soda, 2 cups of borax, and the grated soap. Mix well to ensure even distribution of the ingredients.
3. **Store the Detergent:** Transfer the detergent to an airtight container and label it with the date and ingredients.
4. **Use the Detergent:** Use about 2 tablespoons of detergent for each load of laundry, or 3-4 tablespoons for larger or heavily soiled loads.

Maintenance Tips:
- Store homemade soap and detergent in a cool, dry place to extend their shelf life.
- Label containers with the manufacturing date to track freshness.
- Clean tools used for saponification regularly with warm water and vinegar to remove lye or oil residue.

Creating Your Own Toothpaste

Cost: $5-$10
Time: 10-15 minutes
Crafting your own toothpaste is a straightforward way to utilize natural, non-toxic ingredients, helping you save money while minimizing waste.
Required Materials:
- **Baking Soda:** 2 tablespoons. This gentle abrasive helps clean teeth and eliminate stains.
- **Coconut Oil:** 1 tablespoon (remains solid at room temperature). Known for its antibacterial properties, it also gives the paste a creamy texture.
- **Water:** 1 tablespoon (you can adjust this to achieve your preferred consistency).
- **Peppermint Essential Oil:** 10-15 drops. This adds flavor and also offers antibacterial benefits.
- **Xylitol Powder (optional):** 1 teaspoon. A natural sweetener that can help inhibit tooth decay.

Instructions:
1. **Combine Baking Soda and Coconut Oil:** In a small bowl, mix together 2 tablespoons of baking soda and 1 tablespoon of coconut oil until you achieve a paste-like consistency.
2. **Add Water:** Incorporate 1 tablespoon of water to modify the texture, mixing until the paste resembles conventional toothpaste.
3. **Incorporate Essential Oil:** Stir in 10-15 drops of peppermint essential oil and mix thoroughly.
4. **Include Xylitol (Optional):** If you prefer a sweeter taste, mix in 1 teaspoon of xylitol and blend well.
5. **Storage:** Transfer the toothpaste into an airtight container and use a small amount for your regular tooth brushing routine.

Maintenance Tips:
- Keep the toothpaste in a cool, dry area to prevent the coconut oil from liquefying.
- Prepare small batches to ensure freshness, and remix if you notice any separation of ingredients.

Off-Grid Sanitation Solutions

Introduction to Sustainable Sanitation
Off-grid sanitation methods are crucial for upholding a healthy and sustainable living environment when conventional sewage systems are unavailable. Composting toilets present an effective option, transforming human waste into valuable compost that enriches the soil. This process conserves water and prevents the contamination of water sources. Composting relies on aerobic decomposition, which necessitates proper ventilation and routine maintenance for optimal performance. By separating liquids from solids, these systems minimize odors and accelerate the composting process, making them a greener and more efficient alternative to traditional toilets.

Gray Water Management

Gray water treatment systems represent another sustainable sanitation method, repurposing water from sinks, showers, and washing machines for irrigation or other non-potable applications. Implementing a gray water system requires filtration of solids and careful water management to inhibit bacteria growth. These systems yield a water source rich in nutrients that benefits plants, provided that biodegradable soaps and detergents are used to protect the garden ecosystem. In contrast, off-grid septic systems cater to homes without municipal sewage connections, offering a secure way to treat and dispose of household wastewater. Typically, these systems consist of a septic tank that separates solids from liquids and a drain field, necessitating meticulous planning to prevent groundwater contamination. Regular inspections and tank pumping are essential to avert leaks or clogs that could pose health hazards.

Constructing a Composting Toilet

Building a composting toilet begins with selecting an appropriate container and a well-ventilated, accessible site for maintenance. A sealable container collects solids, while a separator diverts liquids, minimizing moisture and odors in solid waste. A comfortable seat can be installed, and materials such as sawdust or coconut fiber can be used to cover waste and absorb moisture, facilitating composting. The compost produced must mature before it can be utilized in the garden as natural fertilizer. These off-grid sanitation solutions embody principles of self-sufficiency and environmental responsibility, converting waste into resources and reducing the ecological footprint of off-grid living. Through thoughtful planning and implementation, off-grid households can ensure cleanliness, sustainability, and harmony with their surroundings, demonstrating that a lack of modern infrastructure does not necessitate sacrificing hygiene or comfort.

Gray Water Treatment Systems

Gray water systems harness used water from showers, sinks, and washing machines, redistributing it for irrigation or toilet flushing. This approach lowers drinking water consumption and eases the burden on septic systems in off-grid homes. The design of a gray water system begins by identifying water sources, generally excluding kitchen drains due to higher organic content and potential pathogens. Next, select a treatment method, which can range from simple filtration to more advanced biological processes, such as artificial wetlands. The latter utilizes plants and microorganisms to break down pollutants and purify the water. Treated water is typically distributed through drip irrigation, delivering moisture directly to plant roots and minimizing surface contact to reduce health risks.

Establishing a Humanure System

Creating and utilizing a Humanure system involves a commitment to sustainable waste management practices, particularly suitable for off-grid living. The foundation of a Humanure system is the composting toilet, which collects human waste and transforms it into compost through careful management. To initiate a Humanure system, establish a composting toilet if one is not already in place. This can be as simple as using a 5-gallon bucket positioned under a toilet seat within a wooden frame, along with a separate container to collect urine, which helps decrease moisture and odors in the solid waste. The collected waste should be mixed with a carbon-rich material, like sawdust, straw, or leaves, to balance nitrogen levels and facilitate aerobic decomposition.

Next, set up a compost pile or container for depositing waste from the composting toilet. This container should be discreetly located away from water sources to prevent contamination. It's crucial to layer human waste with additional carbon-rich materials to create optimal composting conditions. Cover the pile with a thick layer of straw, leaves, or other insulating materials to retain heat and moisture, essential for the composting process.

Managing the compost pile involves regular monitoring and maintenance to ensure ideal decomposition conditions. This includes turning the pile to introduce oxygen, checking moisture levels, and adding more carbon-rich materials if necessary. The pile should remain moist but not saturated, generating heat as microorganisms break down the waste. If the compost is too dry, water can be added to maintain humidity; if it's too wet, carbon-rich materials should be incorporated to absorb excess moisture and restore balance. After the initial high-temperature composting phase, lasting several months, the material must be allowed to mature for an additional period, often up to a year, to ensure complete decomposition and pathogen elimination. This maturation phase is vital for producing safe and stable compost, which can be used to enrich soil in non-food production areas, such as ornamental gardens or around fruit trees.

When handling humanure, safety measures are essential to prevent contamination and disease transmission. Always wear gloves and wash hands thoroughly after managing compost or working in the composting area. Ensure that the final compost is fully decomposed before use, exhibiting a soil-like consistency devoid of recognizable materials. Employing a Humanure system allows you to close the loop on waste, converting a potential pollutant into a valuable resource for off-grid living. It minimizes the need for water in waste disposal, reduces the environmental impact of wastewater, and enhances soil health and fertility. With diligent management and attention to detail, a Humanure system can serve as a fundamental component of a sustainable lifestyle, showcasing the practical application of ecological principles and resilience in off-grid settings.

Constructing a Humanure Compost Bin

To create a Humanure compost bin, first select a location that is convenient yet distanced from living areas and water sources to prevent contamination. The site should have good drainage and be accessible throughout the year. Required materials include untreated wood, such as cedar or pine (which resist decay), screws or nails, chicken wire for ventilation, and roofing material like tarp or plywood for the top. Begin by cutting wood to form a structure approximately 4 feet by 4 feet, a manageable size for turning compost. The height should be at least 3 feet to provide sufficient volume for composting and enable proper airflow. Assemble the frame using screws or nails to create a sturdy base. For added strength, corner stakes can be anchored into the ground to stabilize the container.

Next, attach wire mesh to the sides of the structure to facilitate ventilation while keeping pests out. The mesh should be dense enough to prevent rodents from entering but porous enough to ensure proper air circulation. If the container sits directly on the soil, leave the bottom open to allow earthworms and beneficial microbes to enhance the composting process. Construct a lid for the container to retain moisture and heat, which are crucial for composting, while also preventing rainwater from saturating the compost. The lid should be easy to remove or open to add materials and turn compost. If using plywood, drill several holes for ventilation or consider a hinged design for convenience.

To initiate the composting process, add a layer of straw or dry leaves to the bottom of the container to absorb excess moisture. After each use of humanure from the composting toilet, cover it with a carbon-rich material, such as sawdust, straw, or dry leaves, to balance nitrogen levels, diminish odors, and promote aerobic decomposition. Turn the compost periodically to introduce oxygen and ensure even breakdown within the container. Monitoring moisture levels is critical; the compost should feel like a wrung-out sponge. If it is too dry, add water or wetter materials; if overly humid, incorporate carbon-rich materials to soak up extra moisture. The composting process may take six months to a year before the material at the base of the container is fully decomposed and safe for use. Once one bin is full, allow it to mature while beginning a new bin to maintain a continuous composting cycle. Safety remains paramount when handling humanure: always wear gloves and be cautious to avoid contaminating water sources. The final compost should be dark, crumbly, and possess an earthy aroma, with no discernible traces of waste. This compost can be used to enrich areas not designated for food plants, contributing to a sustainable nutrient cycle in your off-grid environment. This DIY project not only provides an effective solution for managing human waste off-grid but also enhances soil health by recycling nutrients and decreasing reliance on chemical fertilizers. With careful oversight, a Humanure compost bin can be an essential element of a sustainable lifestyle, transforming waste into a valuable resource.

Creating a Gray Water System

To set up a gray water irrigation system, start by identifying sources of gray water in your household, such as showers, bathroom sinks, and washing machines. Ensure that the water is free from harmful chemicals or solids that could clog the system or harm your garden. Next, design a filtration system to eliminate particulates from the water. This can range from simple mesh filters to more intricate sand and carbon filters for finer filtration. The filtered water should then be directed to a temporary storage tank, known as a "surge tank," which regulates flow to the irrigation system, preventing overflow and allowing sediment to settle.

From the tank, water can be distributed through a pump or via gravity using a drip irrigation system in the garden. Drip irrigation minimizes contact with plant foliage, thereby reducing health risks. It is vital to utilize porous tubing or specialized tubing designed for underground or drip irrigation to avoid clogs. Carefully plan the layout of your irrigation lines, ensuring gray water is exclusively used for ornamental plants or fruit trees where edible parts do not contact the water. Incorporate an overflow route in your design to channel excess water away from the property, preventing stagnation and associated health risks. This path may lead to a designated absorption area or, as a last resort, back into the conventional waste system.

Regular upkeep of your gray water system is crucial: routinely inspect and clean filters, check for leaks, and monitor plant health to confirm that gray water is not adversely affecting your garden. Before starting this project, review local regulations regarding gray water use, as permits may be required or certain systems may not be allowed. Additionally, familiarize yourself with the types of soaps and detergents that are safe for gray water systems, opting for biodegradable products that avoid salts, boron, and harmful chemicals. By following these steps, you can establish a sustainable gray water irrigation system that conserves water and benefits your garden. This initiative not only lessens environmental impact but also presents a practical approach to managing domestic wastewater in an off-grid living scenario.

Off-Grid Waste Management

Managing waste in off-grid living demands innovative approaches to effectively reduce, reuse, and recycle materials, minimizing environmental impact while enhancing sustainability. At the core of efficient waste management is adopting a mindful attitude towards consumption, favoring biodegradable products with minimal packaging or those that can be entirely reused or recycled. By thoughtfully selecting items based on their lifecycle and potential for reuse, you can significantly diminish the amount of waste generated.

Waste reduction starts with conscious purchasing, focusing on essential and eco-friendly products. Buying in bulk, avoiding single-use plastics, and selecting items crafted from renewable resources are vital steps in this direction. Embracing a minimalist lifestyle not only curbs waste production but also aligns with off-grid principles centered on simplicity and self-sufficiency.

Reusing materials is another key facet of effective waste management. Many items typically thrown away can find new life with a touch of creativity. For instance, glass jars can serve as storage containers, while old garments can be repurposed as cleaning rags or insulation. Establishing a compost bin for organic waste reduces landfill contributions while producing valuable compost for gardening, completing a sustainable cycle of consumption and regeneration.

Recycling, albeit more challenging in remote areas, remains a crucial component of waste management. Designate a space for sorting materials such as metals, glass, and some plastics. Since off-grid communities may lack convenient recycling facilities, plan trips to drop off recyclables or research local programs that provide collection services for rural areas. For harder-to-recycle items, seek specialized recycling initiatives that accept materials through the mail. Innovative solutions like crafting eco-bricks from non-recyclable plastics offer a method to repurpose waste into functional building materials. By filling clean, dry plastic bottles with plastic scraps, you create solid blocks that can be utilized in various projects, from paths to small structures, aiding in the containment of plastic waste and preventing environmental pollution.

Promoting personal and community awareness about the significance of waste reduction and sustainable living practices is vital for successfully managing waste off-grid. Workshops, community gatherings, and resource sharing can foster collective efforts toward responsible waste management. By exchanging knowledge and experiences, off-grid communities can develop tailored solutions that address their unique challenges, leading the way in environmental stewardship.

Ultimately, effective waste management in off-grid settings necessitates intentional choices that align with sustainability and self-sufficiency principles. By reducing consumption, reusing materials, recycling where feasible, and educating others, individuals living off the grid can lessen their ecological impact and contribute to a healthier planet. Through creativity and community collaboration, the challenge of waste management in isolated environments can transform into an opportunity for innovation and sustainable living.

Off-Grid Waste Incineration Solutions

Types of Incineration Systems

Incinerators are vital in managing waste off the grid, effectively converting waste materials into ash, gas, and heat. They are particularly beneficial for reducing waste volume, lowering disease risks, and in some cases, generating energy. Various types of incinerators exist, each tailored for different waste categories and operational requirements. The "mass burn" incinerator, for instance, can process mixed or untreated municipal waste without requiring prior sorting or processing. This feature makes it especially convenient for off-grid communities with limited waste management options. Mass burn incinerators function at high temperatures, transforming waste into ash and producing heat that can be harnessed to create steam or electricity.

Another widely used type is the rotary kiln incinerator, which is adaptable and capable of processing a variety of waste types, including hazardous, medical, and chemical waste. This cylindrical system rotates to mix materials, ensuring thorough and even combustion. Rotary kilns operate at higher temperatures than mass burn incinerators, effectively decomposing toxic substances and minimizing harmful emissions. Fluidized bed incinerators represent an eco-friendly and efficient solution for waste disposal. These systems use a bed of hot granular material, such as sand, to suspend and combust waste. This method promotes better airflow and consistent temperatures, resulting in cleaner combustion and reduced emissions. Fluidized bed incinerators excel at processing organic waste and can be tailored to accommodate diverse waste compositions.

Fixed grate incinerators feature a simpler design and are often employed for smaller-scale operations. Waste is placed on a stationary grate, where it burns, and the ash falls into a collection area below. While less efficient than other types, these incinerators require straightforward mechanics, making them easier to construct and maintain, which is ideal for remote off-grid locations. Pyrolytic incinerators, or pyrolysis units, decompose organic materials at high temperatures in an oxygen-deprived environment. This process produces combustible gases that can be captured and utilized as fuel, along with solid ash and charcoal residues. While pyrolytic incinerators effectively reduce organic waste volume and generate energy, they necessitate advanced technologies and meticulous management.

Each incineration type offers distinct benefits and drawbacks, and the choice depends on the specific needs of the off-grid community, including the waste types generated, the waste volume, environmental factors, and available resources for construction and operation. Proper selection, use, and upkeep of incinerators are crucial to minimize environmental impact while maximizing benefits such as waste reduction and potential energy recovery.

Building a Basic Incinerator

Constructing a simple incinerator for off-grid waste management is an effective method for reducing waste volume and minimizing pest attraction and health risks. This project involves creating a small-scale incinerator using readily available materials, designed to safely incinerate non-recyclable waste. The design prioritizes safety, efficiency, and minimizing environmental impact.

To begin, gather the necessary materials, including a metal bin or barrel, wire mesh or grate, metal pipes for ventilation, a drill, and heat-resistant paint. Select a metal bin or barrel that will function as the main body of the incinerator, ensuring it is clean and free of harmful residues. Use a drill to create several ventilation holes around the bottom sides of the bin to facilitate sufficient airflow, which is essential for efficient burning. The size and number of holes may vary, but they should be evenly spaced. Also, drill a few holes in the lid or top of the bin to allow for the safe release of smoke and gases during burning.

Next, prepare a stable base for the incinerator using bricks or concrete blocks to elevate the bin off the ground. This elevation prevents ground burning and enhances airflow through the ventilation holes. Inside the bin, place a piece of wire mesh or grate that fits snugly a few inches above the bottom. This will support the waste while allowing ash to fall below and maintain air circulation. Secure the grate with metal brackets or wires attached to the bin sides if necessary.

To enhance the incinerator's efficiency, consider adding a simple metal pipe as a chimney. Attach this pipe to a hole cut in the lid or the top of the bin. The chimney helps direct smoke upwards, improving combustion. Before the first use, coat the bin's exterior with high-temperature resistant paint to protect it from rust and weather conditions. Allow the paint to dry completely according to the manufacturer's instructions.

When ready to use the incinerator, place it on the base and fill the bottom with dry combustible material, such as paper or small branches, to ignite the fire. Add the waste to be incinerated, ensuring not to pack it tightly to facilitate airflow. Light the fire through the ventilation holes at the bottom and place the lid with the chimney on top. Supervise the incinerator during use and avoid leaving it unattended. After the waste has completely burned and the incinerator has cooled, dispose of the ash safely. This straightforward incinerator serves as a practical tool for managing small amounts of non-recyclable waste in an off-grid context. However, responsible use is crucial, adhering to local regulations regarding open burning and considering environmental impacts. Avoid burning plastics or other materials that release harmful toxins, and prioritize recycling and composting as primary waste management strategies wherever feasible.

Establishing an Off-Grid Recycling System

Creating an off-grid recycling system involves devising a structured approach to effectively manage and repurpose waste materials. Start by identifying the types of recyclable materials commonly produced in your off-grid lifestyle, such as paper, cardboard, metals, glass, and certain plastics. Set up separate bins for each type of recyclable material to streamline the sorting process. Clearly labeling these containers encourages consistent use and helps prevent contamination of recyclables with non-recyclable waste.

To facilitate an efficient recycling process, it's essential to know what recycling facilities are available in your area and their specific requirements for accepting materials. Some facilities may request that materials be cleaned or treated in a particular manner before delivery. If access to recycling centers is limited, consider reaching out to the local community to explore collaborative solutions, such as sharing transportation to facilities or organizing community recycling days.

Creative reuse within the off-grid community can significantly reduce the necessity of transporting recyclables to distant facilities. For instance, glass jars can be repurposed as storage containers, and metals can be gathered and sold to scrap dealers who provide pickup services for larger quantities. Education plays a vital role in the success of an off-grid recycling system. Organizing workshops or informal gatherings to share ideas and techniques for reusing materials can foster a culture of sustainability and creativity. Moreover, staying informed about advancements in recycling technologies and sustainable waste management practices can introduce new opportunities to enhance the system.

For materials that are difficult to recycle or reuse, consider implementing waste reduction strategies to minimize their presence in your off-grid space. Opt for products with minimal packaging, choose reusable items, and avoid single-use plastics to significantly lower waste production. By establishing a comprehensive off-grid recycling system, you contribute to the sustainability of your living environment and the health of the planet. This proactive approach to waste management not only conserves resources but also fosters a sense of responsibility and innovation within the off-grid community, paving the way for a more sustainable future.

Creating a Recycling Station

To construct a waste separation and recycling station for off-grid living, begin by identifying the categories of waste most commonly generated in your environment, such as organics, paper, plastic, metal, and glass. This foundational step is crucial for designing a station that meets your specific needs. Collect materials for constructing the station, which may include recycled pallets, bins, containers, and labels for organization. The design should emphasize durability, ease of use, and adaptability to accommodate various types of recyclables and waste.

Start by building the structure for the station using pallets or other sturdy materials to create a base and shelving to support bins or containers for each waste category. Ensure that the structure is stable and capable of withstanding weather conditions if situated outdoors. For each waste category, select an appropriate container size based on the volume of waste typically produced. Containers should be easily removable for disposing of recyclable materials or waste.

Clearly label each container with the type of waste it is intended to hold. Consider using symbols or images alongside text to make the system easily understandable for all users, including children or guests unfamiliar with your recycling setup. Include a section for hazardous or special waste that requires separate handling, ensuring it is distinctly marked to prevent contamination of other recyclables.

If organic waste constitutes a significant portion of your off-grid waste management, incorporate a compost bin or area into your recycling station. This could be a simple container to transfer compostable materials to a larger composting system or an integrated composting unit that initiates decomposition directly at the station.

To simplify the recycling process, establish a work area equipped with tools to clean and prepare recyclables, such as a sink for rinsing containers, a can crusher, and a paper shredder. This setup will help reduce the volume of recyclable materials and ensure they are ready for transport or processing at recycling facilities.

Consider the potential for expanding the recycling station as your needs evolve or the availability of recycling services changes. Design the station so that additional containers can be added or existing ones repurposed for different waste types. Regularly review and adapt the system based on user feedback to ensure it remains functional and efficient.

By creating a waste separation and recycling station, you take a substantial step toward sustainable off-grid living. This station not only facilitates responsible waste disposal but also promotes recycling and composting, thereby lessening the environmental impact of your lifestyle. Through careful planning and construction, your recycling station will become a central component of your commitment to sustainability and self-sufficiency, making waste management a seamless and efficient part of daily life.

CHAPTER 9:

Home Survival: Techniques for Off-Grid Heating and Cooling

Solar Heating Techniques

Passive Solar Heating

Passive solar heating harnesses solar energy to maintain a comfortable indoor climate during colder months, offering a sustainable and cost-effective solution for off-grid living. This method leverages the orientation and architectural design of a building to absorb, retain, and distribute solar warmth in winter, while minimizing heat gain during summer. Unlike conventional systems, passive solar heating operates without mechanical or electrical components, instead relying on the home's structural elements to manage heat accumulation and release.

To optimize passive solar heating, one must grasp the sun's trajectory and its interaction with various building materials. Thermal mass materials—such as concrete, brick, stone, and tile—play a vital role in this process. These materials capture heat during daylight and gradually release it during nighttime, maintaining a pleasant indoor temperature. Careful window placement is crucial; windows facing south (in the Northern Hemisphere) are ideal for maximizing sunlight intake. Ideally, window areas should constitute at least 7% of the room's floor area for effective results. Additionally, incorporating awnings or deciduous trees can provide shade in the summer, preventing overheating, while allowing sunlight to filter through in winter when branches are bare.

Insulation

Proper insulation is essential for the passive solar heating design, as it minimizes heat loss, keeping the accumulated warmth inside when temperatures drop. Windows, often a major source of heat loss, benefit from double- or triple-glazing, which significantly enhances energy efficiency. For those interested in passive solar heating for their off-grid home, starting with a site analysis is recommended, assessing the sun's path, prevailing winds, and local climate to refine the building design. The goal is to maximize winter sunlight exposure while minimizing exposure to cold winds and excessive summer heat. Integrating thermal mass materials and insulated windows during the construction phase can create a residence that remains warm in winter and cool in summer, negating the need for conventional heating and cooling solutions.

Passive solar heating is not limited to new builds; existing homes can be upgraded to enhance their passive solar capabilities. Adding thermal mass, enhancing insulation, and installing thermal curtains are simple yet effective modifications that can drastically lower a home's energy consumption.

By embracing passive solar heating, off-grid dwellers can not only lessen their environmental footprint but also boost their self-reliance and resilience. This method aligns with sustainable living principles, providing a practical alternative for those wishing to decrease their reliance on external energy sources and coexist harmoniously with nature.

Building Orientation and Window Configuration

Optimal Orientation

The orientation of a building and the arrangement of its windows are critical for maximizing the benefits of passive solar heating, directly impacting energy efficiency and comfort in off-grid homes. Ideally, in the Northern Hemisphere, a house should face south to capture sunlight effectively. This positioning allows living spaces to absorb significant sunlight during winter when the sun is lower in the sky, naturally warming the interior. In contrast, during summer, strategically designed overhangs or deciduous trees can prevent excessive sunlight from entering, helping to keep interiors cool and reducing reliance on artificial cooling methods.

Window Placement

The configuration of windows is also crucial in this energy-saving approach. South-facing windows should be larger and more numerous than those facing north to optimize solar gain during winter. However, it's vital to balance window size with insulation needs since they can contribute to heat loss. High-performance windows, such as double- or triple-glazed models filled with inert gases and low-emissivity (Low-E) coatings, significantly reduce this leakage while still permitting solar energy entry.

East- and west-facing windows require careful consideration as the low sun angles during sunrise and sunset can lead to excessive heat accumulation in the summer months. Reducing the size of these windows or employing shading devices can help regulate unwanted heat. North-facing windows, while not contributing much to solar gain, can be designed to enhance natural lighting, reducing the need for artificial light during daytime hours.

Integrating thermal mass in areas that receive direct sunlight through south-facing windows can further bolster the effectiveness of passive solar heating. Materials like concrete, brick, stone, and tile absorb heat during the day and gradually release it at night, providing a natural source of warmth. This strategic application of thermal mass stabilizes indoor temperatures, fostering a more comfortable living environment without dependence on external energy sources.

For off-grid homes, harmonizing building orientation and window configuration with other passive design features, such as insulation and thermal mass, represents a comprehensive approach to achieving thermal comfort and energy efficiency. This design philosophy not only supports sustainable living principles but also delivers tangible benefits, reducing dependence on non-renewable energy and lowering utility costs.

Thermal Mass and Insulation

Understanding Thermal Mass

In the context of passive solar heating, thermal mass refers to materials within a building that absorb, store, and release heat. Materials such as concrete, brick, stone, and tile can help regulate indoor temperatures by mitigating thermal fluctuations. During daylight hours, these materials soak up heat from the sun, diminishing peak heating demands. As outdoor temperatures drop at night, the stored heat is released slowly, maintaining a cozy environment without the need for active heating systems. The effective positioning of thermal mass is vital; it must be exposed to direct sunlight during winter or indirectly gain heat from the room's air. It is also essential that the thermal mass is insulated from the outside to prevent heat loss, ensuring that the stored energy is utilized efficiently within the building.

Importance of Insulation
Insulation complements thermal mass by minimizing heat transfer between the building's interior and exterior. Adequate insulation is crucial for retaining heat absorbed by the thermal mass, making it an integral part of passive solar design.

DIY Project: Constructing a Solar Heater

Overview

This project focuses on creating a straightforward solar heater that harnesses solar energy to warm air or water for your residence. Solar heaters are eco-friendly, cost-effective, and significantly decrease reliance on traditional heating methods.
- **Difficulty Level**: Moderate
- **Estimated Time**: 1-2 Days

Benefits

A solar heater reduces energy expenses by utilizing free, renewable solar energy. It can enhance your home's heating system, supplying warmth during colder months without relying on electricity or fuel, suitable for both air and water heating systems.

Required Materials
- Wooden planks (for the frame)
- Plywood or OSB panels (for the back panel)
- Clear acrylic sheet or glass (for the front cover)
- Non-toxic black paint (for heat absorption)
- Aluminum foil or reflective insulation (to enhance efficiency)
- Copper pipes or aluminum cans (for water heating) or black PVC pipes for air heating
- Insulation (foam or fiberglass panels)
- Screws and nails
- Silicone sealant (for waterproofing)
- Solar fan (optional, for air heating)
- Pipes or sleeves (for water heater connections)

Necessary Tools
- Electric drill with bits
- Saw (manual or circular)
- Measuring tape
- Hammer and nails
- Brush
- Screwdriver
- Pipe cutter (for copper pipe)
- Heat-resistant tape (for securing tubes or cans)

Alternative Materials
- Recycled items, such as old glass or metal sheets, for the front cover and frame
- Black rubber pipes as an alternative to PVC pipes for air heating

Step-by-Step Instructions

1. **Select and Prepare the Site**
   Choose a south-facing wall or roof that receives ample direct sunlight throughout the day. Ensure the location is easily accessible and structurally sound enough to support the heater. The heater's angle should match your latitude for optimal solar gain.
   - **Time**: 1-2 hours
2. **Construct the Framework**
   Build a rectangular frame using the wooden planks, sizing it according to your available space and heating requirements. Attach a sheet of plywood or OSB to the back to form the base. Ensure the structure is sturdy and all joints are secure.
   - **Time**: 2-3 hours
3. **Prepare the Absorber Plate**
   For a water heater, arrange copper pipes or aluminum cans inside the frame in rows, painting them black to improve heat absorption. Secure them to the frame with brackets or heat-resistant tape. For an air heater,

use black PVC pipes arranged in a serpentine pattern or incorporate metal sheets painted black within the frame. This absorber plate will capture solar energy and convert it into heat.
   - **Time**: 2-3 hours
4. **Add Reflective Insulation**
Line the interior of the frame, surrounding the absorber plate, with aluminum foil or reflective insulation. This step directs sunlight onto the absorber plate, increasing the heater's efficiency. Secure the insulation using heat-resistant tape or staples.
   - **Time**: 1 hour
5. **Install the Front Cover**
Affix the clear acrylic or glass sheet to the front of the frame, ensuring a tight seal to create an airtight chamber. Use silicone caulk around the edges to prevent air or water leaks. The transparent cover allows sunlight to enter while trapping heat inside the heater.
   - **Time**: 1-2 hours
6. **Insulate the Back and Sides**
Attach foam or fiberglass panels to the back and sides of the frame to minimize heat loss. Ensure that the insulation is well secured and covers all exposed areas. This step is critical for maximizing heater efficiency.
   - **Time**: 1 hour
7. **Connect the System**
   - **For a Water Heater**: Connect tubing or sleeves to the inlets and outlets of the copper pipes. The inlet should link to a cold water source, such as a storage tank or main line, while the outlet should direct water to a storage tank or the hot water system in the home. Ensure all connections are secure and watertight, and consider adding a one-way valve to prevent backflow.
   - **For an Air Heater**: If utilizing a fan, install it at the outlet to circulate warm air throughout the home. The inlet should pull fresh air from inside the house, heat it in the solar heater, and then return it warm. Use ductwork to connect the heater to the home's air system, sealing all connections with silicone or heat-resistant tape.
   - **Time**: 1-2 hours
8. **Test the Solar Heater**
Once the system is fully assembled, test it on a sunny day. Monitor the temperature of the heated air or water to ensure efficient operation. Adjust the angle or position as needed for optimal sun exposure and make any necessary modifications to enhance performance.
   - **Time**: 2-3 hours

Care and Maintenance
Regularly clean the clear cover to maximize sunlight penetration. Inspect the system for leaks, cracks, or blockages and repair as necessary. If using a fan, ensure it operates correctly. Drain the water heater in winter if freezing temperatures are anticipated.

Wood Stoves and Biomass Heating Solutions

Varieties of Wood Stoves

Wood stoves come in various designs and functionalities, catering to different heating requirements and preferences for off-grid living. The classic cast iron wood stove is renowned for its durability and excellent heat retention, making it a favored choice. These stoves, built for longevity, often become the heart of the home, radiating warmth even after the fire has extinguished.

Another prevalent type is the steel wood stove, which heats up and cools down more rapidly than cast iron, making it ideal for those who seek immediate warmth without prolonged heat retention.

For those interested in advanced combustion technology, catalytic wood stoves present an environmentally friendly alternative. Equipped with catalytic combustors, these stoves burn smoke and gases at lower temperatures, enhancing efficiency and reducing emissions. They are particularly suited for environmentally conscious individuals looking to decrease their carbon footprint while benefiting from wood heating.

In contrast, non-catalytic stoves rely on design and airflow control to achieve complete combustion. These stoves are simpler to operate and favored for their ease of use and lower maintenance requirements compared to catalytic models.

Pellet stoves represent a modern alternative, utilizing wood pellets or compressed biomass as fuel. They are popular for their convenience, offering automatic fuel feeding and thermostatic control, making them user-friendly heating solutions. Pellets combust cleanly and efficiently, generating minimal ash and requiring less storage space than traditional wood, a crucial consideration for off-grid living.

For those wanting to combine cooking and heating, wood stoves with cooktops are available, allowing for both heating and culinary functions thanks to a cooktop and, occasionally, an oven. This dual functionality makes them a practical option for off-grid homes, reducing the need for separate appliances and maximizing the utility of the stove.

Lastly, portable stoves are designed for easy mobility and setup, making them ideal for temporary shelters, tents, or small cabins. These lightweight and often collapsible stoves provide flexible heating solutions for those prioritizing mobility and simplicity.

Each type of wood stove offers distinct advantages, from the classic cast iron stove known for its charm and prolonged heat output to eco-friendly catalytic models, the convenience of pellet stoves, the multifunctionality of stoves with cooktops, or the portability of lightweight options. When selecting a wood stove for off-grid living, it's crucial to consider space, heating requirements, fuel availability, and personal preferences to identify the best solution for a comfortable and sustainable home.

Firewood Collection and Storage

Efficient collection and storage of firewood is vital for maintaining a sustainable and dependable heating source in off-grid settings. The process begins with identifying local firewood resources, which can differ based on your geographical location. Hardwoods like oak, maple, and birch are preferred for their high energy content and longer burn times compared to softwoods like pine and fir, which burn more quickly and produce more creosote, increasing the risk of chimney blockages.

For those residing near forests, sustainable harvesting methods include gathering fallen branches and trees while avoiding the cutting of live trees, which can disrupt the ecosystem. Alternatively, purchasing wood from local suppliers that practice sustainable logging can ensure a steady supply without contributing to deforestation.

Once collected, proper storage of wood is crucial to maximize its heating potential. The wood should be seasoned, meaning it is left to dry until it achieves a moisture content of less than 20%. This process can take six months to a year, depending on the wood type and local climate conditions. Seasoning wood reduces smoke and enhances heating efficiency. The ideal storage solution is a shed or covered structure that shields the wood from rain and snow while allowing for airflow to aid in drying.

The storage area should be positioned a safe distance from the house to mitigate the risk of pest infestations and minimize potential fire hazards. Elevating wood off the ground on pallets or rails prevents moisture absorption from the soil and enhances air circulation around the logs, further facilitating the seasoning process.

It is essential to stack wood in a manner that allows for adequate airflow, expediting the drying process. Covering the top of the stack with a tarp or a specially designed cover protects it from precipitation while permitting moisture to escape from the sides.

For those utilizing wood stoves or biomass heaters during colder months, maintaining a well-organized and adequately stocked firewood supply is crucial. Keeping a mix of hardwoods and softwoods offers versatility: quick-burning softwoods can be used to ignite the fire, while durable hardwoods can sustain it. Regularly checking the woodpile for signs of pests or rot and rotating the stock to utilize older wood first ensures high-quality fuel for effective heating.

Properly collecting and storing firewood is not just about keeping a home warm; it embodies sustainability and self-sufficiency that requires foresight, planning, and commitment to environmental stewardship. By adhering to these practices, individuals living off-grid can secure a reliable, efficient, and eco-friendly heating source while supporting a self-sufficient lifestyle and minimizing their environmental impact.

Safety and Maintenance

Ensuring the safety and proper maintenance of wood stoves and biomass heaters is vital for both the longevity of the equipment and the safety of users. Routine cleaning and inspection are crucial to preventing fire hazards and maintaining optimal performance. The accumulation of creosote, a highly flammable byproduct of wood combustion, within the chimney and flue can lead to fires if not properly addressed. It is advisable to have these components professionally inspected and cleaned at least annually, preferably before the cold weather sets in.

Additionally, checking for signs of wear or damage, such as cracks in the stove body or flue, loose joints, or deterioration of insulation materials, is essential to avert dangerous situations, including carbon monoxide leaks indoors.

Using wood stoves and biomass heaters correctly is also critical for ensuring safety and efficiency. Always opt for seasoned wood, as burning wet or green wood increases creosote buildup. Avoid overloading the stove, as excessive heat can harm both the stove and the chimney, and never leave the stove unattended while in operation. Installing a stove thermometer can assist in monitoring and maintaining optimal operating temperatures, thereby reducing the risk of creosote buildup.

For biomass heaters using pellets, it is essential to keep the tank and fuel system clean to prevent blockages and ensure a consistent fuel supply. Adequate ventilation is another fundamental aspect of safely using wood stoves and biomass heaters. Proper ventilation ensures a sufficient oxygen supply for combustion and prevents harmful gas accumulation.

In homes utilizing these heating systems, installing carbon monoxide detectors and smoke alarms is crucial, with regular testing to provide early warnings of malfunctions or unsafe operating conditions.

In addition to annual professional inspections, homeowners can carry out simple maintenance tasks. Regularly emptying the ash from the stove, according to the manufacturer's guidelines, prevents airflow blockages and supports efficient combustion. Checking the integrity of door gaskets and seals helps regulate combustion air correctly and prevents smoke leaks into the living area.

For pellet stoves, it is important to clean the hearth, ash traps, and heat exchanger surfaces periodically to ensure safe and effective operation.

By adhering to these safety and maintenance recommendations, users of wood stoves and biomass heaters can enjoy the warmth and comfort these systems provide while minimizing risks. Proper care not only extends the lifespan of heating appliances but also supports a sustainable and self-sufficient lifestyle, ensuring safe and effective use of renewable energy sources.

"Rocket" Thermal Mass Heaters

"Rocket" thermal mass heaters provide an innovative and highly efficient method for heating homes off-grid, utilizing thermal mass principles to store and gradually release heat over time. These systems represent a significant advancement for those seeking sustainable, cost-effective heating solutions, as they combust wood much cleaner and more efficiently than traditional wood stoves.

The core of a "rocket" thermal mass heater consists of a large thermal mass, such as clay or stone, which absorbs heat generated by burning wood in a small, insulated combustion chamber. This design facilitates higher temperature combustion, reducing smoke and enhancing efficiency.

The process begins with igniting wood in a compact, insulated hearth, generating a fierce flame that incinerates most of the smoke and particles that would otherwise remain unburned. This heat warms a vertical chimney, producing a strong draft that draws air into the combustion chamber, ensuring complete combustion. The hot gases then travel through a horizontal metal duct that runs through the thermal mass, transferring heat to it. The thermal mass subsequently radiates this stored warmth into the living area, maintaining a comfortable temperature even after the fire has extinguished.

Constructing a "rocket" thermal mass heater requires selecting materials that can withstand high temperatures and effectively retain heat. The combustion chamber and flue are generally made from firebrick or metal, while the thermal mass may consist of clay, stone, or other masonry materials. The design can be adapted to meet the space and heating needs of the home, with the thermal mass often doubling as a bench or sleeping area.

Safety is a top priority in the construction and operation of a "rocket" thermal mass heater. It is crucial to ensure adequate ventilation to prevent carbon monoxide buildup and to design the system to avoid overheating of the thermal mass. Regular maintenance checks are necessary to clear ash buildup and examine the system for any signs of wear or damage. For DIY enthusiasts, constructing a "rocket" heater is a fulfilling project that provides the opportunity to create a tailored heating solution that aligns with off-grid living principles. With the right tools, materials, and a thorough plan, building a "rocket" heater can be a feasible undertaking for those with basic construction skills. The key to success lies in understanding the principles of rocket design and thermal mass heating to ensure the system is constructed safely and efficiently.

"Rocket" thermal mass heaters exemplify a blend of traditional heating methods and modern combustion technologies, presenting an eco-friendly and sustainable means of heating homes off-grid. By leveraging the combustion efficiency of rockets and the heat retention capabilities of thermal mass, these heaters offer a dependable and sustainable heating solution that embodies the values of self-sufficiency and resilience.

Designing and Constructing a Thermal Mass Bench

Creating a thermal mass bench as part of a "rocket" heating system necessitates careful planning and precise execution to ensure it operates efficiently while seamlessly integrating into the living space. The bench serves as a thermal mass, absorbing and storing heat produced by wood combustion, then gradually releasing it into the room.

The design phase begins with determining the bench's dimensions based on available space and heating requirements for the area. Materials selected for the bench, typically clay or stone, are chosen for their thermal mass characteristics, allowing for substantial heat absorption.

Construction of the thermal mass bench starts with establishing a base that can support the weight of the materials. This base is often created using bricks or concrete blocks, offering a stable foundation for the clay or stone. The next step involves building the core of the bench, where the metal duct from the "rocket" heater will pass. This duct transfers heat from combustion to the bench and must be designed to ensure efficient heat exchange, considering the duct's size and length to maximize the surface area in contact with the thermal mass.

After the core is in place, shape the bench with the chosen material, layering until the desired height and width are achieved. The bench's surface can be smoothed or sculpted for comfort, and additional features like armrests or backs can be incorporated. Allow sufficient drying time for the material to ensure it cures completely before use.

Integrating the thermal mass bench into the living space is crucial for the design. The bench should be situated where it can effectively radiate heat throughout the room, typically positioned centrally or along a wall that facilitates even heat distribution.

Cooling Techniques

Overview

Off-grid cooling strategies are vital for maintaining comfort and preserving food in situations where conventional air conditioning systems are impractical or unwanted. These approaches utilize natural processes and innovative designs to lower indoor temperatures, making efficient and sustainable use of resources like land, water, and air. One effective method involves geothermal tubes, also referred to as ground heat exchangers, which capitalize on the consistent underground temperature to cool air before it enters a building. By burying PVC or metal pipes underground and allowing air to pass through them, you can effectively cool the air during summer and warm it in winter, greatly reducing temperature fluctuations indoors.

Key Components

Insulation and shading are crucial aspects of off-grid cooling, preventing heat absorption from the external environment. Proper insulation in walls, roofs, and floors minimizes heat transfer, while shading solutions like overhangs, curtains, and vegetation can block direct sunlight from windows and walls, significantly decreasing the need for cooling. Thoughtful placement of windows and the use of reflective materials can further enhance these benefits by deflecting heat away from the building.

Solar-Powered Fan Systems

Another innovative off-grid cooling technique is the creation of a solar-powered fan system. This system utilizes photovoltaic panels to power fans that circulate air inside the home or draw in cooler outside air, especially during nighttime when outdoor temperatures drop. Fans can complement passive cooling strategies, such as cross-ventilation and the stack effect, to optimize airflow and heat removal from the building.

DIY projects for off-grid cooling provide opportunities to implement these techniques with hands-on engagement, allowing for customizations tailored to specific needs and different environments. For instance, constructing a basic solar-powered fan system involves selecting suitable solar panels, batteries for energy storage, and fans designed to operate efficiently with the available power. Basic electrical knowledge is necessary to connect components safely and effectively, ensuring the system can deliver reliable cooling without relying on grid electricity.

The installation of geothermal pipes requires careful planning to identify the optimal depth and length of the pipes, along with suitable materials and diameters to meet the building's cooling demands. The installation process includes digging trenches, laying pipes at a slight slope to avoid moisture accumulation, and ensuring the air inlet and outlet are correctly positioned to maximize cooling efficiency.

These off-grid cooling methods not only provide a sustainable alternative to conventional air conditioning systems but also align with self-sufficiency and resilience principles. By harnessing natural resources and renewable energy, individuals can create comfortable living spaces that rely less on external energy sources and are more in harmony with the surrounding ecosystem. Implementing these strategies can greatly enhance the quality of life in off-grid environments by offering effective and eco-friendly cooling solutions.

Geothermal Cooling Systems
The implementation of geothermal cooling pipes leverages the stable temperature of the ground to regulate the climate within buildings, representing a cost-effective and environmentally friendly solution. The underlying principle is straightforward yet effective: a series of pipes are buried at a depth where ground temperatures remain stable, typically around 13°C. Air circulates through these pipes and cools or warms depending on the season before entering the building. This system can substantially diminish the need for conventional heating or cooling methods, offering a sustainable alternative that utilizes the earth's natural thermal consistency.

To establish this system, an initial site analysis is necessary to determine the optimal depth and length of the pipes. The ideal depth varies based on geographical location and soil conditions, usually falling between 2 to 3 meters below the surface. The length of the pipes is also crucial; longer pipes provide greater contact with the ground, enhancing heat exchange. However, overly long pipes can increase airflow resistance, requiring precise calculations to balance efficiency with the system's airflow capacity.

The selection of pipe materials is another vital consideration: polyethylene pipes are often preferred for their durability, corrosion resistance, and relatively low cost. The diameter of the pipes affects the volume of air that can be moved: larger diameters facilitate better airflow but require more installation space. Additionally, it's essential for the internal surfaces of the pipes to be smooth to minimize airflow resistance and allow for easier cleaning and maintenance.

The installation of geothermal pipes necessitates careful planning to avoid interference with underground utilities and prevent radon gas or moisture infiltration into the building. Pipes should be laid with a slight slope towards the building to prevent water accumulation within the system. Installing a condensation drain at the system's lowest point is advisable to manage humidity levels. It is also important to provide filters or screens at the air inlet to prevent debris, insects, or small animals from entering the system.

Once installed, the geothermal pipe system operates passively, requiring minimal energy to circulate air. In larger buildings or regions with extreme temperatures, a small fan may be added to facilitate airflow while still maintaining low energy costs. The system's efficiency can be further enhanced by integrating it into a broader passive design strategy, including effective insulation, natural ventilation, and thermal mass.

Maintaining geothermal pipes is relatively straightforward and primarily involves regularly checking that vents are clear and ensuring the system remains unobstructed. It is also advisable to periodically inspect the interior of the pipes for any moisture accumulation or mold growth, taking necessary action to maintain good air quality.

In summary, the installation of geothermal pipes for heating and cooling offers a viable option for significantly reducing a building's energy footprint. By utilizing the constant temperature of the ground, this system provides an economical and ecologically advantageous method of climate control. Although implementation requires upfront planning and investment, the long-term benefits—such as lower energy costs and enhanced comfort—make it an appealing choice for those dedicated to off-grid living and sustainable building practices.

Insulation and Shading
Insulation and shading are essential factors in regulating the internal temperature of an off-grid home, greatly reducing reliance on active cooling systems and enhancing overall energy efficiency. Effective insulation acts as a barrier to heat flow, helping to keep interiors cool during hot months and warm during colder ones. This is particularly important in walls, roofs, and floors, where the potential for heat transfer is greatest. Materials like fiberglass, cellulose, and foam board are commonly used for insulation, each with a specific R-value indicating their ability to resist heat flow. Higher R-values indicate better insulating properties, making it essential in off-grid living to select insulation with the best R-value possible within your budget to maximize energy conservation and ensure year-round comfort.

Shading helps prevent excessive heat from entering your home through windows and walls exposed to direct sunlight. Exterior shading solutions—such as overhangs, awnings, and deciduous trees—can effectively block significant amounts of solar radiation, thereby reducing cooling demands. Strategic positioning of these elements is crucial; for example, overhangs should be designed to allow low-angle winter sun to enter while blocking high-angle summer sun. Similarly, planting deciduous trees on the south and west sides of the property can provide shade in summer, while allowing sunlight to filter through in winter when the trees are bare.

Using reflective materials on roofs and exterior walls can further deflect solar radiation, contributing to cooler indoor conditions. In addition to these passive cooling strategies, the orientation of your home plays a significant role in optimizing insulation and shading benefits. Homes should be oriented to minimize direct summer sun exposure, with most windows facing north and south to maximize natural light while preventing excessive heat buildup. This orientation, combined with effective insulation and shading, can greatly reduce the need for mechanical cooling systems, fostering a more sustainable and energy-efficient off-grid living experience.

Integrating insulation and shading into the design and construction of an off-grid home requires careful planning and consideration of local climate conditions. By prioritizing these elements, homeowners can create a comfortable indoor environment that remains stable throughout the year, regardless of external temperatures. This not only enhances the livability of off-grid homes but also aligns with sustainable living principles, decreasing energy consumption and minimizing environmental impact.

DIY Project: Constructing a Solar-Powered Ventilation System

Overview
This project involves creating a solar-powered ventilation system designed to ventilate, cool, or circulate air in off-grid settings. The system harnesses solar energy to power a fan, making it an eco-friendly and cost-effective solution for improving air circulation without relying on grid electricity.

Difficulty Level
Medium
Estimated Time: 1 day

Benefits
A solar-powered ventilation system provides air circulation and cooling without drawing electricity from the grid, helping to lower energy costs and carbon emissions. It is ideal for off-grid homes, cabins, greenhouses, or any location where traditional power sources are limited or unavailable.

Materials Required
- Solar panel (10 to 50 watts, depending on fan size and power needs)
- DC fan (compatible with solar panel voltage, typically 12V)
- Charge regulator (optional, to protect the fan and extend its lifespan)
- Rechargeable battery (optional, for operation even when the sun isn't shining)
- Wiring and connectors (for component connections)
- Switch (optional, for turning the fan on and off)
- Mounting brackets or hardware (for securing the solar panel and fan)
- Waterproof junction box (for outdoor setups)

Tools Needed
- Electric drill with bits
- Wire strippers and cutters
- Screwdriver
- Multimeter (to test voltages and connections)
- Tape measure
- Soldering iron and solder (optional, for secure connections)

Alternative Materials
Recycled DC fans from old electronic devices or portable solar chargers with USB outputs for small USB-powered fans.

Step-by-Step Instructions
1. **Select and Prepare the Installation Location**

Decide where to install the ventilation system. For room cooling, position the fan near a window or vent. In greenhouses or similar structures, place the fan to optimize airflow. The solar panel should be mounted in a location with maximum sun exposure throughout the day, such as on a roof or on the ground.
Time: 1 hour

2. **Choose and Install the Solar Panel**
   Select a solar panel with sufficient power to operate the fan. For example, a 10W panel may suffice for a small fan, while larger panels (20-50W) will be needed for more powerful fans. Secure the panel with brackets, ensuring it is angled to capture optimal sunlight.
   Time: 1-2 hours

3. **Install the Fan**
   Position the DC fan in the designated location. Ensure it is securely attached to walls, ceilings, or window frames if indoors. For outdoor installations, make sure the fan is weatherproof or properly protected.
   Time: 1 hour

4. **Wiring the System**
   - **Direct Connection**: If you're not using a battery or charge controller, connect the solar panel directly to the fan. Use wire strippers to expose the ends of the solar panel and fan wires. Connect the positive wires together and do the same with the negative ones, ensuring secure connections with electrical tape or wire nuts. Check connections with a multimeter.
   - **With Charge Controller and Battery**: If you want the fan to operate without sunlight, connect the panel to a charge controller, then connect the controller to a rechargeable battery, and finally connect the fan to the battery.
   Time: 2 hours

5. **Test the System**
   After completing the connections, test the system by placing the solar panel in sunlight. The fan should activate if the panel generates sufficient power.
   Time: 1 hour

6. **Secure Wiring and Fastening**
   Use clips or cable ties to organize the cables neatly. For outdoor setups, use a waterproof junction box to safeguard connections from moisture.
   Time: 30 minutes

7. **Maintenance and Care**
   Regularly clean the solar panel to remove dust and debris that can hinder efficiency. Inspect the wiring and connections for wear and make repairs as needed.

Fuel Efficiency and Maintenance
Enhancing fuel efficiency in "rocket" thermal mass heaters is essential for sustainable off-grid living, ensuring that every piece of wood or biomass utilized generates maximum heat with minimal waste. Fuel efficiency begins with selecting the right wood. Hardwoods, like oak or maple, are denser and yield more warmth per volume than softwoods such as pine. However, it's critical to use dry, seasoned wood, which burns hotter and cleaner than wet wood, decreasing smoke and increasing heat output. For optimal combustion, wood moisture content should be less than 20%.

The size and shape of the wood also impact fuel efficiency. Smaller pieces ignite and burn faster, quickly elevating the temperature in the combustion chamber and maintaining steady heat output. This allows the "rocket" thermal mass heater to achieve optimal operating temperatures more rapidly, where combustion is most efficient and smoke production is minimal.

Maintenance is vital for fuel efficiency. Regularly clearing ash from the combustion chamber and chimney ensures adequate airflow, promoting complete combustion. Excessive ash buildup can insulate the combustion chamber, lowering temperatures and leading to incomplete wood combustion, which not only wastes fuel but also creates more pollution.

It is equally important to check the chimney and flue system for blockages or buildup. A clean chimney facilitates proper draft, drawing air into the combustion chamber and expelling smoke from the home. Any obstructions can impede this circulation, lowering efficiency and potentially causing dangerous smoke to backtrack. Using a chimney brush can help maintain system cleanliness, ensuring safe and effective heater operation.

The design and construction of the "rocket" thermal mass heater significantly influence its efficiency. Properly sizing and constructing the combustion chamber, heat duct, and horizontal ducts according to best practices maximizes heat transfer to the thermal mass while minimizing wood consumption. Any deviation from optimal design can decrease efficiency and increase fuel usage.

Monitoring heater performance can offer insights into fuel efficiency. Observing the amount of smoke produced can indicate combustion quality; ideally, there should be little to no visible smoke when the heater operates at maximum efficiency. Adjusting the quantity and type of wood used, along with the air intake, can assist in achieving cleaner, more efficient combustion.

By focusing on wood quality, routine maintenance, and adherence to optimal design principles, "rocket" thermal mass heaters can attain high levels of fuel efficiency. This conserves resources and supports a sustainable, self-sufficient lifestyle, aligning with the objectives of off-grid living. Proper maintenance guarantees the longevity and performance of your heater, providing a reliable and eco-friendly heat source for your home.

DIY Project: Constructing a "Rocket" Thermal Mass Heater

Overview
This project entails building a "rocket" thermal mass heater, an efficient wood-burning appliance that utilizes a minimal amount of fuel to generate substantial heat. This heater is engineered to absorb and gradually release heat over time, making it an excellent option for sustainably warming homes, cabins, or off-grid workshops.

Difficulty Level
High | Estimated Duration: 1-2 weeks

Benefits
A "rocket" thermal mass heater is exceptionally efficient, allowing for clean wood combustion and significantly reducing the amount of fuel required to heat a space. It delivers enduring warmth, as the thermal mass (commonly a bench or floor) stores heat and releases it slowly. This heater type is eco-friendly, cost-effective, and perfect for sustainable living.

Required Materials
- 55-gallon metal drum (for the heat riser duct)
- Refractory bricks (for the combustion chamber and insulation)
- Clay and sand (to create cob material)
- Insulating materials (such as perlite, vermiculite, or refractory insulation)
- Metal piping or ducting (for the exhaust system)
- Steel rods or wire mesh (to reinforce thermal mass)
- Gravel, stones, or bricks (for the thermal mass base)
- Cob or concrete (for the thermal mass)
- High-temperature mortar (for sealing joints)
- Chimney cap or rain cover (optional, for exhaust)

Tools Needed
- Electric drill with metal-cutting bits
- Angle grinder or metal saw
- Tape measure
- Level
- Trowel
- Bucket (for mixing cob)
- Safety gear (gloves, goggles, mask)

Alternative Materials
Recycled materials like bricks or metal can be utilized to reduce costs. Ceramic fiber insulation can be used for a more efficient heat riser duct.

Step-by-Step Instructions
1. **Site Selection and Preparation**:
   Choose an appropriate location within your home or structure for the heater installation. Consider how close it is to the areas you wish to heat and ensure sufficient ventilation for the exhaust system. Clean the site and prepare a sturdy, level base using gravel, stones, or bricks to support the weight.
   Time: 1-2 days
2. **Building the Combustion Chamber**:

Construct the combustion chamber using firebricks to form a rectangular or square box for burning wood. Insulate the chamber effectively to enhance efficiency. Use high-temperature mortar to seal the joints between bricks, ensuring the chamber is airtight to prevent smoke leaks.
Time: 1-2 days

3. **Creating the Riser Duct**:
The riser duct is a vertical chimney inside the heater that intensifies combustion. Use the 55-gallon metal drum as the outer casing and line the inside with fire bricks or refractory insulation to create a high-temperature environment. Ensure the duct extends higher than the combustion chamber to facilitate proper draft.
Time: 1-2 days

4. **Assembling the Shell**:
Position the drum above the riser pipe. Seal the top of the drum to force hot gases to flow down the sides of the duct before exiting through the exhaust system. This setup enables the drum to radiate heat into the surrounding area. Cut an opening in the side of the drum for the drain hose.
Time: 1 day

5. **Constructing the Thermal Mass**:
The thermal mass, typically a bench or floor, stores heat from exhaust gases and gradually releases it. Create the thermal mass using cob, concrete, or similar materials. Start with a base of gravel or stones, then build the mass using cob or concrete mixed with reinforcement materials such as steel rods or wire mesh. Insert the exhaust pipe into the thermal mass, ensuring a slight upward slope for proper airflow.
Time: 2-3 days

6. **Setting Up the Exhaust System**:
Connect the exhaust pipe from the drum to the chimney or outdoor vent. The pipe should have a gentle slope to facilitate smooth gas flow out of the heater. If possible, install a chimney cap or rain cover to prevent water from entering the system. Seal all joints with high-temperature mortar to prevent leaks.
Time: 1 day

7. **Finishing the Thermal Mass**:
Once the exhaust pipe is secured, complete the construction of the thermal mass around it. Smooth the surface of the cob or concrete to create a comfortable seating area or floor. Allow the thermal mass to dry and harden completely before using the heater; drying may take several days to a week, depending on material thickness.
Time: 2-3 days

8. **Testing the "Rocket" Thermal Mass Heater**:
Before regular use, conduct several small tests to ensure the combustion chamber, riser, and exhaust system are functioning correctly. Monitor smoke emissions and verify that air circulates appropriately. Make necessary adjustments to enhance efficiency and safety.
Time: 1-2 days

Maintenance and Care
Regularly inspect the combustion chamber and riser pipe for cracks or damage, repairing them as needed. Periodically clean the exhaust system to remove soot buildup and ensure proper airflow. Check the thermal mass for signs of wear and repair the surface with new cob or concrete when necessary.

Strategies for Cooling Off-Grid Homes
Efficient cooling of off-grid homes requires innovative solutions that leverage natural resources while minimizing energy consumption. One effective approach is to implement shading and insulation techniques to reduce heat buildup. Planting deciduous trees around the home provides natural shade during summer and, when their leaves fall in winter, allows sunlight to warm the home. Additionally, reflective roofing materials or light-colored paints can significantly decrease the amount of heat absorbed by your home.

Importance of Insulation
Insulation is essential for keeping an off-grid home cool. High R-value materials, such as spray foam, rigid insulation boards, and layered insulation, can be applied to walls, roofs, and floors to minimize heat transfer. Insulated windows or reflective films can also block solar radiation without sacrificing natural light. Passive ventilation methods can create airflow within the home, achieved by opening windows at night to allow cooler air in and using vented skylights to expel warm air from the upper areas of the house. For more controlled ventilation, underground pipes can cool incoming air by passing it through buried ducts, where the consistent ground temperature lowers the air temperature before it enters the home.

Active Cooling Solutions

For active cooling, solar-powered fans provide a low-energy solution for enhancing air circulation and expelling heat. These fans work particularly well in combination with passive cooling strategies, such as utilizing thermal mass, which absorbs heat during the day and releases it at night. Constructing walls or floors with high thermal mass materials like concrete or stone helps maintain a stable indoor temperature.

Evaporative coolers, also known as "swamp coolers," offer an energy-efficient alternative to traditional air conditioning systems in dry climates. These devices cool air through the evaporation of water, consuming significantly less electricity than conventional air conditioners. However, they require a consistent water supply and are less effective in humid conditions. For individuals living in particularly hot climates, a more advanced DIY project may involve creating a small-scale geothermal cooling system. By circulating water through underground pipes, the consistent temperature of the earth is utilized to cool the water, which can then be used to reduce internal temperatures.

Implementing these cooling strategies requires careful planning, taking local climate, home orientation, and available resources into account. By combining various methods, off-grid homes can maintain comfortable living conditions even during the hottest months, aligning with sustainable and self-sufficient living principles.

Enhancing Shading and Insulation Techniques

Maximizing the effectiveness of shading and insulation is vital for sustaining comfortable temperatures in off-grid homes, particularly in areas with extremely hot summers. Strategically utilizing landscaping elements, such as trees and shrubs, can significantly block direct sunlight from entering your home. Deciduous trees are particularly advantageous, providing shade in the summer while allowing sunlight to warm the home in winter once they lose their leaves. Vines and climbing plants on trellises can offer an additional layer of natural shading on walls, significantly lowering the heat absorbed by the home's exterior.

Using reflective materials and paints on roofs and exterior walls can also help redirect solar radiation. Applying light-colored paint or special reflective coatings reduces roof temperatures, and subsequently, those of internal spaces. This method is especially effective in regions with intense sun exposure, where roof temperatures can soar above surrounding air temperatures.

Importance of Quality Insulation

High-quality insulation in walls, ceilings, and floors reduces heat transfer, keeping cool air trapped inside during summer and warm air inside during winter. Materials with elevated R-values are particularly effective at resisting heat flow, creating a barrier that enhances comfort and lessens the need for mechanical cooling systems.

Windows serve as a critical point for heat exchange, making it essential to optimize their performance. Double- or triple-glazed windows filled with inert gases and low-emissivity (low-E) coatings significantly decrease heat buildup while allowing natural light in. For existing windows, reflective films, thermal curtains, or external shutters provide additional solutions to control heat entry.

Passive design features such as overhangs, awnings, and pergolas can offer shade to windows and doors, minimizing direct sunlight exposure. These structures can be engineered to block summer sunlight while permitting winter sunlight to enter, utilizing seasonal changes in the sun's trajectory to gain a natural advantage.

Integrating thermal mass into the home's structure is another effective method for regulating indoor temperatures. Materials like concrete, brick, and stone can absorb and store heat during the day, gradually releasing it at night, thus reducing temperature fluctuations. When combined with passive solar design principles, thermal mass significantly aids cooling efforts by absorbing cooler nighttime air and releasing it during the day.

By employing these shading and insulation strategies, off-grid homes can enhance their comfort and energy efficiency. Each method offers distinct benefits, and when combined, they can create a holistic cooling strategy that reduces dependence on active cooling systems, consistent with the principles of sustainable, self-sufficient living.

DIY Project: Constructing an Earth-Cooled Shelter

Building an earth-cooled shelter leverages the natural insulating characteristics of soil to maintain a comfortable internal temperature, thereby reducing the reliance on mechanical cooling systems. This project entails excavating a partially or entirely underground space to create a shelter that takes advantage of the constant temperature of the subsurface. Initially, it is essential to choose a location with suitable soil, preferably well-draining to prevent issues with water accumulation. Shelter designs can vary based on individual needs and terrain, ranging from simple bermed structures to more complex underground homes.

Planning and Excavation

Begin by outlining the shelter's dimensions, ensuring adequate space for living areas, storage, and other necessities. Excavation can be labor-intensive, so consider renting machinery for larger projects. As you dig, angle the walls slightly inward to ensure stability and prevent collapse. For constructing the shelter, materials such as reinforced concrete, earth bags, or treated wood can be utilized, depending on the project scope and budget. It's crucial to incorporate a waterproof membrane and drainage system around the exterior to protect against moisture.

Importance of Insulation
Insulation plays a vital role in an earth-cooled shelter, enhancing both winter warmth and summer cooling. Install insulation outside the waterproof membrane to protect it from environmental factors while maximizing the natural insulating benefits of the earth. The shelter's roof, often the most exposed section, should be layered with soil over the insulation. This not only adds to the thermal mass, helping regulate internal temperatures, but also helps integrate the structure with the landscape, reducing visual disruption.

Ventilation Considerations
Ventilation is another critical factor. Include ventilation pipes that reach the surface to facilitate air exchange and prevent moisture and radon gas accumulation. These pipes can be concealed to maintain the shelter's discreet profile. For entry, consider constructing a sloped tunnel or vertical shaft with a ladder, which can be insulated and sealed to help maintain a stable internal environment.

Lighting Solutions
For illumination, skylights can be incorporated in areas where the shelter is near the surface, utilizing durable, impact-resistant materials. Alternatively, solar tubes can channel natural light from outside into the shelter, providing lighting without compromising insulation.

Interior Design
The internal layout should prioritize space efficiency and comfort. Use moisture-resistant materials for interior finishes, and consider built-in furniture to maximize space. For energy needs, a solar panel system can be installed on the surface, connected to batteries inside the shelter to ensure electricity without relying on the grid.

Testing and Adjustments
Finally, monitor the shelter's environment for several days to assess temperature, humidity, and air quality, making ventilation and insulation adjustments as necessary. This earth-cooled shelter design not only provides a sustainable living space with minimal environmental impact but also offers a unique opportunity to harmonize with the natural environment, utilizing earth resources to create a comfortable, self-sufficient home.

Sustainable Refrigeration Solutions

Overview
Refrigeration is vital for off-grid living, as preserving food and maintaining a sustainable lifestyle can be challenging without continuous access to electricity. Fortunately, innovative and sustainable alternatives exist that provide effective cooling without relying on traditional energy sources. One such method involves evaporative coolers, including pot zeers. This ancient technique utilizes evaporative cooling, where the evaporation of water from a porous container significantly lowers the internal temperature. A common approach is to place a smaller pot inside a larger one, filling the gap with wet sand and covering everything. As water evaporates from the outer vessel, it extracts heat from the inner pot, keeping the contents cool.

Another time-honored method is constructing underground ice houses or cold rooms. In colder climates, ice can be harvested during winter and stored in insulated underground cellars for use in warmer months. This technique requires strategic planning and effective insulation to ensure the ice lasts as long as possible. By utilizing modern insulating materials, one can enhance efficiency and prolong cooling, providing a reliable storage method year-round.

Natural cellars, often referred to as root cellars, are another effective solution for storing perishable items without electricity. Leveraging the cooler temperatures of the soil, these cellars maintain a consistent temperature ideal for preserving fruits, vegetables, and other foods. Proper ventilation is crucial to prevent moisture buildup and extend the longevity of stored items.

For those seeking a more advanced solution, solar-powered refrigeration is a sustainable alternative that harnesses solar energy. Solar refrigerators and freezers operate on direct current (DC) generated by solar panels, making them well-suited for off-grid environments. Although the initial investment may be higher than traditional refrigerators, the long-term energy savings and reliability in remote locations make solar-powered refrigeration an appealing option for off-grid living.

DIY enthusiasts may also consider constructing a solar-powered ice maker, which generates ice during the day using solar energy. This ice can then be utilized in a traditional cooler or insulated container to keep food and drinks chilled without continuous electricity. This method merges solar energy generation with traditional ice storage techniques, providing a practical and effective refrigeration solution.

Implementing these off-grid refrigeration methods necessitates careful planning, taking into account individual needs, climate, and available resources. By understanding the principles of each technique and adapting them to your specific context, you can ensure a sustainable and reliable solution for food preservation, waste reduction, and comfortable living while minimizing reliance on conventional energy sources.

Evaporative Coolers and Pot Zeers

Evaporative coolers and pot zeers offer an efficient and sustainable means of preserving food freshness in off-grid settings, utilizing the natural process of evaporation to reduce temperatures without electricity. The fundamental principle is that cooling occurs when water evaporates, absorbing heat from the surrounding environment and thereby lowering the temperature. A pot zeer, in particular, is a straightforward yet effective refrigeration device consisting of two clay pots—one smaller than the other—with a layer of wet sand in between. As the water in the sand evaporates through the outer pot, it extracts heat from the inner pot, creating a cooler environment ideal for storing perishable foods. This method is particularly beneficial in arid climates, where higher evaporation rates make it a practical choice for off-grid living.

To construct a pot zeer, gather two unglazed clay pots, sand, water, and a cloth or lid to cover the top. Place the smaller pot inside the larger one, filling the space between them with sand. Once the sand is saturated with water, cover everything with a damp cloth to enhance the evaporation process. Position the pot in a dry, well-ventilated area to optimize cooling effects. Regularly adding water to the sand will ensure continuous evaporation, keeping the contents of the inner pot fresh. This method can significantly lower internal temperatures, extending the shelf life of fruits, vegetables, and other perishables.

Evaporative coolers function similarly but on a larger scale, using a fan to draw warm air through water-saturated panels, cooling the air in the process. The cooled air is then circulated throughout the living space, effectively reducing temperatures. Although more complex than pot zeers, evaporative coolers can serve as an efficient cooling solution for entire rooms in dry climates. Both methods are cost-effective, require minimal resources and maintenance, making them ideal for those living off-grid where conventional refrigeration may be impractical or undesired. By leveraging the natural process of evaporation, these techniques offer practical and eco-friendly alternatives to electric refrigeration, aligning with sustainable and self-sufficient living principles.

Ice Houses and Natural Cellars

Ice houses and natural cellars utilize the earth's inherent insulation properties to create environments conducive to storing perishable items, capitalizing on the consistent underground temperatures to keep food fresh year-round. Constructing an ice house involves digging into the ground or up a slope to take advantage of the thermal stability found below the frost line. Insulating the walls with materials like straw or sawdust helps preserve the ice harvested during winter, allowing it to last through the warmer months. This historical method, used before modern refrigeration technology, offers a sustainable way to maintain food freshness without electricity.

Natural cellars, in contrast, are specifically designed to store fruits, vegetables, and other foods at a stable, cool temperature, prolonging their shelf life. By excavating the storage area deep enough into the ground, one can benefit from the earth's natural cooling properties. Proper ventilation is a crucial element in the design of natural cellars; strategically placed vents create airflow that helps maintain a cool internal environment while preventing the accumulation of ethylene gas, which can hasten spoilage. The ideal temperature for a natural cellar typically ranges between 0°C and 4°C, with humidity levels kept between 85% and 95% to avoid product desiccation.

Constructing a natural cellar can range from simply burying an old freezer to creating a dedicated underground room. Location is critical; in northern climates, a north-facing slope is ideal as it receives less direct sunlight. Insulating the cellar roof with soil, straw bales, or contemporary insulation materials can further stabilize internal temperatures. Shelving and containers inside the cellar should be arranged to maximize airflow around stored foods, thereby reducing the risk of mold or moisture damage. Regular monitoring of temperature and humidity is essential for making necessary ventilation adjustments and ensuring optimal food storage conditions.

Ice houses and natural cellars offer practical, low-tech refrigeration solutions for off-grid living, allowing for food storage without reliance on electric cooling systems. These methods not only minimize energy consumption but also enhance food security by providing a dependable means of preserving crops and bulk purchases. As part of a sustainable living strategy, they provide valuable insights into harnessing natural resources and adapting traditional techniques to meet modern needs.

CHAPTER 10:

ESTABLISHING A COMMUNITY NETWORK

The Role of Community Networks in Emergencies

Building community ties and cooperation are essential aspects of off-grid living, as they cultivate a support network for resource sharing and knowledge exchange, bolstering the group's resilience and sustainability. The foundation of a robust community lies in shared values and objectives among its members, such as mutual aid, environmental stewardship, and a dedication to self-sufficiency. To foster an effective community, open communication is crucial, creating environments where everyone feels heard and appreciated. This can be accomplished through regular meetings, social events, and online forums that promote transparent sharing of ideas, concerns, and achievements. Collaboration within the community often takes the form of joint initiatives, such as building communal spaces, community gardens, or cooperative water systems. These efforts not only enhance the group's infrastructure but also strengthen social ties and cultivate a sense of belonging and pride among members. Skill-sharing workshops are another vital aspect of collaboration, allowing members to learn from one another and impart valuable knowledge, ranging from traditional craft techniques to contemporary technologies. This exchange not only enhances the community's self-sufficiency but also deepens interpersonal relationships.

Conflict resolution is a critical component of community building and requires a proactive and empathetic approach. Establishing clear, shared guidelines for addressing disputes and forming a neutral body to facilitate dialogue can help maintain harmony. Encouraging restorative practices, which focus on understanding, healing, and rebuilding relationships rather than punishment, transforms conflicts into opportunities for growth rather than sources of division.

Sustainable initiatives, like collaborative renewable energy projects or waste reduction programs, showcase how teamwork can lead to innovative solutions that benefit both the community and the environment. Often, these projects become models for other communities, extending the impact of collaboration beyond local boundaries. Creating partnerships with neighboring communities, participating in regional sustainability programs, and engaging with online networks can provide invaluable resources, inspiration, and support. These connections can spark larger collaborative initiatives, shared learning experiences, and a stronger collective voice for promoting sustainable living practices.

Promoting a culture of collaboration also entails celebrating the community's accomplishments and acknowledging the contributions of its members. Celebrations—whether recognizing project completions, personal milestones, or seasonal events—foster a sense of belonging and gratitude among members. These moments of joy and collective success reinforce community bonds, reminding everyone of the strength derived from unity.

Ultimately, community building involves weaving a network of relationships that support both individual and collective well-being. It is a dynamic process that evolves with the community, necessitating continuous commitment, adaptability, and a shared vision. Through collaboration, communities can exhibit remarkable resilience, sustainability, and deep connections during emergencies, embodying the principles of mutual support and environmental stewardship that define this lifestyle.

Steps for Building a Community Network

Creating a community network begins with identifying individuals and families who share a common vision of sustainable, self-sufficient living. The initial step is to seek like-minded individuals through various channels, such as social media groups, to connect with those in similar circumstances. Once a group is formed, the next crucial step is establishing shared goals and values that will guide the community's development and functioning. These could include commitments to renewable energy, organic farming, and communal living arrangements.

Involving local authorities early in the planning process can facilitate development and ensure compliance with relevant laws and regulations. A key aspect of maintaining harmony and ensuring democratic decision-making is establishing a governance structure that reflects the community's values. This could involve forming committees or councils responsible for various facets of community life, such as resource management, conflict resolution, and event planning. Regular community meetings provide opportunities for open discussion, decision-making, and shared responsibilities among members.

Utilizing expertise within the group to design and construct homes, community spaces, and systems for energy, water, and waste management not only lowers costs but also reinforces community ties. Sustainable building practices should be prioritized to minimize environmental impact and ensure infrastructure longevity. Fostering a culture of learning and skill-sharing within the community enhances self-sufficiency and resilience. Through collaboration, shared values, and a commitment to living harmoniously with the environment, communities can offer a fulfilling and sustainable alternative to conventional lifestyles, reflecting principles of mutual support, environmental responsibility, and self-sufficiency.

These initiatives not only capitalize on the diverse skills and resources of members but also strengthen social bonds and collective resilience in the face of challenges. Participating in communal projects, such as constructing community structures, developing shared renewable energy sources, or establishing community gardens, allows individuals to utilize their unique abilities and acquire new skills, enriching the community as a whole. These projects require careful planning, coordination, and effort, providing opportunities for members to work collaboratively, fortifying relationships, and generating a sense of belonging and fulfillment.

Mutual aid extends beyond structured projects, representing a spontaneous and organic form of support that arises in response to the immediate needs of the community. It may manifest in assisting a neighbor to rebuild after a storm, sharing excess crops during bountiful harvests, or providing care during times of illness. Such acts of kindness and support form the foundation of community life, ensuring that no member faces adversity alone. The principle of mutual aid is predicated on the understanding that each individual's well-being is intricately linked to that of the community as a whole. It transcends mere transactions, fostering a culture of generosity and empathy.

The effectiveness of collaborative projects and mutual aid largely hinges on efficient communication and the ability to mobilize community resources effectively. Regular meetings and open communication channels are essential for sharing ideas, resources, and feedback in a transparent manner. Technology can play a pivotal role in facilitating this process, with online platforms and communication tools enabling coordination even when members cannot be physically present.

Leadership within these projects often emerges organically, with individuals stepping up to lead based on their skills, experiences, or passions for particular initiatives. In this context, leadership is not hierarchical but rather focused on promoting collective action and ensuring that every voice is heard and valued. Decisions are generally made democratically, aiming for consensus to ensure that aid projects and efforts reflect the collective will and needs of the community.

Evaluation and reflection are critical components of collaborative projects and mutual aid, allowing the community to learn from each experience and enhance future initiatives. Celebrating achievements and acknowledging the contributions of all participants bolsters the community's positive spirit and the value of collective effort toward shared objectives.

Community support off-grid

DOWNLOAD THE COLOR VERSION HERE

NAVY SEALS BUG-IN GUIDE

NAVY SEALS BUG-IN

CHAPTER 11:

STRESS MANAGEMENT

Mental Readiness: Equally Vital as Physical Preparation

Importance of Psychological Readiness
When embracing off-grid living, mental preparation is just as crucial as physical readiness. The challenges of isolation, unforeseen difficulties, and the necessity for self-sufficiency can greatly affect emotional well-being. Cultivating a resilient mindset and effective coping strategies is vital for managing the stress and unpredictability that accompany this lifestyle.

Identifying Psychological Hurdles
The first step toward effective mental preparation is acknowledging the emotional hurdles that may arise, such as feelings of isolation, anxiety from lacking immediate support, or stress related to the daily demands of self-sufficiency. Accepting these emotions as part of the experience enables proactive management.

Establishing a Support System
Even in remote locations, it is essential to create a support network. This can be achieved through regular communication with individuals who share similar lifestyles, community groups, or online forums. Sharing experiences and solutions with those familiar with off-grid living can provide emotional support and help alleviate feelings of isolation.

Managing Stress through Physical Activity
Effective stress management techniques are indispensable for psychological preparedness. Practices such as mindfulness, meditation, and deep breathing help maintain emotional stability and mental clarity. Engaging in physical activities, such as crafting, gardening, or walking, supports not only physical health but also enhances mental well-being, reducing stress and promoting a positive mood.

Setting Realistic Objectives and Celebrating Progress
Establishing achievable goals is crucial for avoiding frustration. Life off the grid presents numerous challenges, and accepting that not every plan will unfold as intended can alleviate feelings of disappointment. Recognizing and celebrating small achievements along the journey to self-sufficiency fosters a sense of accomplishment and motivation.

Problem-Solving and Adaptability
Cultivating problem-solving skills and adaptability allows you to creatively tackle the challenges of off-grid living. This includes addressing technical issues related to off-grid systems and managing the unpredictability of weather and natural resources. Viewing challenges as opportunities for learning nurtures a positive and resilient mindset.

Emergency Preparedness
Having an emergency plan is essential for alleviating anxiety. Being prepared for unforeseen circumstances, such as medical emergencies or natural disasters, instills a sense of security and peace of mind. Engaging in personal hobbies and interests outside of daily tasks can offer mental respite and help prevent burnout.

Coping with Loneliness and Maintaining Mental Health in Isolation
While off-grid living provides a unique sense of freedom and connection to nature, it can also lead to mental health challenges, particularly loneliness. The solitude that many seek in this lifestyle can transform into feelings of depression or anxiety if left unaddressed. Recognizing early signs of these issues is vital for maintaining mental well-being.

Establishing Routines and Social Connections
Creating a daily routine that includes regular social interactions, even through technology, is essential. Video calls or social media platforms can help maintain connections with the community despite physical distance. Additionally, practices like journaling and meditation facilitate ongoing reflection on one's emotional state.

Physical Activity as a Natural Remedy
Regular physical activity enhances physical health and has positive effects on mental health, alleviating symptoms of depression and anxiety. Incorporating physical tasks into daily routines, such as gardening or walking, can serve as a mood booster, offering immediate gratification and long-term benefits.

Pursuing Hobbies and Acquiring New Skills
Engaging in hobbies that bring joy or learning new skills can counteract feelings of isolation. Exploring local flora and fauna, for instance, provides a sense of purpose and encourages personal growth, bolstering self-esteem.

Building Companionship and Support Networks
Creating a support system, even if virtual, is a crucial strategy for maintaining mental health in isolation. Regular interactions with friends, family, or online communities provide important emotional support. Additionally, having pets can offer valuable companionship, providing structure and comfort in daily life.

Recognizing the Need for Professional Support
Knowing when to seek professional assistance is essential. Online therapy has become increasingly accessible and should not be stigmatized. Prioritizing mental health is just as critical as physical health for successful off-grid living.

Cultivating Resilience
Developing resilience is key to managing the daily challenges of off-grid living. Resilience encompasses the mental capacity to deal with stress, overcome obstacles, and recover from setbacks. Fostering this mindset involves maintaining a positive outlook, viewing difficulties as chances for growth, and developing emotional and mental flexibility.

Techniques for Stress Reduction
Utilizing stress reduction strategies, such as mindfulness, meditation, and physical exercise, can help maintain focus and tranquility even in challenging situations. Developing problem-solving abilities and learning from mistakes enhances your capacity to confront future challenges.

Setting and Achieving Goals
Establishing realistic objectives and making gradual progress toward them instills a sense of purpose and direction. Celebrating accomplishments, no matter how small, boosts self-confidence and motivation. Remaining adaptable and ready to respond to changing circumstances is essential for navigating the complexities of off-grid life.

Managing Emergencies and Stress
In an off-grid context, addressing emergencies necessitates careful preparation and a resilient mindset. Life off the grid can be unpredictable, with unexpected events ranging from severe weather to health crises. Formulating a comprehensive emergency plan is the initial step in effectively responding to crises.

Techniques for Stress Management During Emergencies
Stress management strategies are vital during emergencies, just as they are in daily life. Regularly practicing breathing exercises, yoga, or meditation can help maintain calm during crises and enhance overall well-being.

Building a Supportive Community
Establishing a supportive community can significantly alleviate the challenges faced during emergencies. Sharing resources, knowledge, and experiences with neighbors and friends can mitigate the impact of crises. Additionally, personal preparation, such as acquiring first aid skills or learning to maintain off-grid systems, builds confidence and capacity to cope with difficulties.

Embracing Adaptability and Lifelong Learning
Being willing to adapt and continuously learn is essential for navigating the unforeseen circumstances of off-grid life. Staying informed about new technologies and strategies for self-sufficiency allows you to tackle challenges more effectively.

<u>FINAL THOUGHTS</u>

Everyday life often leads us to overlook the importance of security, resources, and modern conveniences, yet this book serves as a reminder that the unexpected can occur at any time. Building long-term resilience fundamentally relies on both mental and physical preparation. We have examined strategies, techniques, and mindsets focused on the "bug-in" approach, which emphasizes the decision to remain at home and transform it into a secure and self-sufficient haven during emergencies. Beyond technical skills, this journey has encouraged a deeper contemplation of safety and the responsibilities we hold towards ourselves, our families, and our communities.

A key takeaway from this guide is the necessity of adopting a comprehensive approach to preparation. It's not merely about stockpiling resources or fortifying the physical defenses of our homes. Genuine security arises from our ability to adapt to changing circumstances, maintain composure in stressful situations, and develop a robust plan for navigating crises at multiple levels. In this framework, our home evolves into more than just a physical space; it becomes a fortified sanctuary, a command center, and a place where we can rely on our capabilities and resources.

In an increasingly unpredictable world, where natural disasters, economic upheavals, and social unrest can occur, self-sufficiency and readiness have become vital skills. We have discussed how to establish food supplies, manage water resources, produce energy autonomously, secure our homes against intrusions, and respond to health emergencies. These techniques are not solely for survival in extreme scenarios; they also serve as tools to enhance daily life quality, diminish reliance on external infrastructures, and promote a more conscious and sustainable lifestyle in harmony with the environment.

Mental preparation emerged as another critical aspect of our exploration. In times of crisis, the ability to remain calm and respond swiftly can mean the difference between success and failure. Simulations, well-practiced emergency plans, and continuous training should be woven into the fabric of family life. Engaging loved ones in this process not only boosts their awareness but also fosters unity and cooperation—essential elements during any emergency. Mental resilience, the capacity to manage stress, and the willingness to confront the unknown are the true assets that keep us secure in challenging times.

Perhaps the most significant insight conveyed by this book is that preparation should not be viewed as a solitary or exclusive act. We are not merely preparing ourselves; we are contributing to the creation of a stronger and safer community. Being prepared entails the ability to assist those around us, safeguard our neighbors, and ultimately enhance collective stability. Support networks, collaboration, and cohesive communities are vital during and after a crisis, and the knowledge gained from this guide can become a meaningful resource for the common good.

Finally, preparation must be an evolving process. The world is perpetually changing, along with the nature of the threats and emergencies we may encounter. It is imperative to remain informed, refine our skills, adjust plans to align with new realities, and foster a spirit of continuous learning. Every situation presents an opportunity to grow, improve, and learn. Preparation does not conclude with the completion of this book; rather, it marks the beginning of a journey that necessitates dedication, flexibility, and an ongoing commitment to growth.

As you reflect on this journey, remember that being prepared does not equate to living in fear or paranoia. It means embracing a sense of responsibility and awareness, living confidently with the knowledge that you have control over situations even when chaos reigns. Transforming your home into a sanctuary is the first step toward a freer, safer, and more tranquil life. Continue to implement the lessons from this guide, share your insights, and help foster a more resilient world, where each of us is equipped to tackle the challenges ahead.

Thank you for taking the time to read
"Navy Seal Bug-In Guide".
I sincerely hope you found the insights and strategies helpful in preparing your home for any crisis.
If you enjoyed the book and found value in its content, I would greatly appreciate it if you could share your thoughts by leaving a review. Let me know what stood out to you or what you found most useful—it would mean a lot!

Made in the USA
Monee, IL
16 October 2024